Cristina Pelizzatti

COACHING THE ESSENCE

THROUGH THE POWER OF LOVE

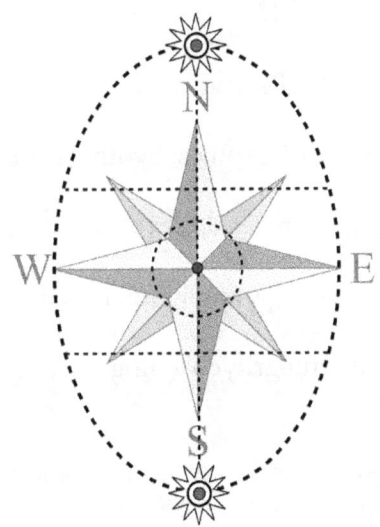

Transpersonal Leadership- from the multidimensional perspective of Psychosynthesis

© Cristina Pelizzatti

English edition: March, 2023

ISBN: 979-8-9875223-2-5

Synthesis Insights
Easton, Maryland 21601
USA

Editor: Nicholas Pearne

Layout & Cover Graphics: Synthesis Insights

Cover Illustration: *Shadows* (Elio Pelizzatti)

Author's website: www.syntegritycoaching.com

Email: cris@syntegritycoaching.com

Full-color versions of the illustrations in this book are available on the synthesis-coaching.com website:

*To Bianco, my Maestro, my son, trusted to me
for a brief period of the One Life.
Ever in my heart.*

*From non-Being, lead me to Being.
From the Shadows, lead me to the Light.
From Death, lead me to Immortality.*
                    Bṛhadāraṇyaka Upaniṣad (1.3.28)

COACHING THE ESSENCE

FORWARD

My name is Bill. I am a licensed commercial pilot, engineer, technologist, holder of black belts in three martial arts, musician, and Psychosynthesis Life Coach. As Executive/CTO and leader of various trade associations, I traveled the world for over thirty years, working in teams that contributed to the development of technologies and processes in the field of microelectronics that made possible the miniaturization of the devices that we all know today.

Cristina is one of the most authentic people I have ever met.

Possessing a spirit forged in the fires of adversity as she faced "sink or swim" challenges throughout her life, she emits a lovely, golden energy, a joy that still shines despite profound tragedy and personal loss.

This book places that story in the spiritual context that characterizes her life and worldview. Profoundly authentic, her spirituality comes from deep within and manifests itself in a myriad of simple, unaffected ways of relating to the world around her-from her beloved Huskies and other friends within the animal kingdom to a deep resonance with the planet we all live on, and those she knows as friends. She brings honesty, clarity, and a forthright approach to her coaching practice, and possesses the ability to transmit difficult concepts and even more difficult messaging in a disarming and empathic manner.

As this book will relate, her spiritual pathway began at a very early age, thrown out onto the streets of Paris during summer vacation visits with her paternal grandmother. Learning French was a matter of survival as she and her brother dealt with the local kids, and all through those formative years she demonstrated a toughness and resilience which served her well in the trials that followed, leading to achievement of World Championship awards in her chosen sport of sleddog racing. This achievement was gained at considerable personal cost and continuing difficulties in her life including the premature death of her father, renowned Valtellina artist Elio Pelizzatti, and her questioning spirit guided her on a multifaceted voyage of spiritual discovery ranging from scaling the highest peaks of Italy's Valtellina to accompanying others in their own journey of "psychological mountain-climbing" through transpersonal psychology. She had just begun Masters level studies of the ancient, Millennial Vedic wisdom with the Bhaktivedanta Institute in Ponsacco (Pisa) when her beloved son was diagnosed with bone cancer. She lost him a year later after an epic battle against both the illness and the regimented, narrow approach of the national healthcare system. The innovative therapy we brought over from the MD Anderson Cancer Center (Austin, TX) was too late to save him.

Rather than sink into a morass of self-pity, Cris drove ahead with her studies, working as a professional sommelier and taking on work-from-home computer assignments. Her desire to make a significant contribution to those in the throes of suffering, while at the same time not categorizing suffering as a pathology but as a difficulty which offers the opportunity to discover a meaning of life over and above the psychological trauma was the driving force in that difficult period.

She gained her Masters in Indovedic Science in 2010, and shortly after discovered Psychosynthesis. It was a chance-meeting on a train into Milan, and some drawings on a fogged-up window that contextualized the concept of spiritual development of the Vedas with the Egg Diagram of Psychosynthesis which launched her into a new world and a new perspective on psychology and spirituality.

Ever grounded, she first volunteered as a librarian at the local training institute, and eventually enrolled in the program, becoming a certified Psychosynthesis Counselor three years later. This was followed by another chance-meeting which led to Psychosynthesis Life Coach training with The Synthesis Center (Amherst, MA). After graduating from this program with her PLC certificate, she collaborated with The Synthesis Center for another year, honing her teaching and coaching skills, building

Forward

the experience and hours which eventually led to credentialing with the International Coaching Federation (ICF) as a Master Certified Coach (MCC).

In 2016 Psychosynthesis Life Coaching was a specialty within the nascent field of Life Coaching, and still mostly unknown in Italy, the birthplace of Psychosynthesis. Seeing the power that the Psychosythesis vision of the human psyche could bring to coaching, Cris spent over a thousand hours translating the Synthesis Center materials into Italian and launched a training program with this as a core curriculum in 2017. The immediate success of this program led to the foundation of Synthesis Coaching Associates (SCA), headquartered in Easton, MD with operations in Northern Italy, and Cris' credentialing as an ICF Master Certified Coach was a major contributor to accreditation of SCA as an ACSTH program provider in 2019 and successively as an ICF-accredited Level 1 and Level 2 Coaching Education Provider in 2022.

During this time Cris has expanded her studies, gaining certifications in specialties including the application of Neuroscience in Coaching, Positive Psychology, Neuro-Linguistic Programming, Green Coaching, Rational Emotional Education and Heart Intelligence, among others. Throughout all this she continues to question, to innovate, bringing together concepts from a multiplicity of fields and molding them into a practical, coherent vision of humankind's psychic and spiritual world. She is very careful about "spiritual bypassing" in its various forms: shortcuts to obtaining transpersonal experiences without first understanding the personal realm and developing one's innate abilities and potentials.

Her exposure to my martial arts training has grounded her belief in the value of meditation in action and what we call "dynamic immobility"- an expression of profound mindfulness built on an intense awareness of the world around us.

This book is not a "how-to" manual, nor is it a treatise in Psychosynthesis or a history of it. It is a free-flowing meditation on Life and Cris' experience of how spirituality as expressed

COACHING THE ESSENCE

in Psychosynthesis, the Vedas, and other works of profound wisdom weaves itself in everything we do. Were it formatted differently, this book would resemble the approach taken by my Great-Uncle, R. Buckminster "Bucky" Fuller- who, despite his ground-breaking contributions to architecture and sustainability towards the middle of the last century, always considered himself first and foremost a poet.

This book is poetry in prose, and I am honored to have been invited to write the Forward.

William Burr, PLC, ICF, FinstCT
"Castle Farms", March, 2023

PRESENTATION

Dorothy Firman, Ed.D., LMHC, PLC, BCC-
"It is a rare gift to be invited into the inner world of this author, while also being guided through the deep, complex, and powerful work of being a Psychosynthesis Life Coach. The weaving of the two worlds- Cristina's life long personal journey, and the elaboration of being a PLC works magically. Cristina is an amazing teacher and coach and she has taken Psychosynthesis Life Coaching into new and deepened territory, as she draws on not only the source of Psychosynthesis (Roberto Assagioli), but into the many spiritual and psychological streams that have informed Psychosynthesis, joined with Psychosynthesis and helped to create the beautiful, wide river that is Transpersonal Psychology. This is a book that will most assuredly strengthen any coach's work, and it is an essential book for all Psychosynthesis coaches. Thank you Cris!"

Dorothy is a Licensed Mental Health Counselor, Board Certified Coach, a pioneer in Psychosythesis Life Coaching, the founder of the Synthesis Center in Amherst, Massachusetts, a trainer of PLCs, and author of a number of books including (as editor), *The Call of Self: Psychosynthesis Life Coaching*.

Dr. Patrick Williams, Ed.D., MCC, BCC-
"Cristina Pelizzatti has written an opus in COACHING THE ESSENCE, in my opinion. I was first introduced to Psychosynthesis and the work of Assagioli in 1976 as I was completing my doctorate in Transpersonal Psychology. I, of course, studied the theories of Jung, Adler and then Assagioli, all three of whom broke away from Freud's inner circle since they all had a more theological and spiritual bent to the human journey.
Jung and Assagioli both studied other cultures and practices especially those of the EAST such as Buddhism, Vedic scriptures

COACHING THE ESSENCE

and more. Even after Assagioli completed his thesis on Psychosynthesis in 1911, he was not widely known outside of Italy due to few publications. His work has been rediscovered and fits well in the Life and Wellness Coaching profession today.

Pelizzatti, in this very comprehensive book, shares her personal journey, and the profound and deep understanding when Psychosynthesis came into her life. She shares those stories and her way of synthesizing the knowledge, theories and personal yearnings into a practical method and course of learning for those in the profession of coaching, counseling, or personal transformation. Read it slowly, digesting the content a few bites at a time…then come back and read it again. It will resonate to your body, brain and being, applied to your personal journey… which is the essence of psychosynthesis."

"Doc Coach" Pat Williams is a Coaching Pioneer, Adventurer, Life & Leadership Coach, Founder of the Institute for Life Coach Training (ILCT), Inaugral Member of the International Coaching Federation's Circle of Distinction, and prolific presenter and coaching advocate. Pat has authored multiple articles and co-authored a number of books, including *Becoming a Professional Life Coach* and *Getting Naked with Your Clothes On*.

PREFACE TO THE ENGLISH EDITION

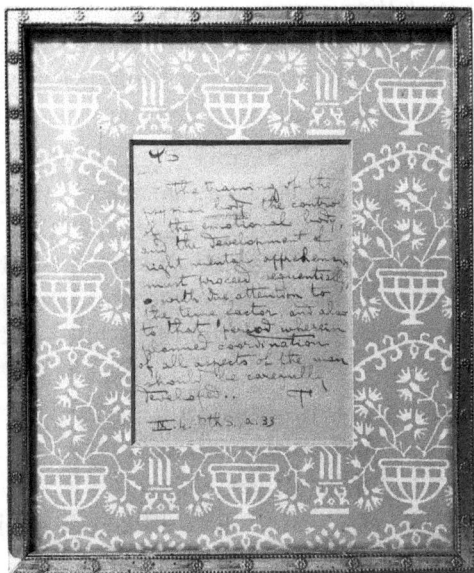

Photo: "Assagiolino"- orignial note handwritten by Roberto Assagioli

Why did I want to write another book on coaching when there are already so many? How do I think I can contribute in this field considering that so much has already been published on this topic? What can I add in the field of Psychosynthesis considering that here much has already been published?

I didn't have the honor of knowing Roberto Assagioli personally. I had the opportunity to read his texts, articles, manuscripts and to hear about them through people who knew him, but even if I never met him personally, it is as if there was a connection between us that nevertheless brought us together.

I encountered Psychosynthesis and subsequently Roberto Assagioli in the most painful moment of my life, discovering that we shared the same pain: the loss of a child.

There are many questions that pass in front of the screen of my multiple personality. I could go on and on listing the inner voices that I hear and that constantly raise their volume, confusing me and slowing me down, even pulling me backward rather than moving forward. Yet despite the incessant buzz, fatigue and demotivation that they sometimes bring me, I feel something stronger coming from within, urging me to forge ahead and through them, laboriously bringing their positive intention to light and then going Beyond.

So I decided to get involved once again and this time with another piece in the huge puzzle that I've always tried to compose, an illustration that slowly manifests itself and that I feel belongs to me, still veiled but not obscured, which transmits enthusiasm and strength, keeps me focused on the moment and allows me to creatively recompose the events of my life in a precise and sensible order.

Synthesis, making synthesis, putting together the messy parts that belong to this puzzle, giving them the right location, value, and meaning: if I'm missing one, the drawing would be incomplete. To then see, through the union of the parts, the Beyond- the great image that underlies them.

"If I'm not for me, who is for me? And if I'm only for myself, what am I? And if not now, when?"

- R. Hillel (Hillel the Elder), Pirkei Avot, I.14.

This work is for me to make a synthesis. I write it for me and I do it now, to then share it with others. If I don't do it now, when will I do it?

In this English edition I am pleased to welcome one of our graduates, Andy Lyde, PLC and ICF Professional Certified Coach, to Chapter 13 "Original Research". Andy's work is important because it is exploring the parallels between Psychosynthesis and other coaching skillsets, opening the door to a broader and more inclusive application of Psychosynthesis to coaching. I am also pleased to welcome one of our PLC students, Laura Williams, to Chapter 14 "Reflections". Thank you, Andy and Laura!

I dedicate this work to my many teachers whom I have had the honor of meeting along my life's path, who one day, while I was groping in the dark, led me to meet the Light through

Preface

Psychosynthesis. It is not my intention to write a scientific treatise or even a book on the history of coaching or an academic text on Psychosynthesis. This writing is a practical manual that comes from the desire to share, with anyone interested, how I became a Psychosynthesis coach, putting together the various pieces of my life: a life that has been marked by my aptitude for transpersonal coaching since the very beginning, being an essential tool for living soulfully in everyday life, implementing the highest potentials that are seeking to come to light and be activated.

The words written by Roberto Assagioli in his original Assagiolino (literally "little Assagioli"- the term used for the small, handwritten notes on which he jotted down reflections and insights), now framed and hanging on the wall in my small studio, are a daily reminder of the emphasis Psychosynthesis training places on the development of a right mental attitude through a project that needs to find an ideal program with which to coordinate the various elements of Being. The time has come for me to synthesize and give meaning to my life, according to a plan that becomes increasingly clear along the way.

In synthesis this is my "Journey Beyond. A History of Self-Leadership and Resilience".

In particular, I dedicate these reflections to my father Elio who dedicated his life to Art and to my son Bianco, the Master Child, who in his brief manifestation in this life taught me that the way of Love is the way to move, at any cost.

I further dedicate this work to my daughter Carmen, who teaches me that being a mother is a splendid and very difficult task; and to my mother who is a masterful example of the will in all its aspects and qualities.

I also dedicate this writing to those who have been present in my life in a very significant way, teaching me how to become "World Champions" by working together in the arduous sport of sleddog racing, following the paths of life as well as the snowy trails, learning how to deal with extreme events and not get discouraged through reliance on one's own psycho-physical resources; to my mentor Bill (William Burr): without his gentle, strong presence none of this would have been written; to my guide Dorothy (Didi) Firman, Ed.D., who showed me how Psychosynthesis can truly be embodied with congruence as solid as granite. Lots of gratitude also to my MCC coaching mentor Patrick Williams Ed.D., MCC, a living example of "Conscious Living Mastery".

And finally, I dedicate it to all the people and companion travelers who have been present during my life's journey, including my four-legged brothers and sisters, each with their own uniqueness and energy, value and peculiar way of manifesting their essence, to which I am deeply grateful. A lot of gratitude also goes to all those who have made me grow through overcoming the obstacles they have kindly placed in my path. Without these, how could I and can I train my varied skills?

Cristina Pelizzatti, PLC, MCC

Castello Dell'Acqua, Sondrio, Italy
March, 2023

CONTENTS

1. **THE JOURNEY BEYOND**
   A Story of Self-Leadership and Resilience 1
   Psychosynthesis- the Journey Through and Beyond 4
   Being Who I Am 6
   Training Myself to be a Conscious Coach 10

2. **PSYCHOSYNTHESIS**
   Brief Introduction and Transpersonal Themes 13
   Transpersonal Psychology 17
   States and Stages of Development of Consciousness 30

3. **THE ESSENCE OF PLC**
   Psychosynthesis Life Coaching 33
   The Path Towards the Transpersonal 39
   PLC as a Transpersonal Process 46
   Accepting Vulnerability as an Opportunity for Growth 51

4. **KNOWING HOW and Knowing Why** 55
   Motivating Action 61
   Living in the Fullness of Being in the Moment 64
   The Value of the Extraordinary in the Ordinary 71

5. **PSYCHOSYNTHESIS COACHING**
   The Stages of the Process 83
   Being Who We Already Are 84
   From Personal Leadership to Transpersonal Leadership 86
   The Ideal Model for the Self 90

6. **DUKKHA: SUFFERING- A brief exploration** 97
   Realizing the Seed of Divine Intention 101

COACHING THE ESSENCE

7. **THE SCIENCE OF CONSCIOUSNESS**
   Involution and Evolution of the Psyche: the Cascade
   of Samkhya 109
   - *Being Manifest Consciousness* 123
   - *Psychoenergetics Sampler* 125
   - *Ideal Model Visualization Exercise* 128
   - *Don't Lose Sight of Your Own Spiritual Identity* 130
   - *A Kind Love which Motivates and Moves* 132
   - *The Phases of IDA* 137
   - *Paradoxically We Are Already a Self* 138

8. **KEY CONCEPTS**
   Synthesis of Maps and Concepts of Psychosynthesis 141
   - *The 10 Laws of Psychodynamics* 141
   - *The Egg Diagram- the Psychic Cell* 145
   - *What is a Subpersonality?* 148
   - *Ideal Model or Idealized?* 150
   - *Silence- the Word of the Self* 153
   - *The Neuroscience of the Psychological Functions* 157

9. **THE PSYCHOSYNTHESIS LIFE COACH (PLC)**
   Guiding the Entelechic Process 183
   - *Entering into the Void* 187
   - *The Will to Go Beyond- from Sleddog Racing to Psychosynthesis* 195
   - *The "Will to Run"* 198

10. **BEING PLC- The Self, Leader of the Process** 207
    - *Replying to My "Call of Self"* 207
    - *The Will to Want What I Want* 212
    - *Presence: "Being Flow"* 219
    - *Fantasy or Reality?* 225
    - *We are Universes on a Journey, Toward the One* 229
    - *How Do We Work with the Will in Psychosynthesis Coaching?* 231

Contents

11. **FROM DOING TO BEING**
    Embodying Awareness — 239
    What, then, is the PLC's Role? — 243
    Embodying Awareness of "Being a Self" — 249

12. **WITH THE GOAL IN THE HEART- The Blessed Joy** — 255
    From the Naradha Bhakti Sutra: Bhakti- Bliss, or Power of Love — 258
    Dutiful Joy — 270
    In Synthesis — 286

13. **ORIGINAL RESEARCH**
    Psychosynthesis and Positive Psychology Coaching — 293
    Levels of Sophistication in Strengths Coaching — 294
    The 7 Steps of Synthesis — 296
    Some Psychosynthetic Reflections, 2008-2022 — 301
    Using a Popular Strengths Assessment within the Framework of Psychosynthesis Life Coaching — 305

14. **REFLECTIONS- Experiencing Psychosynthesis** — 317
    Serena: *Awakening* — 317
        Self-Awareness — 318
        Relationships — 322
        Eyes of the Bear — 324
    Silvia: *The Cabin in the Woods, The Guiding Wolf and my Encounter with Psychosynthesis* — 329
    Clio: *The Heartbeat- A Journey in Discovery of Self* — 339
    Laura: *A Return to Self: Self-Validation and Healing through Psychosynthesis* — 343

EPILOGUE — 351

COACHING THE ESSENCE

CHAPTER 1

THE JOURNEY BEYOND
A Story of Self-Leadership and Resilience

"There are certain fundamental facts and their related conceptual elaboration, profound experience and understanding are central and constitute the sine qua non of Psychosynthetic training."
                                                            -Roberto Assagioli

"The Journey Beyond" is a central theme of my life and refers more generally to the natural course of life. The Psychosynthesis that I am about to describe here is an experience lived deeply within myself, which includes perspectives and elements from many other disciplines, beginning with the ancient, millennial Vedic Wisdom tradition which was a source of inspiration for Italian psychiatrist Roberto Assagioli M.D., the founder of Psychosynthesis. My work is guided by his belief that "the only limit of Psychosynthesis is it has no limits", and adheres to an essential criterion- to maintain rigor and scientific discipline, any innovation or development must further the realization of Self. Every single technique that I use with my clients or that I teach my students has been tested on me first, time and time again.

Going Beyond is the continuous pathway onward, towards something that attracts, and in the process learning from obstacles in order to bring into play one's aptitudes and abilities to overcome them and grow stronger.

But how are we equipped to make this movement? Do we

look back as we go forward? Are we stuck in the present and is this the only reality we focus on as we inevitably have to move forward? Or do we focus on the future as we move forward, drawing on the past as a resource while staying steadfast in the present?

The simple passage of time and its effects mean we are constantly moving forward, towards a destination which is often only vaguely defined but needs to be clarified. One of the key elements which runs through the ICF Core Competences, especially Core Competency No. 3, is that if at the beginning of the coaching process there are unclear or ambiguous definitions, topics or objectives, as a coach we have to explore until the ambiguity is resolved.

Essentially, we're going "Beyond" in a journey that both the coach and the coachee are taking, moving constantly forward in the session towards the goal, with the objective of achieving a clear result.

There can be no ambiguity.

But how do we know that the goal has been truly clarified, to the point where the mists have lifted and the summit is there in all its beauty, waiting to be reached? It is a task that requires a great deal of preparation and rigor on the part of the coach, who is about to accompany another human being on the path to his or her goal, traversing his or her own inner territories, moving toward the heights which lead to his or her own more profound awareness.

There is a movement forward towards the goal through a process of inner discovery that both coach and coachee are involved in undertaking.

As human beings, we are inevitably moving forward in the larger context of life, as well as in coaching, but the question is what are we really moving towards and how?

The destination or outcome of the session is not always clearly defined, just as achieving the goal does not always guarantee the desired satisfaction.

By viewing the coaching process as a forward movement and

1- The Journey Beyond

as an ebb and flow in the context of a journey beyond one's limiting beliefs, then the forward movement takes shape and meaning.

We have a space to cover and a destination to reach in a specific period of time that flows together with our clients in the session. We want to get to the end of the session in a partnership founded on a positive attitude which maximizes efficiency and performance, actualizing the client's potential to be brought into responsible and ecological action. At the end of a successful session, something will have changed in the way the client perceives themself. They will be different from the person who entered coaching, as they will have realized more about themself and their abilities. They will have reached the awareness of being much more than they thought they were when they started the coaching journey. The client will have learned that in order to be authentically themself they need to be so in their entirety, thanks to the empathic acceptance of their own vulnerability related to their inner multiplicity. This multiplicity is also an immeasurable resource of potential the masterful management of which is necessary to achieve any joyful result, the outcome of which is being oneself completely. Being authentically oneself by showing oneself masterfully through the multiplicity, according to time, space and circumstance.

It's not exactly a walk in the park. It is a journey forward, towards a significant achievement, and we want to get to the end of the journey successfully, having shared with clients this progress towards their desired goal, honoring and celebrating this achievement, both for reaching the destination and for having the willingness to explore more about themselves, putting themselves "out there" sincerely.

From a psychosynthetic point of view, the frame of reference from which I operate, the "Journey Beyond" is the fascinating and complex path towards Self-realization, the realization of one's essential True Nature, the Self, immersed in the multiplicity of our psyche through Its reflection, the "I" or personal self.

Psychosynthesis, or "synthesis of the psyche" is the process of transforming our inner multiplicity into the essential Oneness that furthers our spiritual and physical evolution: attaining and moving beyond Personal Leadership to Transpersonal Leadership, through the creation of a synthetic Ideal Model that facilitates the emergence of the Self in action.

"Truth: Truth is not received, but conquered, realized. We must render acts worthy of it. If we could fully realize Truth, the Eternal Wonder, Holy Truth, which is the essence of all things and all beings, we will be transformed, regenerated. Truth is the good, the perfection behind the whole id model ....Abiding in Truth"

— Roberto Assagioli

Psychosynthesis: the Journey Through and Beyond

"Life as a work of art. Emphasizing the artistic element in inner work. Creating ourselves. Sculpting ourselves. Develop"

— Roberto Assagioli

Elio Pelizzatti: "Gabbiano" (1975)

It was love at first sight. His fascination to this day remains a mystery to me, our relationship is sincere and not always easy, sometimes I've tried to take a break from it, but then I find myself always returning. I have often wondered what it is about the core of Psychosynthesis that exerts such magnetism on me. Why is it so important for me to continue on this path? What in it

1- The Journey Beyond

motivates me, despite the fatigue and isolation I sometimes feel? If something stronger, something greater that I cannot clearly define, overwhelmingly defines my life today, there must be a why, and if that why exists, then it is worth finding.

I do not have an answer, only many, many questions. I have learned to use them for a noble purpose, to help those like me at some point in their lives who have found themselves groping in the dark or making difficult and decisive choices in their existence. I use questions as a powerful transformational tool, a stimulus to search beyond the surface to the vital, pulsating core that keeps one alive. A powerful question is vital and wields power.

A professional coach knows how to ask the right questions at the right time to stimulate his or her client to overcome obstacles, tapping into his or her inner resources to see beyond and learn more about himself or herself, thanks to the valuable collaboration between two human beings.

In the Millennial Vedic Tradition, the Master accepts the disciple only when the disciple is able to ask the ideal questions. An ideal question is powerful and vital. From this perspective, the Master is the client and the disciple is the coach, who asks the ideal questions of the client, such that the present and powerful, often latent Essence emerges.

The examples and tools you will find in this book are the result of years of study and passionate work that I still do in the field of professional help using a transpersonal, Essence-centered approach through Psychosynthesis applied to counseling and coaching.

Among the fundamental fields in which Psychosynthesis operates are personal integration and actualization. The realization of our own highest potentials is the area I have been involved in for many years: in my younger days through the competitive sport of sleddog racing, then, since 2008, through Psychosynthesis counseling and since 2015 through Psychosynthesis coaching.

Coaching is for me the "Master Way to Self-Realization," and through Psychosynthesis this way has found its Essence, placing me at the service of people who wish to realize themselves. My "mission" is to make coaching an Art for the manifestation of intrinsic Beauty through the use of questions that provoke a ripple effect in the client's mental field, catalyzing critical thinking in the sedimented pattern of beliefs about oneself, facilitating the emergence from the heart of a creative and stimulating reflection, to be actualized with an Ideal Model for the Self.

Being Who I Am

"The art of living" is "living as an art" <u>Develop</u>
- Roberto Assagioli

I'm Cristina, Psychosynthesis Coach.

"Being and Doing" find synthesis in who I am. Through me, an Ideal Model that I have built piece by piece along my life, that of the coach, has shaped a self-image aligned with my feeling, through which I can do what I love and love what I do. A dynamic and synthetic model that has many facets and evolves over time, without changing the center around which the dynamism takes place.

In this book I'm sharing with you my reflections on Psychosynthesis and coaching applied to Psychosynthesis, going through my own experience and perspective, sharing this journey together with others who, like me, have found in Psychosynthesis the ideal synthesis of their own inner realm, unifying Being and Doing through the methodology of coaching applied to Self-realization.

Strictly adhering to what Roberto Assagioli left us as a legacy, the seven psychosynthetic cornerstones as existential facts are always present in my work and life.

They are dynamic, taking strongly into account the "multidimensionality" of the human personality and maintaining awareness of the chronic inner conflict which exists in all of us due to the latent energies related to each psychic content and

1- The Journey Beyond

self-image, each of which demands the satisfaction of specific primary needs for their survival.

In my youthful years spent walking, climbing, skiing, practicing the competitive sport of sleddog racing, and deeply loving my Valtellina mountains, I learned so much about myself and my abilities as I faced my limits. I learned that every achievement is strenuous, and that once you reach a peak and contemplate the vastness that unfolds from that perspective, then you have to descend and return to the valley. That "downsizing" was the recurring gift I carried with me as I returned to the valley after each ascent, and I realized that once I conquered a peak or a podium, another challenge, another conquest to be made was already there waiting for me.

Step by step I was walking more and more within myself, with the peak in front and the goal in my heart. Always going Beyond, exceeding my limits, but without losing sight of the guidelines and fundamental distinctions that Assagioli set in Psychosynthesis, starting from the principle that he himself emphasizes in his writings: maps are not a finite but approximate representation of a territory that is the inner nature of the human being, plastic, complex, elusive, fed by a complexity that if not modulated, produces confusion and undesirable results.

A climb without flights of fancy to the peaks of one's personality, traversing a territory that must be approached with the right equipment and preparation, together with an experienced guide who knows the terrain and is equipped to deal with obstacles along the way. Together traversing territory that leads step by step to the coveted summit, which once reached, adds to one's ability to tackle further, possibly more difficult ascents, and then descending back into the personality with a transformed awareness, with new talents to apply in daily life.

In short, I would say a path of Active Resilience, built by going toward desired goals, going beyond one's limits by recognizing the opportunities presented by and surmounting the inevitable obstacles, putting into play and training one's skills, acquiring others, and then going Beyond.

Beyond the limits of personality exists the dimension of

COACHING THE ESSENCE

Being, the dimension of the Self, the transpersonal dimension that underlies and provides a foundation for the personality. Achieving awareness of the existential reality within us, of this subtle, a-temporal, a-spatial dimension, leads to an ability to tap into the highest potentials, qualities, values and energies emanating directly from the Source, the Self, and knowing how to responsibly bring these transpersonal energies into practical action, in daily life.

Assagioli defines this achievement as Self-realization, an arduous, coveted, strenuous, and forever transformative path from which to live one's existence by drawing from the Source in every moment of one's life. Self-realization is basically the attainment of the heights of our most profound awareness that puts us in touch with the intelligence of the heart, enabling us to manifest ourselves as human beings with the capacity for self-determination. I define it as "Self-Leadership"- an awareness that allows mastery over one's abilities within the various bio-psychic "layers" of Being, reaching the essential spiritual layer, the substratum at the foundation of the historical personality- as Assagioli has been defining in his Psychosynthesis for almost a century.

"Unmastered multiplicity can produce confusion, the wealth of details can hide the whole picture and prevent one from discerning the connections of the different parts and their varied meaning, function, and value."

- Roberto Assagioli

I graduated as Counselor in Psychosynthesis and Psychoenergetics in 2013, with a certificate of Professional Competence from the Italian national certifying authority AssoCounseling, subsequently reaching the highest level of Supervisor Counselor. I taught at the "GEA" Psychosynthesis Counseling School in Sondrio until 2015, when I started my studies with The Synthesis Center (Amherst, MA). I completed training as a certified Psychosynthesis Life Coach (PLC) in May, 2016, under the guidance of Dorothy Firman, Ed.D., and participated as an assistant trainer in her "Will to Grow"

1- The Journey Beyond

program for a year. Since Psychosynthesis Life Coaching was relatively unknown in Italy at the time, we teamed up to bring "The Will to Grow" to Italy, in the Italian language. This cooperation provided the foundation for Synthesis Coaching Associates' extensive portfolio of Psychosynthesis Life Coach training programs, and since then my path in Psychosynthesis has evolved from the single Italian reality, taking its own distinct direction and bringing Psychosynthesis Life Coaching into the professional structure of excellence in world coaching through the International Coaching Federation (ICF).

Elio Pelizzatti: "Pizzo Scalino" (2002)

To date Synthesis Coaching Associates (SCA) is the first and at the moment only school of Life Coaching in Psychosynthesis (PLC) accredited as an ICF Level 1 and Level 2 Coaching Education Provider, with its own unique and well-structured format. You can learn more about our work and programs here
www.synthesis-coaching.com

For details of the ICF and a definition of Coaching:
www.coachingfederation.org

COACHING THE ESSENCE

Training Myself to be a Conscious Coach

*"The **duty** of Wisdom"*

– Roberto Assagioli

Psychosynthesis has always unknowingly belonged to me.

Beginning with the artistic context in which I was born and raised by my father Elio Pelizzatti, artist and painter, Beauty through Art forged me. Nobility reflected in the essential values of which my mother Luisa carries the seeds as daughter of an ancient noble lineage- the Italian Besta family; Fascination as I walked the streets of Paris where I lived alternating between Paris and the mountains of Valtellina for over 40 years. World-class competitive sleddog racing and climbing the peaks of my Valtellina "brought me home" through deep contact with Wild Nature, and during the moments of joy as well as in the deepest desolation of my existence, I was unknowingly but inexorably training myself to be a coach.

Essentially I was walking my way step by step, drawn by a mysterious but overpowering "Calling" just as I am still doing, fully living my varied experiences, learning through action, knowing myself more and more, fine-tuning the pieces that thanks to the encounter with Psychosynthesis I was able to synthesize and bring into service through a self-image, a role that I truly feel belongs to me: the Coach.

Fate brought me to Psychosynthesis at the darkest moment of my life. In the deep darkness the Light found me and the Power of Love allowed me to be reborn to a new me and gather the essential fragments of life that restored meaning to my existence.

The resilience I'm referring to, having experienced it, is based on this Power of Love.

In a special way I love Psychosynthesis because it allows me to practice Vedic Wisdom, the ancient Science of the Spirit, in

1- The Journey Beyond

today's reality of immediate and simultaneous communication, where time becomes condensed and seems to be never enough to arrive at goals which themselves seem to be ever further from one's Self.

Carmen Lenatti: Lago Palù (Valmalenco, SO)

COACHING THE ESSENCE

CHAPTER 2

PSYCHOSYNTHESIS
Brief introduction and main themes in Transpersonal Psychology

"The Magnetic Power of Love and the Dynamic Efficiency of the Divine Want"

— Roberto Assagioli

"Transpersonal" is an "ideal" term to indicate what is gone through to then go beyond the personality, the path indicated by personal Psychosynthesis. This lays the necessary foundations for moving on to the next phase of Transpersonal Psychosynthesis, towards the towering peaks of personality where the highest qualities reside, the universal values, the latent potentials that can be brought into the field of the consciousness of the "I". By transforming the multiplicity of representations which make up the personality, the image and likeness of the intrinsic work that requires to manifest itself will emerge: an Ideal Model for the Self.

Step by step through the journey of life we can resonate with this great underlying image, sometimes glimpsing it, hearing its whisper, sometimes turning our gaze away and diverting our listening, but always feeling its effect.

As in a kaleidoscope, the changing self-images, the transient forms of roles to which we give so much importance and adherence, filter our perception and change continuously, revolving around themselves and around a pivot that cannot be seen but

COACHING THE ESSENCE

which is perceived by the effect of its force, without which there would be no movement.

This fixed point around which our transient self-images inevitably carry out their revolution remains present but latent, a potential whose essential forces are Love and Will. Bringing the latent potential to light and manifesting it into conscious action in line with the Ethical Cosmic Order (Dharma) can be likened to the process of Transpersonal Leadership, a path that leads to the unveiling of the Essential Image, composed of the nucleus of each individual superficial image, and to action grounded in one's highest potentialities related to Essence.

A process that requires two major Leadership skills: Love and Will.

```
Vorrei dormire sulle pene amare
Vorrei riposare come una foglia morta
Vorrei scendere nel profondo
e muto mare della mia anima -

Vorrei aggrapparmi a te
sull'altalena della vita,
simile ad un gioco senza inizio e
                    - senza fine

Vorrei,vorrei,vorrei chiudere gli occhi
e vedere i tuoi occhi,
la tua bocca
e la mia anima mentre ti guardo.-
```

Elio Pelizzatti: Poesia (1960). For a translation of this text, use the QR code:

What is meant here by "Love" is not the romantic version "à la Madame Bovary", but the power of Love according to Dante in his Divine Comedy and the *Bhakti* Yoga in the Millennial Ve-

2- Psychosynthesis and Transpersonal Psychology

dic wisdom. This is the potent force that acts with motivation and intention, proceeding from the depths to the heights, from object to subject, in many different forms. Love as the engine of action, a driving force that with a masterful design makes the sun and the other stars revolve around a central point, and within ourselves is a process that leads to positioning at the center of oneself, in the "I" rooted in the Self, in the flow through the here and now, governing our inner dynamics at will. Through the repeated use of an ideal image emerging from the synthesis of the essential qualities of multiplicity, realignment with the Source takes place. At this point the "I" can finally re-position itself in the pure Volitional Awareness to which it ontologically belongs, using the multiplicity, the subpersonalities at will as allies aligned with its essential values, purpose, and meaning, to achieve the desired destination in line with destiny.

In Psychosynthesis coaching, the coach positions themself in the pure Consciousness of the Self, through an Ideal Model for the Self in the moment, whose bridge is the personal "I" which has a mission to achieve: realizing itself, i.e. attaining the realization of Being already a Self, in expression through a certain personality, composed of a chronically conflicting multiplicity. The Ideal Model is an essential instrument and one of the seven psychosynthetic cornerstones, an evolving image, ideal for awakening us to the awareness of "Who" we already are. As Assagioli underlines, The Ideal Model is an experiential fact.

The Self is not a result to be achieved, but the realization of already Being that Self.

From the standpoint of Psychosynthesis the process of Personal Leadership becomes the actualization of the Self by the "I", its reflection immersed in the personality. To be a "Leader" means to attain the realization that each chosen action has the potential to manifest the Self through the reconnection of each subpersonality present in the personal self's field of consciousness at a given moment with its essential purpose, positioning it in the service of the "I" as a resource through its nuclear energetic quality. The shift of subpersonalities from obstacles to resources occurs when the "I" can dis-identify from

COACHING THE ESSENCE

them, balancing the two ontological forces of the Self: Love and Will.

Balancing Love and Will requires practice and effective techniques to develop awareness and maintain the psychological distance from the inner dynamics of which we are bearers. The antidote used in Psychosynthesis Life Coaching as a primary coaching skill to bring out the Self is disidentification. This is a constant process rather than a technique, which enables the balance of the two ontological forces of Love and Will in the process of obtaining a psychological distance from the mental field, the system represented by the Egg Diagram, one of the primary maps in Psychosynthesis which we'll see later in more detail:

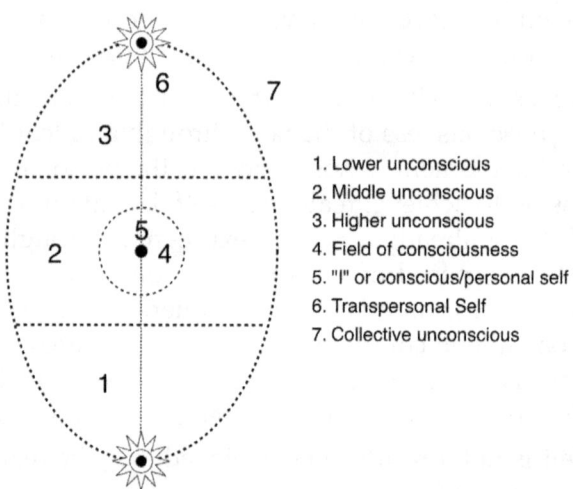

1. Lower unconscious
2. Middle unconscious
3. Higher unconscious
4. Field of consciousness
5. "I" or conscious/personal self
6. Transpersonal Self
7. Collective unconscious

Graphic: Synthesis Coaching Associates

From this positioning, it is possible to observe the larger picture from a different and higher, holistic perspective: the view from the Self. From here an ideal action plan through the "I" can be brought out which allows us to arrive at an ecological, sustainable result starting from ourselves: the action par excellence that brings transpersonal energies into manifestation, procuring as a "side effect" lasting satisfaction and a profound sense of self-esteem, ultimately "Joy".

This awakening provides the basic foundation for a personality more solidly rooted in the "I", the directing agent of the

2- Psychosynthesis and Transpersonal Psychology

transient and impermanent self-images residing in the personality, and for the next step of Transpersonal Psychosynthesis. This step enables access to the highest dimensions of the psyche, where the qualities and potentials of the Self reside with a higher energy valence.

Knowing how to access these highest dimensions and how responsibly to bring them into manifestation through the "I" requires the primary and basic competence of managing one's inner resources, a personality, and mindset built around a realistic and viable Ideal Model. This model is synthetic and non-static, in constant evolution, forming a bridge between the "I" and the Self: an Ideal Model for the Self that is a driver of Leadership at the Transpersonal level.

<u>The seven key concepts in Psychosynthesis</u>

From the notes dictated in English by Assagioli in 1974 in the essay on Psychosynthesis training entitled "Training", here are the seven cornerstones or fundamental factors:

- disidentification
- the personal self
- the will (good, strong, skillful)
- the ideal model
- synthesis (in its various aspects)
- the superconscious
- the transpersonal Self

Transpersonal Psychology

"We must bring together 'all that we are now' to facilitate the path to all that we 'can become' in the future <u>if we want to</u>"
- Roberto Assagioli

Transpersonal Psychology deals with the study of higher human potentials through a methodology that integrates science with the study of ancient spiritual traditions, validating non-ordinary states of consciousness, states, and stages of awareness, spiritual emergence, the study of transpersonal experiences, and related phenomena. It also deals with disturbances which are understood as states of discomfort of the personal self due to the unawareness of one's True Ontological Nature, and a perception of not being in line with one's Essence, the Self.

Through studies of the states and stages of consciousness Transpersonal Psychology offers a scientific approach to spirituality, a synthesis of science and ancient wisdom, creating a bridge between the millenary traditions of wisdom and modern science. It is a spiritual science that studies the "Ultimate Reality" by experiencing what Psychosynthesis terms the *"recognition, acceptance, traverse, integration and going beyond the masks of the personality"*, highlighting and activating human potentials in line with one's essence, the Self.

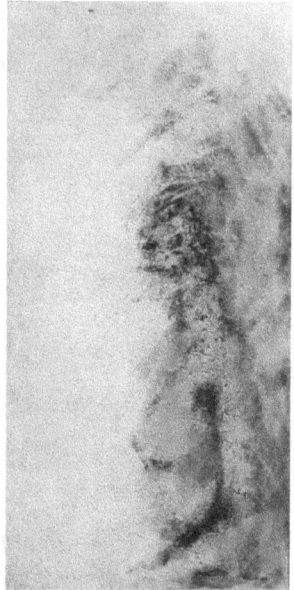

Elio Pelizzatti: "Figure of a Woman" (1960)

Transpersonal Psychology invites a pluralistic and integrated approach. It researches and strives for integration between psychological principles and methods and spiritual, shamanic, and ritual practices. It is a study of the mind and the tools for its

2- Psychosynthesis and Transpersonal Psychology

transcendence, reaching the boundaries of the "I" encapsulated in a psycho-physical manifestation and then going beyond, toward the Source. Transpersonal psychology is phenomenological, inclusive, and optimistic.

The term transpersonal literally means "beyond the mask". It refers to transcendance of the personal self, evolution of a sense of identity which is mostly separated from the Source to one that is deeper, broader, higher, more inclusive, and unified with a more comprehensive Whole.

The core concept in transpersonal psychology is oneness or nonduality: the awareness that each part or the whole person is fundamentally and ultimately a part of a higher and vast whole. Transpersonal psychology is a field of inquiry which includes theory, research, and practice, providing insights and applications based on research and experience, utilizing methodologies for evaluating and confirming or disconfirming its results.

Founded by Roberto Assagioli in the early 1900s, Psychosynthesis may be considered a forerunner of transpersonal psychology. Growing interest in the psychological implications of Buddhism, Yoga, shamanism, psychedelic states, and holistic medicine fueled its development. Transpersonal studies are arising in a number of fields, including medicine, education, anthropology, and organizational development. There are strong interconnections between transpersonal psychology, ecopsychology, and deep ecology.

Transpersonal psychology involves study of the mind and its transcendence, up to the boundaries of the "I" encapsulated in a psychophysical manifestation and then beyond, towards its Source. Among only a few others, for more than a century Psychosynthesis can be considered a precursor of this psychological discipline, as is the Millennial Vedic Wisdom tradition from time immemorial.

Consciousness is the focus of research in the transpersonal field, not as a result of the mental process but as the foundation and engine of it. This represents a shift in point of observation and paradigm from Western thought: the observer is the subject observing the field of action, as masterfully described millennia ago in the Vedic Tradition and particularly in Patanjali's *Yoga Sutras*, the *Upaniṣhad*, the *Puranas* and the *Bhagavad-Gītā*.

In the Millennial Vedic Tradition the transpersonal state or the achievement of the awareness of Being a Self corresponds to the Self-realization postulated by Psychosynthesis: the awareness of the existence of pure spiritual energy that manifests itself through the "I" immersed in the psyche, possessing the ability to experience the objective world thanks to the psycho-physical tools, the psychological functions used by the subpersonalities with which it identifies.

This state of consciousness is referred to as *Caturtha, Turia* or *Quarto*, pure awareness, paradoxically absolute while at the same time relative.

Psychosynthesis defines the "I" as the reflection of the Self in the personality, pure awareness and will, free from contents, whose realignment or positioning in the Presence of the Self depends on the awareness available at any given moment of one's ontological identity, the Original Image.

This state of Being in one's ontological awareness, the Presence we aim for in Psychosynthesis, is realized during the journey toward the Self. This occurs once one recognizes, accepts, traverses and supersedes the limitations inherent in personality-related psychic contents, achieving the awareness of already being a Self in manifestation through its image reflected in the personality, the "I", which is in turn acted upon by its sub-agents, the subpersonalities, impermanent and transitory self-images associated with objective reality.

These psychic contents, the subpersonalities, distort the "I" from its path towards the Source, diverting it towards the satisfaction of their primary needs, binding the "I" to impermanent reality. An imprisonment that results in the perception of suffering.

This "dynamic and magnetic game" of self-images (subpersonalities) belonging to objective reality that takes place in space-time, causes a shift of the "I-Self" axis towards the "I-self-image" axis. This shift is caused by the attraction exerted by the subpersonalities on the "I" as described in the "Ten Laws

2- Psychosynthesis and Transpersonal Psychology

of Psychodynamics" defined by Assagioli in *The Act of Will*, one of the major texts in Psychosynthesis and a masterful coaching manual.

Due to the ignorance of one's True Nature, defined in the Vedas as the state of *Avidyā*, the "I" unconsciously identifies most of the time with the variegated impermanent self-images, following their ends which are driven by their primary needs that demand satisfaction as also defined in the Ten Psychological Laws. The result is the subject moves mainly in the objective dimension of doing, which has as its objective the impermanent, transitory state of happiness that does not find fulfillment.

Psychosynthesis can be described essentially as an educational path of self-awareness that aims at Leadership from the Self, a positioning that leads to the power to govern one's inner world made up of multiple chronically conflicting parts, each with a specific mission to fulfill that is linked to the laws of the physical world to which they belong, the first of which is survival.

The personal interest connected with the goal that brings a person into coaching moves from the inside out in an unconscious way, with motivation to act on the choice of walking the path to achieve it. This unconscious motivational drive stems both from the desire of one or more superficial self-images (subpersonalities) to satisfy a particular need as well as from the "I"'s unconscious drive to access a higher level of meaning and purpose through adherence to values that increasingly coincide with one's existential vocation.

The path to achieving a goal is ultimately rooted in the need to understand and integrate at ever-increasing levels that which we do not know but from which comes the unconscious desire (the motive) to bring into manifestation, through concrete, meaningful and positive action, that image emerging among the many. This image, represented in Psychosynthesis by concept of the Ideal Model, is more authentic and allows one to reflect one's Source, made in the likeness of the Self.

An Ideal Model for the Self is built step by step, synthesizing the past in the present, in order to enable the future to emerge which calls for its manifestation in the here and now.

COACHING THE ESSENCE

The Ideal Model is a winning self-image, designed in detail and chosen to be worn acting as if you already are this model. It condenses past, present and future into an idea-force made up of a dynamic balance of contrasting, sometimes opposing tendencies, having an attractive flux that draws its energy from the dynamic tension between the parts. In this interplay of forces, the integrity of the Essence is preserved and manifested through the interacting multiplicity of the energetic nucleus present in each pole.

I define this dynamic model *Syntegrity*: the integrity of the Essence emerges through the synthesis of multiple divergent forces, in an image that resonates energetically with the energy of the Self and which has the purpose of acting as an Ideal Model, so that the "I" enters into resonance with the Self. An Ideal Model that uses contrasting forces with an evolutionary intention, which exerts a attraction on the "I", with intensity (governance of the personality) and direction (tension towards the Self) thereby facilitating the emergence of the Self and subsequently manifesting it in ecological and sustainable actions starting within the inner system.

"Syntegrity"- W. Burr/C. Pelizzatti

"Tension is the Great Integrity"
- R. Buckminster Fuller

Generally the Ideal Model, one of the seven key concepts of Psychosynthesis, is defined as "of the 'I' or of the Self". Personally, from my experience I prefer to call it <u>the Ideal Model "for</u>

2- Psychosynthesis and Transpersonal Psychology

the 'I' or for the Self", simply because the Self belongs to the transcendent dimension and cannot be represented with a single, static, defined image. This image can instead be applied to the "I" immersed in the personality which, while evolving in awareness, transforms the various superficial self-images into a single image that synthesizes them and that can best represent the ideal instrument for manifesting the Self at any given moment and context.

This synthesis is in a state of constant dynamism, evolving, revealing through each experience in which the interacting self-images appear and disappear, the Essence that underlies everything.

The Self remains unmanifested, unmoving, unchanging, ontological, belonging to the transpersonal dimension, intrinsically satisfied, beyond the objective historical personality. Its counterpart, the "I" or personal self, a subjective reality encapsulated in an objective bio-psychic form, becomes increasingly manifest in its authenticity when, consciously and through the disidentified state, it chooses to wear at will an Ideal Model in order to facilitate the representation of the Essence in the moment.

Once identified, this Ideal Model must be updated through a detailed and ongoing project, and consciously manifested through the rigorous methodology which Psychosynthesis provides.

The first step consists of Personal Psychosynthesis: getting to know one's personality and its components, overcoming the limitations of beliefs related to superficial self-images, unveiling the positive intention that is to be subsequently integrated into the "I" so that in its role as "Director" it puts the potentials of multiplicity into action toward the goal, while harmonizing the personality and empowering itself through their synthesis.

From this dynamic synthesis emerge the necessary skills for the next step of Transpersonal Psychosynthesis, a passage that takes the subject's awareness to the higher levels of the psyche, into the realm of subtle energies emanating from the Self in the higher unconscious or superconscious. This region, absent from most psychological theory of the time, was introduced by Psychosynthesis in the early 1900s.

COACHING THE ESSENCE

At this superconscious level, the image that emerges as a role model to be acted upon consists of the essence of the positive qualities synthesized earlier and now empowered by the luminous energies of the Self. The empowerment of the "I" at this level goes beyond the limits of the objective dimension, drawing directly from the Source, the Essential Subjective Reality.

The human/Cosmos relationship is at the heart of Transpersonal Psychology and takes into account the evolutionary potential of non-ordinary states of consciousness: rather than being cataloged exclusively as pathological, transpersonal experiences are studied with psychological and scientific rigour. The objective is to affirm the validity and truthfulness of what exists beyond manifest reality, with particular emphasis on the here and now, the field of infinite possibilities and the direct experience of non-ordinary states of consciousness.

I like to define the field of Transpersonal Psychology research as the "web consciousness", defined in detail thousands of years ago by Vedic science. In the *Māṇḍūkya Upaniṣad*, to name one, the states of consciousness that I have previously referred to and more specifically as waking, dreamless sleep, deep sleep, *Turiya/Quarto* or pure Consciousness, are defined in detail.

"The fourth aspect of the Atman or Self is Turiya, literally the Fourth. In this fourth state, consciousness is neither turned outward nor inward. Nor is it both outward and inward; it is beyond cognition and the absence of cognition. This fourth state cannot be experienced through the senses or known by comparison, deductive reasoning, or inference; it is indescribable, incomprehensible and unthinkable with the mind. This is pure consciousness. This is the true Self. It is the cessation of all phenomena. It is serene, tranquil, full of bliss, and it is one without seconds. This is the true Self that is to be realized"

- Māṇḍūkya Upaniṣad, 7

The subtle boundaries that isolate the "I" from the awareness of Being a Self embodied and encapsulated in the psyche, are constituted and represented by the psychic contents with which the "I" unconsciously and incessantly identifies itself. Due to the unconscious identification with subpersonalities, the energies

2- Psychosynthesis and Transpersonal Psychology

coming from the transpersonal region of the psyche are distorted from evolutionary to selfish ends, or for the satisfaction of the needs related to the "I" unconsciously identified with subpersonalities- better known as ego.

Due to the attraction exerted by each psychic content which takes the form of a partial, superficial self-image aimed at a precise objective relating to a primary need, the conditioned "I" solidifies its roots in manifest reality, thinking that it is whatever shape or identification that provides a certain sense of identity in a given moment, tying itself to the pursuit of satisfaction and happiness by following objective needs, basically deviating from the Joy which is its essential birthright.

Millennia ago the Vedas confirmed that we are, in our Essence, composed of Conscious Awareness and Bliss. In Psychosynthesis, Joy is the barometer of Presence or alignment with the Self. The more we perceive this state of consciousness, the more we are in touch with our core, our essential nature.

Each self-image, or subpersonality as defined by Psychosynthesis since the early 1900s, is both limiting and empowering. When the "I" is not aware of the presence and exercise of power by a subpersonality, it is dominated by it, limited and confined to an idealized self-image or model that can divert or block the passage of transpersonal energies. These are hijacked by the subpersonality for its own use, for its own purposes and objectives. This can occur even against the will of the "I", as confirmed by the Laws of Psychodynamics described by Assagioli in his landmark treatise *The Act of Will*, in particular, the eighth:

"All the various functions, and their multiple combinations in complexes and sub-personalities, set in motion the realization of their aims outside of our consciousness, and independently of, and even against, our will."

- Roberto Assagioli

From the perspective of Psychoenergetics, defined as the fifth force of psychology by Roberto Assagioli in the early 1900s, the inner and outer dynamics are energetic interactions at various levels of manifestation. The Self, purely spiritual, transpersonal

COACHING THE ESSENCE

energy, radiates Its energies in the material-objective dimension. We come into contact with It and experience It through the "I" which is immersed in the personality, composed of a condensed or collapsed energy in the subpersonalities, multiple evanescent and overbearing forms, and in a particular mental system or psychic field, represented by the Egg Diagram or Map of the Psyche, as we will see later.

If we do not have a clear understanding of this passage, it will remain difficult to understand the various psychosynthetic key points that mark the evolutionary and iterative process of the journey of Self-realization, beginning with the "I", expanding the boundaries limiting its field of awareness, limits derived from the active presence of self-images with which the "I" constantly unconsciously identifies.

This process is masterfully defined thousands of years ago in the Vedas, in particular in the *Samkhya* "Involutionary Cascade of Consciousness" and the subsequent phase of the "Evolutionary Cascade of Consciousness" which I will refer to in more detail in Chapter 7: how Consciousness passes from the unmanifest state to manifestation, proceeding through Self-Realization.

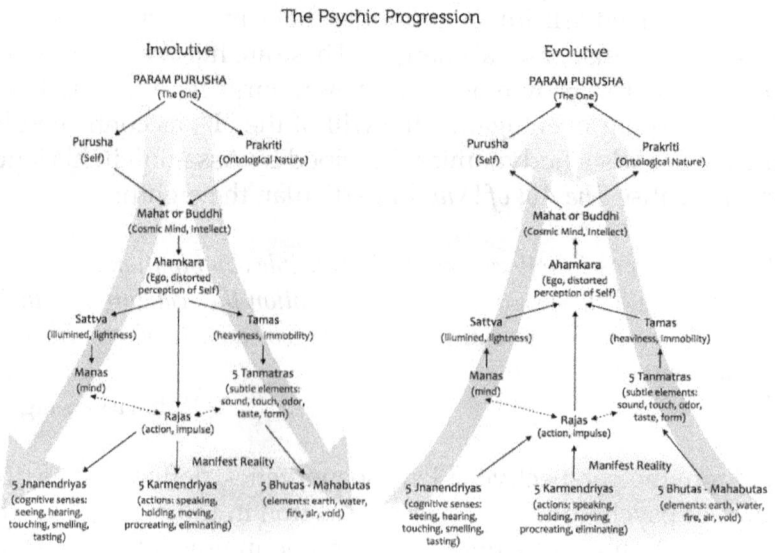

Graphic: W. Burr

2- Psychosynthesis and Transpersonal Psychology

The process that leads to Self-realization is the essence and the heart of Psychosynthesis: becoming more and more ourselves as we act in life: whatever the direction, the goal is always "One", to become who we essentially are already- an observing consciousness, according to Patanjali's *Yoga Sutras*, which knows itself through the use of the mind, when the exploration of the vast world of Being passes through the awareness of Being Consciousness.

The Millennial Vedic Tradition places the Self in the metaspace of the heart and it is in the heart chakra that we perceive the correspondence between consciousness and states of being. This understanding takes place through symbolic images, where each image contains within it qualities of consciousness and qualities of the notion of the world, which together make up perception. This "intelligence of the imagination" resides in the heart, as James Hillman also states in his book *The World Soul and the Intelligence of the Heart*:

"The expression -intelligence of the heart- connotes the act of knowing and loving simultaneously by means of imaginary help."

- J. Hillman

"My friends, sons of asuras, know that the Supreme Personality of Godhead is always present as the Supreme Soul in the hearts of all living entities. Verily He is everyone's benefactor and most sincere friend and it is never at all difficult to worship Him. Why, then, do people not engage in devotional service to him? Why is she so attached to producing all sorts of artificial objects, meant for sense gratification?"

- Śrimad-Bhāgavatam, 7,7,38

It is through the subtle sense organs, the <u>Psychological Functions</u> represented by Assagioli's Star Diagram, that each self-image comes into contact with the external objective world through the "I". This contact renders the experience subjective, generating an awareness separate from ontological reality, reinforced throughout the experiences of life and creating a sense of personality that seems solid, but actually consists of a manifold representation of superficial, impermanent and ever-changing self-images.

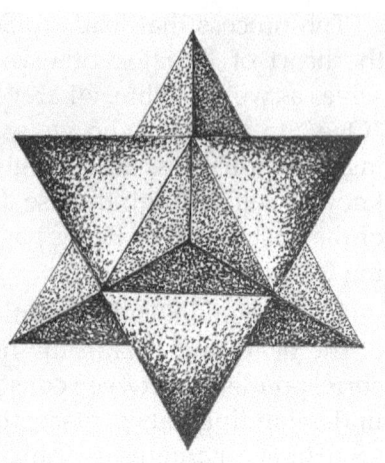

The multiplicity is composed of the subpersonalities within the true essential identity, which consequently ends up lying latent in the unconscious, due to the attraction exerted by the self-images with which the "I" mostly unconsciously identifies itself, binding the subject to the dimension of doing, and veiling, even to the point of precluding, the awareness of the dimension of Being.

Carmen Lenatti: "Stella" (2010)

A subpersonality with specific goals and powers binds the subject to manifest reality; when worn repeatedly it is defined as dominant or the most mature. The subject defines himself as: "I am an artist, an architect, a teacher, a worker, a peasant woman, I'm rich, I'm poor, etc.".

It is as if the "I" implodes into a single self-image that defines all of its relative identity, encapsulating itself in a specific mental set-up, functioning one-way- using the psychological functions only through the lens of that subpersonality. Behavior is conditioned to beliefs that feed on that mental attitude: a superficial subpersonality or self-image metaphorically resembles an Ouroboros or infinite loop.

"Om! In this city of Brahman, there is an abode, a small lotus flower. There is a small space inside it. What is found in this small space is what must be sought, what must be aspired to understand."

"That does not age with old age and does not die if the body is killed. This is the real city of Brahman, which contains all desires. This is the Self, free from evil, old age, death, pain, hunger, and thirst. His desire for him is the truth, what he conceives is the truth."

2- Psychosynthesis and Transpersonal Psychology

"Those who leave here without having found the Self and the desire for truth, for them, in all worlds, there is no freedom. But those who go hence having found the Self and the desire for truth, there is freedom for them in all the worlds."
- Bṛhadāraṇyaka Upaniṣad 8.1.74-75

The Self is the resource to draw on: the daily contact with its energies takes place through a volitional act. The Self that incarnates is very vulnerable, it is not vulnerable in its Essence but in its manifestation in the field of consciousness, the "I", since, due to unconscious identification, the "I" is subject to the dynamics of subpersonalities.

"A skilled geologist can figure out where the gold is and by various methods can extract the gold from the ore that contains it. Similarly, a spiritually elevated person can understand that the spiritual fragment exists in the body and that by cultivating spiritual knowledge, it is possible to achieve perfection in spiritual life. But as the person who is not skilled cannot understand where the gold is, so the fool who has not cultivated spiritual knowledge cannot understand that the spirit exists within the body."
- Śrimad-Bhāgavatam, 7,7,21

In Psychosynthesis coaching the attitude of the coach is inclusive and synthetic, present moment by moment from the coach's Self to the client's Self, through a transcendental relationship in which the awareness of one's True Nature is grounded and encapsulated in the personality.

The awakening of one's essential reality, that of already being a Self that experiences Itself through the "I", immersed in a bio-psychic reality, is forever transformational at the transpersonal level. At that stage, the subject tends to manifest its essential purpose (of life) with ecological and sustainable, significant and positive actions, in line with its Essence.

Following is a definition of Transpersonal Psychology that I encountered in my studies at Naropa University (CO-USA) in 2013 in Transpersonal Ecopsychology, with Prof. J. Davis:

COACHING THE ESSENCE

"Transpersonal psychology stands at the interface of psychology and the spiritual disciplines. It builds on other psychological perspectives which it generally sees as useful but incomplete and limited. Thus, it is inclusive of other psychological approaches, culturally diverse wisdom about psychopathology and mental health, and various states of consciousness. Transpersonal psychology is not a set of beliefs, a dogma, or a religion, but an attempt to bring a full range of human experiences into the discourse of psychology. Transpersonal psychology focuses on self-transcendence and mystical states of consciousness as they are understood within a psychological framework." (Davis, 1999).

Moreover:

"Many definitions define transpersonal psychology in terms of the study of altered states of consciousness (see Lajoie & Shapiro, 1992). Probably most transpersonalists would agree that altered states are important, but they do not necessarily define the field... Other definitions assume the field is centrally concerned with psychological health and well-being (Hutchins. 1987; Walsh & Vaughan, 1980)." (Walsh and Vaughan, 1993).

In the Vedas:

"Where there is duality, we see the other, smell the other, hear the other, talk to the other, think of the other, understand the other; but when all has dissolved in the Self, how and who can we smell? how and who can we see? how and to whom can we talk? how and of whom can we think? how and who can we understand? how is it possible to understand that through which everything is understood? how is it possible to understand the One who understands?"

- Bṛhadāraṇyaka Upaniṣad 2.4.28

"Two birds with light-colored wings, intertwined with bonds of friendship, perch on the same tree. One of the two eats the sweet figs; the other who doesn't eat keeps watch. Where those beautiful birds ceaselessly sing their share of eternal life, and the sacred synods, There is the mighty Keeper of the Universe, who, wise, has entered me in my simplicity. The tree on which the beautiful birds eat the

2- Psychosynthesis and Transpersonal Psychology

sweetness, where all rest and procreate their offspring; On its summit they say that the figs are very sweet, whoever does not know the Father will not attain it."

- Rigveda 1.164.20 - 1.164.22

States and Stages of Development of Consciousness

"Daily life is a constant testing and training"
- Roberto Assagioli

In the field of Transpersonal psychology, a distinction is made between States and Stages of development of consciousness.

The American psychologist Frances Vaughan, Ph.D. provided further perspective on Context, Content, and Process.

Context: Looking at these three elements in the context of coaching, the transpersonal context implies that the experienced professional coach in this field is aware of the centrality of consciousness to the successful outcome of coaching. In the transpersonal view, consciousness itself is both the subject and object of change and the instrument of the process.

The experienced coach in this field operates in the knowledge that it is the client who learns how to solve the obstacle to achieving their goal (the contingent situation) meanwhile both the coach and the coachee move toward their ideal future. In contrast, solving a particular situation for the client means to deprive them of the process of learning and evolution in consciousness as well as the assumption of responsibility for the action taken.

The transpersonal approach of Psychosynthesis Life Coaching (PLC) enables people to draw on their highest inner resources rather than expecting the solution to be provided perhaps by the coach or somebody else or limiting themselves to drawing on resources related to the personal dimension.

As Assagioli says, we have a vast, immense potential energy reservoir in our unconscious that we do not use because we are

COACHING THE ESSENCE

not aware of it, or possibly we limit ourselves to grasping the smallest part of it, the one of which we are aware through the filters of perception linked to the subpersonality that dominates at the moment the field of consciousness of the "I".

Going beyond, into the superconscious region of the psyche and returning to the here and now, in the middle unconscious, actualizing through the "I" realization of the transpersonal potentials related to the energies of the Self is the uniqueness that the Psychosynthesis approach has been providing for over a century. This methodology finds synthesis and effectiveness in coaching, to act in line with Self-realization, the Yoga of Action defined in the Vedas.

Content: any experience in which the individual transcends the limits of exclusive identification with the personality encapsulated in the body-psyche form; mystical, archetypal, and symbolic realms of deep psychological experiences (in non-ordinary states of consciousness) that procure well-being and healing, and are valuable for evolutionary development in consciousness.

Process: contemplates specific methods, techniques, and practices applicable in the field of action in the relationship of helping the person to facilitate conscious access to the transpersonal dimension.

CHAPTER 3

THE ESSENCE OF PLC
Psychosynthesis Life Coaching

"One does not give a man wings by casting off his chains"
— Roberto Assagioli

To be a Life Coach is to one who has made the professional and personal choice to serve others as a trainer in key areas of life, becoming a living example using inner strengths and resources to face difficulties with a positive attitude. Life experiences are a gym where we train our existing talents and acquire new ones, providing a great opportunity to both learn and grow and nourish our resilience.

Inevitably there will be times when your motivation as a coach is weak, you just won't feel strong enough to provide for someone who comes to coaching needing our support.

There will be times when clients bring topics with them that resonate with their life issues. You'll feel the urge just to say 'No, I can't help here! How can I train a person to support their psychic baggage when I struggle to support myself?'

For me, the beauty of being a Psychosynthesis Life Coach (PLC) emerges especially in these challenging times. At these junctures, I, in turn, get support from my supervisor as an external resource and simultaneously bring myself within myself, into the inner resourceful center of wisdom and power, my Self.

As a PLC I'm are aware that, as human beings, we have

immeasurable inner potentials, strengths and higher resources, waiting to be discovered and utilized.

In my role as a PLC, I'm focused on the present with an orientation toward the future, spotting the client's strengths, respectful of the purpose and life objectives the client wishes to achieve. I work together with the client to create new possibilities to realize these potentials in ecological and sustainable actions, beginning with managing one's inner dynamics, in the here and now.

In the PLC process, we work with our clients in a transpersonal partnership to enhance the awareness that every element present in the psychic field (history, events, memories, self-images/subpersonalities, mistakes, crises, joy, suffering, positive and negative aspects, high and deep realities and much more) has a meaning and a reason, with a right to exist and to be valued.

We will manage the timing and circumstances in the best possible way to arrive with our client at the "greatest goal" of life through the ongoing and irreversible process of evolutionary growth, which occurs through the transformation of inner dynamics and conflicts, integrating and metabolizing them into the disidentified "I". This is a process that implies not only the change of a mindset used to downloading from the past but, above all, a flexible mindset that allows access to the transpersonal dimension of the psyche, where synthesis takes place.

As professional coaches, we are prepared to guide the client in this process, honoring past experiences and living fully in the present. We set out to ensure a positive attitude founded on a flexible mindset, heart-connectedness, and will to put in motion the Essence with meaningful and purposeful actions which become a source of joy.

We believe that human beings are complete and essentially capable of optimizing their inner dynamics once they awaken to their inner core of synthesis. With unconditional positive regard, we confidently assume that the client is the expert and that they can determine the best for their own lives in all circumstances.

We work with the client to maximize their highest human potential, strengths, and resources, accessing these to create a life in line with the client's core values, bridging the gap between

3- The Essence of Psychosynthesis Life Coaching

where they are in the present moment and where they want to be. The reconnection with one's Self, the immense source of inner wisdom and power, is the larger goal we are seeking together: enabling the Self to become the Leader of the whole person.

We help our clients to recognize and name, therefore becoming increasingly aware of, the "Field of Infinite Possibilities" related to the dimension of the Self. They will probably already have partially perceived this in certain circumstances as a nameless sensation: the transpersonal dimension that leads to its realization and subsequent actualization.

By activating their creativity, we stimulate them to give a name and a form to this transcendental dimension and root it in the personality through the "I". We will help them find an appropriate affirmation to anchor the transpersonal energies in their personality as a driving force to move towards their desired goals.

We maintain a presence with our clients with gentle curiosity to find out more about their mindset, beliefs, vision, desires, talents, basic needs, interferences, qualities, values, strengths, and whatever else may be necessary in the coaching partnership for success in reaching their goal.

With empathetic presence and firm determination, we pose questions to our clients to get them to consider what is fundamentally true for them, not just dwelling on the first thing that comes to their minds. We listen for the deep purpose of their life that wants to emerge, broadening their perspective with a flexible attitude and positive unconditional regard, increasing their awareness of standards, and highlighting their talents and resources available to the achievement of excellence, thereby creating purposeful lives in line with their authenticity.

The first essential phase of the psychosynthetic coaching process focuses on creating maximum clarity of the goal brought into session, generating more and more space for the "I" of the client to become "Director" of their personality- what is defined in Psychosynthesis as "Personal Psychosynthesis". This first phase is followed by a second- that of "Transpersonal Psychosynthesis" which involves realization, grounding, and utilization of higher,

COACHING THE ESSENCE

Transpersonal potentials in daily life through reconnection with one's Essence, the Self. This takes place through a specific process masterfully outlined by Assagioli in *The Act of Will*.

The PLC works in partnership with the client to reach this ability to act in line with the Self, the action par excellence or "Yogic" action as described in the *Bhagavad-Gītā* millennia ago.

The realization of the Self as the foundation of Being and the realignment of the I-Self axis is essential to act in line with the Essence, which provides the highest and most effective pathway to reach Transpersonal Leadership.

The realignment of the "I"-Self axis and the achievement of the ability to act according to one's own Essence occurs in a lifelong dynamic balance of harmony through conflict, goal after goal, freeing the subject one step at a time from unconscious attachment to outcome-related expectations.

This is a key point in that the object is the journey towards the goal, savoring every step and paying attention to the development and employment of one's previously unknown or unused talents, capabilities and resources in the attainment of the higher goal: acting from the Self for the Self.

This realignment is a critical step, as the purpose of the process is to savor the journey toward the goal, appreciating each step with care and attention to the enactment of one's talents, strengths, abilities, and activation of previously untapped inner resources heading toward the highest goal: acting as a Self.

By remaining attached to the expectations inherent in the desired outcome, one loses sight of the small steps and the path to goal achievement, the enactment of one's higher abilities, aptitudes and potentials, which, when taken for granted or denigrated return from where they emerged: buried and latent in the unconscious.

Savoring each moment as unique and valuable is the attitude that we seek as a PLC and we live this attitude with congruence as an example of authenticity or as an Ideal Model for our coachee.

Because Every Moment Matters.

3- The Essence of Psychosynthesis Life Coaching

Photo: C. Pelizzatti (Cambridge, Maryland)

The path to the goal becomes the gym in which we train our abilities; while at the same time broadening and amplifying the "I"'s field of consciousness, through the realization that the Self is the Source from which the highest qualities, the "meta-potentials," emerge.

From this perspective, obstacles along the way and possibly the non-achievement of a goal will provide ideal opportunities to redefine the path, to train certain talents and acquire others, to inhibit some that are not necessary for the intended good end and to learn to prototype, to explore obstacles from a positive and purposeful perspective. Each obstacle or hurdle provides a developmental opportunity rather than a failure.

Remaining conditioned by attachment to the outcome without considering a broader and higher perspective when the desired goal is not achieved means that the onset of frustration and negative emotions is inevitable. This approach will disempower the client, decreasing their self-esteem, and will simultaneously empower a subpersonality that reverts to its natural tendency to keep the "I" under its dominion.

COACHING THE ESSENCE

This subpersonality's purpose is always to protect the subject, however it is the modality with which they replicate a dynamic that becomes obsolete, as it does not evolve. It remains crystallized at a given moment in the personal history of the subject: they are generally unaware of this dynamic and repeat it until it becomes a "comfort zone", a limiting mindset that is difficult to change.

In the short term, the purpose for which each subpersonality arises is positive and good. It aims to keep the "I" in its (the subpersonality's) comfort zone. This is, however, an attitude that over time becomes imprisonment, constraining the personal self by the dynamics of the subpersonality itself, which in turn are driven by satisfaction of a primary need.

During the psychosynthetic coaching conversation, we work with an emphasis on the client's "I". We will be expanding limiting identifications, exploring limiting beliefs, and pushing the boundaries of a subpersonality's comfort zone related to and circumscribed by specific convictions. With empathy and gentle determination, we facilitate the emergence of the client's basic needs and the positive intention at the subpersonality's core.

We are committed to positive transformation, facilitating the client's awareness to find their innermost motivation. We actively participate in the transformational change taking place from within the client themself through the awareness and use of the will in every aspect, phase, and quality necessary to move successfully toward the goal brought into the session.

We support with care the client's process of becoming the Director of their inner system through the realization of the presence of a luminous center on which to position and from which to draw, thereby articulating a more positive intention while moving toward the desired goal and simultaneously achieving what is truly meaningful in the client's life.

We affirm together with the client that the "I" is pure consciousness and will, by definition not colored by any content. The "I" includes the intrinsic attributes of awareness, wisdom, power, and freedom.

The Self is the deepest reality. The personal sense of self or

3- The Essence of Psychosynthesis Life Coaching

"I" exists as a relational emanation of the Self, forever linked to It: the link between the "I" and the Self is never lost or interrupted, but each person has a different level of awareness of this ontological relationship, sometimes even to the point of being completely unaware of it.

Therefore, it is essential to establish the I-Self reconnection, sensitizing the client's awareness of the inherent ontological Self-relationship while moving toward the goal of the session in the time and space of the coaching relationship. Our objective is the design of an action following the mind-heart alignment, the metaspace where the Self resides.

This process is at the core of Psychosynthesis Coaching as a transformational pathway at the transpersonal level.

In synthesis, it is a priority for the PLC that the coachee, as well as successfully achieving their goal, leaves the session motivated to take the SMART step (Specific, Measurable, Attainable, Realistic, Time-based) defined in the session. This SMART step emerges from the awakening of a renewed self-awareness and a new self-image to wear at will which forms an Ideal Model allowing the Self to manifest through the "I", becoming the Leader of the internal human system.

The ideal outcome is a successfully actionable first step that can put one's highest potential into action, responsibly, first for oneself and consequently to meaningfully impact the context in which one interacts, *"adding positive valence to the Universe."* (W. Burr)

The Path Towards the Transpersonal

"The Self. Trends to Motivational theory"
- Roberto Assagioli

The transpersonal process implies the crossing through and beyond the personality, towards the Universality that resides deep within us, to the point where we can perceive or "see" as "I" through the vision of the Self. The perception of ourselves expands to merge with the world as One, the Non-dual state of Being, then returns to the personal dimension having embodied this awareness, manifesting it with congruent, ecological, and sustainable actions.

At this point, Self-realization corresponds to becoming aware of the responsibility to act for the Self in any desired goal, as the deepest desire emerges from the Self in its call for manifestation, trending in line with Dharma, the Ethical Cosmic Order described in the Vedas. By acting in this context, we do not create karma- reactions that return corresponding to the actions we have taken, which require resolution.

A goal is also a desire related to a specific amount of time: the path to the goal that is generally traveled is the one corresponding to the most frequented brain pathway, established as a deep belief. The self-image from which the goal is generated determines the success in achieving the goal, based on its feeling of satisfaction. From neuroscience, we know that the brain constantly tries to predict the outcome and that we ultimately decide emotionally. I'll describe more of this mechanism in Chapter 8.

From what subpersonality, then, does the decision-making process of goal choice emerge?

The transpersonal path includes the sequence of going beyond the personality through a process of energy transmutation to the depths and heights of the psyche, then back into the personality by anchoring in the "I", thus becoming more and more humanly adherent to one's Essence, manifesting action in line with Dharma.

Along this path, one develops a greater awareness of one's shadowy parts, the bits we know about ourselves that we may not be particularly proud of, which we, therefore, keep hidden even from ourselves. But we also gain an awareness of our highest potentials that we dare not admit to possessing since we associate a sense of pride with them that we cannot permit ourselves to accept or a sense of responsibility for putting those potentials into practice that we don't want to take.

We also bear in mind that, as represented in the Egg Diagram,

3- The Essence of Psychosynthesis Life Coaching

everything that is not under the spotlight of consciousness, in the field of consciousness of the "I", is and remains in the shadow of the unconscious.

"You cannot light up a dark room by driving out the darkness, but only by turning the light on."
- Foster Bailey 1947

From this perspective, the shadowy parts do not exclusively take on a negative connotation, but an objective reality that justifies the fact that the latent potential of psychic contents is not immediately available by choice as the person is not immediately aware of their presence.

The individual is therefore involuntarily subjugated to their dynamics until these elements are brought under the spotlight of the I-Self through direct attention.

It is this attention that is the switch that turns on awareness, which increases in proportion to the ability the subject possesses to maintain a presence to themself and simultaneously to the object on which they focus. This ability is defined in Patanjali's *Yoga Sutras* as *Ekagra*- the ability of keeping the mind fixed on a point, a state of mind undisturbed by the incessant flow of contents entering the mental field represented by the Egg Diagram that impact the conditioned "I".

When the subject can bring complete attention back to a specific point and hold it for the necessary and chosen time, in addition to easing the tension related to inner dynamics, they begin to perceive the energy of the Self as belonging to themself, of being "One". This is leads to a perception of being complete and self-sufficient with their own Source, able to use the intuitive tool of the mind as an effective ally, thanks to the realization of the ontological I-Self relationship.

Presence as a key competence in coaching and the maintenance of this state can be summarized by the concept of *Ekagra*. The ability to remain incessantly focused on an intentional point, to extrapolate the essential core of the contents is an essential element of coaching, leading to effective direction of the

COACHING THE ESSENCE

synthesized energies towards the goal.

This attitude of Presence is obtained through the process that Psychosynthesis defines as "disidentification": the ability to create a neutral space at will, a state of consciousness in which the modifications (*Vṛtti*) of the mental field (Egg Diagram) are stilled (*Nirodhaḥ*). From a broader and practical standpoint this means remaining in Yoga, the ability to still the waves of the mental field and realize the uninterrupted relationship between the individual spiritual spark and its Source.

As Patanjali explains in the *Yoga Sutras*:

> "yogaś cittā vṛtti nirodhaḥ"
> *"Yoga consists of the suspension of modifications in the mental field."*
> - Samādhi Pāda v1.2

The next step beyond the mental state of focused attention (*Ekagra*), is referred to as *Niruddha*, the place of silence, of emptiness between psychological contents. This is the goal of the Yoga state i.e., the I-Self reconnection, a mastery over the bio-psychic system by the Self manifesting through the "I", activating Transpersonal Leadership. This is the process we aim for in PLC, as we journey together with our clients toward their goal for the session.

The simultaneous maintenance of Presence and attention focused on one point leads to concentration, the act of controlling the psychological functions, which is the primary role of the will, facilitating the ability to remain steadily fixed in one's center or barycenter of the personality, the "I".

This ability opens the door, emerging from the interaction of the senses with the objects of the senses, to the experience of being the Observer and Director of one's inner dynamics from a neutral, disidentified state of consciousness while simultaneously participating in the realization of the Self, the silent, motionless spiritual Witness.

Even thought is a psychic object if we take the perspective of considering the mind as an object of a subject that participates and perceives through psychological functions.

3- The Essence of Psychosynthesis Life Coaching

When the "I", the subject, manages to keep the mind fixed on its essential reality, the Self, it becomes skilled in observing the dynamics related to the subpersonalities at play moment by moment from a higher perspective. In the process it acquires the ability to dominate and manage them with a compassionate, loving, caring attitude, once they are recognized as important components in the psychic system.

The act of maintaining awareness of the flow of contents in and out of one's field of consciousness and focusing attention on the particular self-image that exerts a greater attraction on the "I" at a given moment increases observant concentration through the flow of presence from the Self, reducing the attractive tension exerted by the subpersonality on the "I" as confirmed in the 8th Law of Psychodynamics.

Maintaining focused concentration on a point from the "I", also referred to as meditation on a seed (*Bīja*) or the skill of maintaining Presence referenced in ICF Core Competency No. 5, simultaneously on the client and the coaching process eases the attractive tension exerted by subpersonalities and leads to a change in the level of consciousness: from the personal level to the transpersonal.

To clarify further, each word has power and represents the manifestation of thought (a psychic object) that once expressed takes on a specific sound-form (idea-form) with intention and direction. The *Bīja* is a sound-seed with the power to transform subtle energy into matter (from thought to word to deed); moreover, each form corresponds to a unique sound, which, through its particular vibration, informs the idea-force, which is then manifested objectively.

Maintaining Presence through an act of will in the Self (*Bīja*) simultaneously with the client's Self during the coaching process facilitates the transformation of the energy of the word related to a specific mental set-up (subpersonality) from limiting belief to potential. We do this by posing stimulating questions that emerge spontaneously (intuitively) through contact with the energetic vibration of the enunciated word, in a continuous flow of space-time from the beginning to the end of the coaching conversation.

COACHING THE ESSENCE

By carefully focusing on subtle, non-verbal communication and on the sound energy that unfolds its true potential, the positive intention of that seed sound finally conveys the Self-Intention, previously confused with subpersonality-related content.

This passage is fundamental to understanding the meaning of "Self-Leadership" from the perspective of psychoenergetics. Thus emerges the importance of self-awareness in focusing attention and maintaining fixed concentration on one's center as we participate in the incessant flow of psychic contents entering and leaving the various regions of the mental field outlined in the Egg Diagram during the coaching process.

The ability to position oneself in the "I" from the Self, the silent, welcoming, nonjudgmental, empathetic, and dynamic Witness, increases awareness of the vibratory energy of contents entering the field of consciousness, through the contact of the psychological functions with what is perceived and thereby becomes the focus of the senses.

This positioning and the choice to direct attention to one content at a time allows us to increase awareness of the focused object and develop a greater understanding and perspective on it. The ability to bring out the intrinsic quality contained in the heart of the object itself, called in the Vedas "*Svarūpa*", the essential, substantial idea-form, increases in proportion to the intensity with which concentration is maintained on the focused object.

Through constant practice, this skill becomes an unconscious ability that emerges naturally when needed.

The Form tells us of Substance; it takes on its features and characteristics, basically resembling that which informs and has no form since it is Substance. Through form we go beyond what can potentially become, actualizing and becoming the Substance that underlies all manifestations. In the space of contentless silence, composed of Substance fertile with every possibility of objective becoming, we can quiet the modifications (*Vṛtti*) of the mental field by facilitating the emergence of the psychological function "Intuition."

Intuition is the psychological function with which the "I" realizes its Substantial reality, equal to and simultaneously

3- The Essence of Psychosynthesis Life Coaching

different from the Source, participating in the unitary or non-dual state of Being. It is a receptive awareness dominated by the energy of Peace, maintained through a constant willful act with the intention of remaining the Observer who observes themself in the process of gaining the Directive skills on form needed for evolutionary purposes.

I, as "I", want the "I" to be the Source of my thought.

The goal, then, is to create a state of peace while maintaining a state of silence, until a sense of deep stillness, of inner calm, emerges in the fog of the incessant flow of content that veils awareness. Maintaining this state of dynamic balance is a skill that requires constant practice and trust in the process one has carefully constructed.

Attention becomes an action chosen by an act of will, the action of the mind under the dominion of the "I" related to the Self, which is directed on external phenomena through the psychological functions. These are the tools the "I" has at its disposal to experience itself in objective reality, make it subjective and bring it into action in the service of the common good as opposed to being exclusively subjected to the dynamics of subpersonalities.

By developing awareness of the unique I-Self relationship, self-empathy emerges, which is essential to bring out the highest potentials hidden in the shadowy parts, finally illuminated by the Light of the Self and available to the "I".

I define this process as "I" empowerment at the transpersonal level, moving from identification to the transformation of psychic contents that are metabolized in the disidentified "I", once their essential quality emerges and is anchored in the subject's awareness, procuring well-being in the entire bio-psychic system through the realization of the unique I-Self relationship.

Through this transpersonal empowerment, the subject acts in line with their evolutionary process, according to their specific and unique nature (*Svadharma*), following the way of Dharma.

COACHING THE ESSENCE

PLC as a Transpersonal Process

"The invariable mark of wisdom is to see the miraculous in the Common."

- R.W. Emerson

As a transpersonal process Psychosynthesis Life Coaching recognizes a hierarchy consisting of developmental stages of consciousness: pre-personal, personal, and transpersonal, and states of consciousness varying from individual to individual. These stages are not always linear, and all this is within a framework that contextualizes context, content, and process, involving methodologies, strategies, and modes of intervention specific to each client.

As coaches, we are the experts of the process; the client is the content and context expert of their own experience. The transpersonal process that occurs in Psychosynthesis Life Coaching is nurtured by the presence that the coach maintains from his or her Self to the client's Self, creating an environment of resonance with the highest regions of the psyche. This is facilitated by the coach's transpersonal orientation, which encourages the unfolding of the client's essential potentials and qualities.

As a PLC we accompany our clients in relaxation of the rational mental dimension, expanding the space of the field of consciousness in all psychic regions, facilitating access to the intuitive mind, and rooting and anchoring the awareness of transpersonal contents in the "I". These will be used as motivators towards chosen goals, maintaining awareness of the uninterrupted "I-Self" relationship during the journey towards achieving the client's goal.

With empathy and strong determination (Love and Will), the PLC accompanies the client in this ongoing "I-Self" effort to find for themselves the appropriate answers within themselves, as well as the solutions to move forward by committing to realistic and valuable goals within a given time frame.

We guide people toward reaching their most intimate and

3- The Essence of Psychosynthesis Life Coaching

essential nature as they achieve their desired goal, simultaneously enhancing the "I-Self" relational connection as the "External Center of Synthesis", having ourselves made the personal experience of our transpersonal yet material nature, of being therefore paradoxically, simultaneously, immanence and transcendence.

"Think of the example of the two or three geometric dimensions, which Einstein has made popular with his Relativity. For the flat, two-dimensional Being, the psychic circle is everything, it is immense for it with plenty of room to wander around. But the three-dimensional Being enters and exits."

— Roberto Assagioli

We position ourselves as guides with empathy, presence, kindness, beginner's mind, positive attitude, unconditional acceptance devoid of judgmental attitude, and awareness of each individual's self-actualizing tendency, starting with us. The transpersonal qualities that the coach brings into the session act as a mirror in which the client can mirror themselves and recognize the presence of these and many other qualities.

We become an "External Unifying Center" holding the I-Self space as a transpersonal context in which the process takes place, moved by the energy of the Self. The relationship becomes a Self-to-Self partnership generating and driving the transpersonal process, emphasizing the client's awareness in the here and now as a volitional being, empty of values, a witness without content.

Our positioning as the "External Center of Synthesis" becomes the channel through which the energies of the Self flow into the field of the coaching relationship and from which we connect with our clients who, in turn, stimulated by this positioning, experience connection with their Source.

During this process, we are accompanying clients in a collaborative and cooperative partnership, in line with their agenda, toward their goals, going about fulfilling what they essentially lack: the fundamental desire of the Self to manifest Itself, upon which the needs of the subpersonalities relate to the client's personal history. This is a shared journey of moving together from the dimension of doing to the dimension of Being.

We remain centered in our Presence, in the here and now, aware of being bearers of a history associated with particular events and ways of presenting oneself through various masks/roles/self-images depending on the circumstances. Yet we are transformed through our reconnection with the inner ontological Reality, which enables the creation, at the level of active imagination, of a new model to be "worn", suitable for achieving the desired future- an Ideal Model that allows the subject to "function" from the Self or, even better, to Be functional for the Self.

Once the empathic and compassionate acceptance of the multiple parts of which we are bearers has taken place, each one can emerge with its nuclear potential to be brought to synthesis as the authentic completeness of the image that wants to emerge: the Ideal Model for the Self. At this point, the transformation of the unconscious contents, from obstacles to resources, takes place from the Self, illuminating them.

The awakening of reserves of transpersonal energy empowers the person with motivation and the ability to find solutions within themselves to overcome obstacles, turning these into opportunities to practice their skills and evolve in consciousness as they head toward the achievement of the chosen goal. This process has as an outcome the generation of new perspectives on the direction to follow in the future, nurturing their sense of self-worth. In this journey, the personality becomes more and more consciously rooted in the personal "I", becoming the pivot around which, from there on, the subpersonalities will revolve.

In other words, the Self bears witness to this experience through the development of the "I" or Self-realization. When we enter the energy field of a dominant subpersonality, we push its limits with empathy and firm determination so that its evolutionary transformation can take place. This transformation occurs in proportion to how well the client can accept the reason for its presence and dynamic. At this point through the creation

3- The Essence of Psychosynthesis Life Coaching

of a space of content, which we achieve in Psychosynthesis through the technique of disidentification, the "I" emerges from the multitude of self-images, and as the Observer and Director, the client is coached to maintain or return to this inner positioning of presence, stimulating their abilities to become aware, moment by moment, of the dynamics to which they were previously unconsciously subjected and, therefore, to decide how to manage them at will, for the successful completion of the desired outcome.

Once the power related to the inner dynamics of subpersonalities is identified, the realization that without psychological detachment from this power evolutionary growth cannot take place enables the subject to accept that they are not just a particular self-image with corresponding dynamics, but have that as well as many others. They realize that it becomes possible to choose them at will and to coordinate them at the appropriate time as powerful allies to achieve the desired end.

This shift of "command position" so to speak, or Leadership, can occur when the subject is positioned in the disidentified "I", and from there reaches the ability to access the transpersonal qualities present at the core of subpersonalities.

At this point, the previously conditioned "I" transcends its conditioning and its ontological characteristics of awareness will emerge, increasing the ability to discern the transpersonal qualities at the core of the subpersonalities from the mechanics related to the needs inherent in the personal dimension.

It's important to note that subpersonalities are not abandoned or removed but rather emerge in a more integrated and complete way in the contentless "I", metabolized in a creative synthesis, thanks to the established and solidified I-Self connection.

The result, as suggested millennia ago by Patanjali in the "*Kaivalya-Pāda*" of the *Yoga Sutras*, is that from the moment liberation from the vicious hold of contents on the "I" takes place, the Light of the Self shines through the "I", refracted within the multiplicity of self-images which become powerful energy resources.

COACHING THE ESSENCE

"The immovable, unchangeable, pure awareness of one's true nature is attained through self-awareness; at this point, the mind assumes the stability between one state and another, the consciousness of pure awareness."

- Yoga Sutra, Kaivalya-Pāda, IV.22

"Don't fight forces, use them."

- R. Buckminster Fuller

The discovery, as Assagioli suggested, of being fundamentally a Self that expresses itself through the "I", emphasizes the importance of the path of self-discovery as the golden way toward any goal. The experience of attaining awareness of our infinite nature as Self and bringing subtle transpersonal energies into the personal "I", conditioned by the limitations of the form we wear, requires training, humility, and courage to recognize and then face our vulnerability.

In the PLC setting we create, through our Presence to the Self, a transpersonal space, sacred as belonging to the dimension of Being. In the role of guide or "External Center of Synthesis", we enhance the field of the coaching relationship with Self Presence, the space in which the client can mirror themselves and allow themselves to confidently and safely let go of the many masks they wear, often unconsciously, in daily life, gradually unveiling their authenticity that is intimately linked to vulnerability, on a personal level.

During the transpersonal coaching process, the client begins to realize and show their vulnerability, the core at the heart of itself, the vulnerable self. This Self is not vulnerable in substance, but in the form through which it manifests: the "I" immersed in the personality, also referred to as the personal self or historical self, and more commonly known as ego, identified unconsciously and acted upon incessantly by the multiplicity of superficial (belonging to the personality) self- images.

This realization enables the person to achieve the freedom to "Be" and find the courage to be that Self, to be brought into action through the will, with the ability to respond rather than

3- The Essence of Psychosynthesis Life Coaching

react impulsively to situations that arise in daily life, through empathetic acceptance of the limitations imposed by the unconsciously clothed and interpreted form.

Working on vulnerability awakens and leads the client to the awareness of the power of resilience. This is the inherent ability to learn from crisis, personal history, and one's wounds and, during the process, become stronger and more flexible through the use of one's inner resources, personal skills, and strategies chosen in line with Purpose, Meaning and Values related to the Self. From this perspective, resilience is also the ability to get more and more in touch with one's Essence and ability to choose responsibly and activate the intrinsic transpersonal qualities of each subpersonality, while at the same time dealing with obstacles in the pathway toward the goal, accepting them as evolutionary opportunities to learn and grow.

Accepting Vulnerability as an Opportunity for Growth

"We all have latent potentials that are infinitely greater and higher than we believe. It depends on us, on our decision, to implement them."

- Roberto Assagioli

Graphic: Carmen Lenatti (2010)

COACHING THE ESSENCE

Resilience becomes the driver of an intention, rooted profoundly within the psychic peaks, to become stronger and more flexible by learning to view obstacles as a training ground for putting one's psycho-physical faculties into action on a personal level. At the same time, resilience is also that evolutionary drive that comes from the transpersonal dimension, the engine to self-realization and enactment of the intrinsic ontological potentials present in the vast psychological universe, moving from a depowering state to empowerment, through mastering one's inner dynamics from the Self.

Coming to accept vulnerability as an evolutionary opportunity and daring to get in touch with one's authenticity requires courage, the action emerging from the heart (from the Latin- "cor"- heart and "agere"- act), which is empathic by nature. Perception of the mind-heart alignment can be immediate and uses emotional intelligence for application strategies. We often hear about "heart", "acting from the heart", "having a heart". The heart is at the center of the Egg Diagram system, the energetic meta-space in which the Self resides.

As indicated millennia ago by Vedic wisdom, particularly in the Ayurveda, the mind resides not in the brain but in the heart, where the Self also resides. Rooted in the heart, the mind expands its activity through the brain, blending the influence of both.

In other words, it means resonating with one's Essence that resides in the metaspace of the heart, which is empathic, exerts unconditional Love, accepts without judgment, and allows the subject the freedom of choice (also known as free will) to be, in some way, authentically oneself.

Not accepting one's vulnerability means accepting masks (and related dynamics) as idealized models which cover and hide the authentic image in the likeness of the Source, the Ideal Model for the Self.

Accepting as a strong potential the weakness we often feel correlated with vulnerability requires a flexible mind predisposed to resonate with the heart, a heart predisposed to communicate with the mind, and a will manifested at every stage. The

3- The Essence of Psychosynthesis Life Coaching

volitional act is only as strong as the weakest link, and often the goal-setting phase is not only not the easiest, it's the weakest.

Sometimes there are inconsistencies between the goal of the initial session and what emerges during the coaching process: the goal the client really wants to achieve. This inconsistency depends on with which self-image the client enters coaching and how this self-image gets transformed along the way, revealing its positive intention and qualitative energy that can be used to empower the client's "I" in achieving their goal.

At the same time as this transformation occurs, there is a change in the client's way of perceiving themselves. They begin to see themself as much more than they thought they were at the beginning of the journey together, a change related to the dynamics of the subpersonality with which they entered into coaching and the related inner and outer expectations.

The transformation of the subpersonality on a personal level amounts to the release of its energetic qualities useful for solidifying the personality around the client's "I" in its ontological role as Director.

The next step is to bring the subpersonality integrated into the "I" under the spotlight of the Self, so that the higher potentials present in its core will emerge.

The client at this point will have qualities at their disposal that were previously used to primarily to achieve meaningful goals (satisfaction of one or more primary needs) for one subpersonality as opposed to another. The subpersonality or subpersonalities are now present as evolutionary directional factors for the "I", empowering the transpersonal process, to be acted upon immediately as if they were already functional to arrive successfully and enthusiastically at the "great goal": one's authenticity.

In other words, the psychosynthesis of superficial self-images- the subpersonalities, also defined as complexes formed by multiple elements of various natures, mental patterns, well-established beliefs, and personal values, first takes place at the personal level then at the Transpersonal level. The energetic qualities emerging during the coaching process constitute significant elements to be brought to synthesis in a self-image that can act as a bridge between the two dimensions, personal and transpersonal: the Ideal Model.

Definition of an Ideal Model for the Self is the principal technique I use in my coaching approach. It is certainly not the only one, but it is the primary- a work that leads to clarifying any ambiguity inherent in the desired goal, starting with the evolution and transformation of the client's initial self-perception that they brought with them into coaching.

In synthesis, the PLC process revolves essentially around the unveiling of the client's "Who" (their I-Self) among the "what" (the subpersonalities and related contents) with which they unconsciously identify, leveraging the essential image that seeks to emerge as an Ideal Model for manifestation of the Self.

CHAPTER 4

KNOWING HOW
and Knowing Why

"The minute you begin to do what you really want to do, it's really a different kind of life."

- R. Buckminster Fuller

Change is part of the process of life. Sometimes it is chosen and desired, and other times it is unexpected and unwanted: in these situations acting as pro-active participants in the flow of change with the ability to "know how to act" makes the difference between letting oneself just survive or actually live a given moment. Knowing how and why to act in one mode rather than another makes the essential difference.

The "why" emerges through the discovery of being simultaneously "Will and Vulnerability": two inevitable facets of the human condition. As Viktor Frankl teaches with his Logotherapy and "Will to Meaning" approaches, even in the most extreme situations we can always freely choose our inner attitude, a freedom that does not depend on circumstances.

The coach's ability to be fully present to the two ontological forces of the Self- Love and Will- during the coaching conversation allows the coach to accompany and support the client in the process of building resilience. This is accomplished by using and balancing these forces so the client can emerge more solidly anchored in their Self as they go through their vulnerability as an "I" encapsulated in the personality, experiencing the quality of this transpersonal Presence within themselves.

The client thus feels not only seen and heard but deeply understood, contained in a space of deep trust, supported and accompanied toward their freely chosen solution, growing in awareness, training their abilities while realizing more and more of themself.

Basically, as PLCs we accompany people in the realization of their Self as they achieve their chosen goals; in our leadership role, we are guided by our Self that creates and contextualizes the coaching process at the transpersonal level. Through partnership at the transcendental level, clients learn to use the qualitative resources within their subpersonalities: high qualities related to values that emerge from reconnecting with their Source, as they achieve their goal.

There are three fundamental steps along this path:

- <u>Identification</u> the recognizing and naming of psychic contents and parts (subpersonalities/superficial self-images) in play, related mental models within the personality corresponding to inner dynamics, specific beliefs, behaviors, and particular use of psychological functions.

- <u>Disidentification</u>: the emergence of the "I" through a process that leads to an awareness of the roles in play corresponding to superficial self-images, emotional detachment from these psychic contents, creating at will a neutral space between the "I" and the contents it experiences, positioning itself as an "Observer" with the ability to see in a detached way the dynamics emerging from identification with psychic contents and acquiring the ability to direct them at will as "Director".

- <u>Self-identification</u> with psychic contents through the "I": self-images, roles in play/subpersonalities, that are now chosen by the "I" to be functional in achieving a purposeful goal.

The act of de-identifying or disidentification is a process that leads to the ability to create a voluntary distancing from the contents present in the field of consciousness, an inner action that

4- Knowing How and Knowing Why

the subject performs, a shift possible only at the moment they become aware of the presence and effect on their personality of these contents. In practice, disidentification can occur after having identified the contents present in the field of consciousness and having observed how they cause a specific effect on psychological functions.

Once the contents have been identified, in particular the superficial self-images/subpersonalities with related mental, emotional, and behavioral dynamics, the act of positioning oneself in a neutral position allows the subject to observe them from a different perspective as they arise in the field of consciousness. It therefore becomes possible to accept these contents with an empathetic, nonjudgmental attitude, with unconditional positive regard and recognition of the freedom to exist, not by interpreting them but by evaluating how they can be applied as resources or otherwise in achieving the desired goal and then choosing, metaphorically speaking, which one and when to wear it at will and for which end.

The creation of this voluntary neutral inner space and mindful positioning within it allows the subject to direct attention at will, to choose among the multitude which subpersonality to use as the best ally to achieve the desired goal, thereby activating the psychological functions related to it and training its will to successfully continue toward the desired outcome.

The "deconditioned" personal self acquires a renewed ability to overcome obstacles thanks to the empowerment that the specific subpersonality provides it, training its skills while simultaneously growing in awareness. This is a journey that has resilience as its context, the ability to become more and more oneself through discovering and putting into action one's talents and abilities for ecological and sustainable purposes, starting with one's self.

Then let go, return to the neutral space, and in a constant flow repeat the same process, observing and directing attention to which subpersonality to focus on and choose to wear again at will, and which field of energy emerges from one subpersonality to use. In this flow it is possible to explore other subpersonalities

COACHING THE ESSENCE

and eventually use them as needed, so that the "I" can be empowered by the transpersonal quality present in their heart instead of being imprisoned by the volitional dynamics related to the basic needs each subpersonality carries and tends toward.

When the "I" voluntarily identifies with the subpersonalities, it assumes their power, having access to their essential quality and positive intention. This positioning of the "I" as Observer and Director corresponds to the strengthening of the subject or Personal Leadership: the dominion over one's personality through successive phases of identification and disidentification, in an iterative process that leads to a state of dynamic balance, a state of harmony through conflict also known as Personal Psychosynthesis.

From this positioning at the center of itself, the "I" that has realized its ontological nature: that of Being a Self, equal in substance and simultaneously different in quantity, becomes the means for radiating the energies of the Self on the subpersonalities which it focuses on. These are thus transformed in their essence, their intrinsic value and positive intention, thanks to the emanation of transpersonal energy in the personality through the "I" which is forming a bridge, creating and using an ideal image that combines the two dimensions

The core qualities of subpersonalities can now emerge to be metabolized and brought into action by the "I" under the direction of the Self, for the highest ends.

This process of "Self-Identification" in synthesis allows the subject to wear, from time to time, the ideal subpersonality for the goal to be achieved, voluntarily assuming its strengths and then letting it go in a constant flow that now occurs consciously, since the subject has activated the ability to observe and direct their inner multiplicity at will without being trapped in the dynamics linked to the personal dimension. This is the key to inner freedom.

This process leads to the awareness of being an "I" that has the power of choice, that wants to participate in the experience of being the Observer with the power, when it assumes the Director's role, of being able to direct at will one's inner strengths

4- Knowing How and Knowing Why

related to the richness of the multiplicity.

Diversity now enriches the I, which is positioned in the Self, in its Essential Reality as the Internal Unifying Center, a positioning in which Synthesis can take place. Self-Identification: the realization of the Self and putting Its energies into action through the "I" is the basis of "Transpersonal Leadership" or "Self-Leadership", the "meta-goal" to which we aspire in PLC.

The realization by the "I" of the existence of the multiplicity of subpersonalities, the "diversity", through the stages mentioned before: Identification, Disidentification, Self-Identification in the psychosynthetic process of *Knowing, Possessing and Transforming*- enables the subject's awakening to the Oneness state of Being, the Unity in diversity.

The awareness of the personal self as a non-duality with the Source to which it essentially and ontologically belongs leads to appreciation of the inner multitude as an immense energy reservoir, available now to the conscious subject for purposeful actions.

Listening to personal meaning, value, and purpose, as the framework of the goal brought into the session by the client, means listening to the authenticity that wants to emerge: seeing the larger picture beyond any goal. This is the positioning we seek as PLC, the position of being in the moment-to-moment flow state, anchored from our Self to the client's Self. We listen for the larger context in which clients place themselves as they move toward meaning, value, and purpose, thus providing the potential for connection to something larger than the personal self encapsulated within the personality.

As an "External Center of Synthesis" we resonate with the client's "Internal Center of Synthesis" and, through our congruence, we function as bridges, thus allowing the client to build their own bridge towards their ideal future, reaching their highest, ontological capabilities, that are intrinsically waiting to be manifested.

During Psychosynthesis coaching sessions, in our role as experts in the tools and techniques and the client in their role as experts in their inner territory, we guide them along the path of discovering their authenticity. They begin to see they are becoming capable of achieving their goals successfully, of finding their own solutions, possessing the skills needed to deal with obstacles along the way to the goal brought into the session.

The partnership that is established from the very beginning takes place at the transpersonal level, creating an interactive field between coach and coachee. In the transpersonal flow of interaction the contents are transformed in the sequential process of knowing, then possessing, and finally transforming them through presence to the Self, the True Guide of the whole process, which begins, takes place and ends in the personal dimension.

In this movement that takes place in the personal dimension, with a context grounded in the transpersonal dimension, we are positioned as the External Center of Synthesis. From here, together with the client we traverse their inner territory- the various psychic regions represented by the Egg Diagram Map. This positioning or state of Presence facilitates the coachee in becoming increasingly self-confident and secure as we experience together, one step at a time, the journey into the deeper and higher regions of the unconscious, gaining knowledge of some of the many parts (subpersonalities) that inhabit them, their history, the dynamics of their interactions, and the primary needs they carry.

This leads to an increase in the client's awareness and confidence to emerge safely from the comfort zone they brought into session, recognizing the "I" in its freedom as their true comfort zone, a secure place from where to invite the many parts as welcome guests, whose arrival now empowers the "I" rather than weakening it. The control that subpersonalities exert over the will, which is diverted toward the fulfillment of the primary needs they carry, and that traps the "I" in one subpersonality or another, is no longer dominant. The "I" is now free to perceive the underlying meaning of its truly desired goals, no longer limited in its development to the personal level and free of the urge to fulfill desires related to the basic needs of the subpersonalities.

However, gaining the awareness that such needs have the

4- Knowing How and Knowing Why

right to exist as real in the personal dimension and that at the same time, there is another dimension that calls for manifestation, increases the subject's ability to make ideal choices for his or her "well-Being", finding a synthesis in the goal brought into the session, which allows the satisfaction of both personal and transpersonal dimensions.

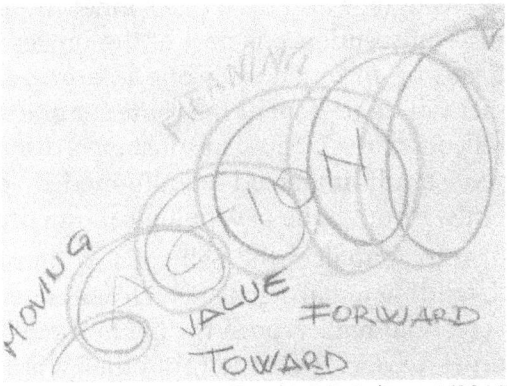

Graphic: C. Pelizzatti (2016)

Motivating Action

Motivation is an essential component of the coaching process. It is the coachee who drives the session to achieve their goal, and as partners, we coach them to stay in touch with the deeper meaning that lies hidden within the superficial motivation, with powerful questions designed to stimulate and manifest the "Purpose of the Self", the intrinsic motivator.

We partner with our clients to trust and recognize their intuitions as valid, going through a cognitive process that evaluates the inclusion of intuitive function in the personality.

This process involves directed and meaningful use of the rational mind to translate what emerges from Intuition and subsequently to integrate the new awareness into the vehicle of expression of the personality, the psychological functions, through the "I" that moves towards an ever wider Purpose, Meaning, and Value. These steps are necessary to sustain the manifestation of the Self as the foundation of any goal in life.

It is by maintaining a presence in the Self, with the awareness of this Presence in us and with the will to act congruently with It, that the process of Self-realization of the client is contextualized so that the inner wisdom of the organism can emerge as a strength that can be relied upon with confidence.

Learning to recognize and trust one's inner impulses toward wholeness and transcendence is part of the process that can be identified as getting in touch with one's Source, the Self. The Self is the inner Guide present at the center of one's personality through Its reflection, the I, equal in substance, different in magnitude, and constantly impacted--conditioned by contact with psychic contents, through the psychological functions.

The impulse to Actualize the Self calls to Its manifestation through the I, tending toward goals which are more and more in line with its essential reality, once the "I" becomes empowered in its function as Observer-Director, in other words, becoming the Leader of oneself.

The person thus learns to harmonize their personality around their internal unifying center, the I, now aware of its True Ontological Nature, at each stage of the their journey, which sometimes wears one self-image and at times another, as their transpersonal essence or *Svārupa*, is empowered through these. *Svārupa*, as explained in the Vedas, means the personal expansion of the Original Natural Transcendental Identity, the true nature of manifestation.

Maintaining Presence at the center of oneself, present to one's Essence in the dynamism of the multiplicity that inhabits the psyche, one maintains homeostasis, the ability to self-determine, self-regulate (knowing how to consciously direct one's inner world). The positioning readies one for the evolutionary use of the dynamics between the various opposing tendencies, synthesized in the Ideal Model for the Self.

The coach stimulates the client through powerful and provocative questions designed to activate their interest, provide alternative perspectives, and experience the various subpersonalities in the coaching setting. The client becomes aware of their effect

4- Knowing How and Knowing Why

on the personality, bringing out the deeper latent desire and nuclear quality present in each motivated by the Self to the point where they reach always more profound and higher inner spaces: the infinite "field of possibilities".

The attainment of an expanded state of consciousness, as well as a broader sense of identity and awareness of being able to actively participate in one's transformation, leads to a new vision of possibility, acceptance, and willingness to loosen limiting beliefs related to the past, contextualizing the chosen goal with the larger life outcome, through maintaining a presence to the Self.

"The past and the future are immanent in an object in the present, they exist as different representations of visible forms, in the same flow of experience of the properties of the Substance."
- Patanjali, Kaivalya-pāda, VI, 12

The experience of the present moment occurs in the field of consciousness of the "I", the psychological region in the middle unconscious shown in the Egg Diagram. We need to learn to appreciate, in the process of becoming who we essentially are, each moment and experience as precious and meaningful. We are Self-present, more and more in line with our inner project that we are called to manifest: an Ideal Model from which to live our life from the transpersonal level, and manifest the Self in ecological and sustainable actions.

Accessing the transpersonal dimension means opening ourselves with confidence to inspiration-intuition at the moment when we doubt our abilities. We do this by connecting to the universal energies and transpersonal values that are always available to us, preparing us to receive them, metabolize them and use them for evolutionary purposes.

It is the degree of self-awareness of the "I" that allows us to access the deeply elevated unconscious regions and sustain the emerging contents, transforming them in line with the Ideal Model we have chosen to "wear" and forming the bridge between the two dimensions of Being (personal-immanent and transpersonal-transcendent).

COACHING THE ESSENCE

The return to the personal level, in the middle unconscious, occurs through an act of will motivated by the Meaning of the Self. At this point in the coaching conversation, the client is guided through the process of creating a SMART step to bring the new awareness into action, acting it out through the self-image that ideally increasingly represents the ontological I-Self relationship.

Living in the Fullness of Being in the Moment

Elio Pelizzatti: "Donna e Gabbiani" (1984)

Non-Duality - Synthesis:
"Where there is duality, we see the other, smell the other, hear the other, talk to the other, think of the other, understand the other; but when all has dissolved in the Self, how and who can we smell? how and who can we see? how and to whom can we talk? how and who we can think? how and who can we understand? how is it possible to understand that through which everything is understood? how is it possible to understand the One who understands?"

- Bṛhadāraṇyaka Upaniṣad 2.4.28

By the "disidentified personal self" we mean a self-image as the organizing principle in the individual field of consciousness

4- Knowing How and Knowing Why

that evolves through the experiences of life, or one could say, that ideally makes the journey of life evolve by maturing (evolution in awareness).

Transpersonal psychology and PLC propose that we can take a further step in this evolution: a person who reaches the level of Transpersonal Psychosynthesis by passing through personal Psychosynthesis has consolidated a solid personal structure formed around a transpersonal level of development of the personal self or I, emerging from this transformational process with an identity in line with one's Ideal Model, useful for the "I" to reflect the Self more and more clearly and move beyond impermanent individuality.

Beyond, it means having a consciousness free from psychological contents due to the realignment of the "I" with its Source, and maintenance in this neutral space, acquiring the appropriate tools to connect with the transcendental subjective dimension at the foundation of personal objective manifestation.

In the *Bhagavad-Gītā* this passage is defined in Chap. 11, verse 8:

"But you cannot see Me with your eyes, so I give you divine eyes. Contemplate My mystical opulence."

Krishna (the Self) explains to Arjuna (the "I") that only with new "eyes" is it possible to see Beyond: through the vision of the spirit it is possible to perceive the eternal meaningful Essence in the relative transitory representation. This ability is acquired through the process of Self-Realization.

This is the transcendental level of realization described throughout the world in the Spiritual Traditions of all ages, all of which require the attainment of abilities developed through arduous training to contemplate the transcendental Reality, going beyond the limits of manifest reality.

Each step toward a further stage of consciousness represents a successive stage of personal transcendence: the structure of the superficial self-images with which the "I" ceaselessly identifies: the subpersonalities, is transcended as experiences are transformed and metabolized into the dis-identified "I". This process allows the emergence of the essential intrinsic quality of each representation, or *Svarūpa*.

An unconsciously identified "I", generally known as an ego, has no awareness of its "True Nature" and is a particular organization of the personal self. It is rooted in deep and conditioning beliefs, having the assumption of being separate from the rest of the context and consequently presuming to be the center of control of the life of the individual.

The person may appear integrated and balanced, but fundamentally their ego or personal self, under the power of unconscious identifications, is based upon the fragmented and distorted view of their essence, their Self and the creation of defensive boundaries from suffering. This creation is rooted in the Great Ignorance or lack of spiritual awareness, defined in Patanjali's *Yoga Sutras* as *Avidyā*, limiting the subject's ability to live life joyfully and fully, with simplicity, naturalness, creativity, authenticity, and freedom.

This fragmentation is due to the unconscious identification of the "I" with the multiple contents present in the unconscious and their related dynamics, as described by Assagioli in the Ten Laws of Psychodynamics. Superficial subpersonalities/self-images tend incessantly to assume control and guidance of the personality, linking the subject to the dimension of doing.

Through the technique of disidentification, the egoic identification is gradually transformed and transcended, thanks to the empathetic attitude towards oneself supported by the coach's role as the External Center of Synthesis. Acting becomes congruent with one's transpersonal values, and identity and the awareness of the Self are increasingly rooted in the present, with a compassionate attitude towards oneself and towards others, gradually freeing oneself from conditionings thanks to their transformation at the transpersonal level.

This emergent authenticity is congruent with transpersonal ontological identity. When we are identified with the personal self through subpersonalities, we live in a kind of prison, as we are trapped in the dynamics of a role, a superficial self-image

4- Knowing How and Knowing Why

that gravitates around a primary need. We are inhibited or precluded from the true ontological nature and the personal freedom to manifest our fundamental need for Self-realization.

We, therefore, consider the value of the "I" or personal self, unconsciously identified with psychic contents, as well as its limitations due to identification: in the Transpersonal process the personal self/ego becomes understood, transcended, integrated, and synthesized- not eliminated. This process provides a mature basis for access to the higher stages of consciousness and elevated transpersonal manifestations, for the responsible enactment of the highest values and strengths, in an integrated personality revolving around a solid center of synthesis.

Through the development of the personal self and access to the higher faculties of the transpersonal realm of one's psyche, we will have a greater ability to know and express these potentials in the course of achieving goals. We are also keeping in mind that, when identification occurs unconsciously, the personal self is the greatest obstacle in this process and in transpersonal development.

"By suffering from our weaknesses and offering this suffering, we transmute it into strength."
- Roberto Assagioli

The distortion-disconnection of the personal self from the Self is the origin of suffering, called *"Dukkha"* in the Vedic Wisdom Traditions.

"Our 'I' derives its identity, its existence, from the level of activity in which it actualizes itself. Our 'I' moves into the soul, like the 'I-of-the-dream' in the house dreamed by Jung and the consciousness lights up now on one level or on another."
- J. Hillman

Imagine a candle lit in a space surrounded by mirrors: the flame of the candle represents the Self; the reflection generated by the mirrors represents the field of consciousness of the "I", in the myriad facets, surfaces, and changing images that Assagioli

COACHING THE ESSENCE

calls subpersonalities. The resultant sum of the mirrors is the personality; the I, the personal synthesis that varies according to the reflection with which it unconsciously identifies, the Self as Transpersonal synthesis. If the mirrors are not clean, the reflection is veiled or obscured, if they are broken, the reflection is scattered and the light is diffused in a distorted and dispersive way, not directed toward a focused point that amplifies its power. When the mirrors are clean and undamaged, the reflected candlelight is equal to the light emitted by the Source and amplified.

"There is no Bhodi tree, no support for a bright mirror. Since everything is empty, where can the dust rest?"

- Hui Neng

When it realizes its Real image, that of being a spark of the Self reflected into the personality and having the power to govern the various representations at will the "I" can act as an amplifier for the energies of the Self and make them available to the subpersonalities. This enables the definition and achievement of goals in line with one's transpersonal Purpose, Meaning, and Values, therefore facilitating evolution in consciousness.

The Ideal Model catalyzes this authentic self-image and related transpersonal energies so that the subject can begin to train meta potentials through the "Acting as If" technique used in Psychosynthesis. This technique was described millennia earlier by Patanjali, and Assagioli was an avid student of the Vedic Wisdom Traditions.

From this perspective the "I" simultaneously observes itself and the superficial self-images as psychic objects by assuming the role of Observer and, depending on the desired end, the role of Director. This gives the "I" the power of choice to act through the multitude of parts, while at the same time empowered by them.

This movement of energy originating in one's Essence is the empowerment that we want to bring to light while working as a PLC, in a process of developing Leadership starting from the personal dimension and then rising to the transpersonal one.

4- Knowing How and Knowing Why

The technique of disidentification, which represents the key to inner freedom, is a constant process of maintaining a solid position at the center of oneself, in the "I" that has realized itself as Self, and, at the same time, in the subpersonalities.

This ability is accessible through the change of attractive power of the "I" that, having realized that it is that Self, chooses to position itself in the Self, the Flame through which its reflection can experience manifest reality from an elevated perspective, remaining consciously neutral.

The Self always remains the silent and motionless Witness. It participates in experience through its reflection, the "I" immersed in the bio-psychic form, which has the psychological functions as tools for experiencing objective reality along the evolutionary journey whose goal is Love.

All this happens when the field of consciousness of the "I" is purified from the unconscious conditioning contents, as Patanjali taught us in the *Yoga Sutras*, millennia ago.

"Liberation is the establishment of the energy of seeing, of consciousness, in its true nature (Svarūpa pratisha), the return of the manifestation which is empty."

- Patanjali- 4.34 Kaivalya-Pāda

By transcending the separate sense of self, we realize the non-dual relationship with one's Source or Synthesis. This does not mean a loss of consciousness or personal identity but an increase in awareness, with greater clarity of one's life purpose, as the conditioning and mental limitations of an egocentric conception are transformed and absorbed by the "I", integrated, metabolized, and transcended into a dynamic synthesis.

In the flow of experience, the essential identity emerges integrated from a profound and elevated perspective, where the personal self and the Natural Essence are no longer divided but united in a synthesis of dynamic tensions.

This does not mean that everything becomes fused together and undifferentiated but, rather, expanded, more open, and inclusive in the non-dual vision of oneself and the surrounding

COACHING THE ESSENCE

environment. What needs to be transcended is the identification of the consciousness of the one who is seeing with the thing seen. Once again I quote Patanjali in his *Yoga Sutra*, where he explains how confusion (*Sam*) dissolves through the light of knowledge, arriving at "seeing" (*Vid*) with the eyes of the Self.

From the *Sadhāna Pada*:

2.17 *The foreseeable cause of suffering is due to the apparent invisibility of pure awareness in what is visible.*

2.20 *Pure awareness is the knower itself; it appears to operate through the perception of the mental field.*

2.23 *Personal power over the forms in their essence is acquired through awareness of the causal reason for their union.*

2.24 *Lack of wisdom, the cause of Ignorance (Avidyā) confuses the reality of things.*

2.25 *Confusion with what has no existence seizes the moment the one who sees distances himself from the thing seen, obtaining Liberation.*

2.41. *From the purification of the mental field emerge happiness, one-pointed concentration, mastery over the sensory faculties, and the ability to realize the Self.*

Everything is energy: depending on the speed of the energy vibration, one has manifestation ("mass"- in the Vedas: *Vyakta*) or the subtle state not perceptible with the senses ("non-manifest"- in the Vedas: *Avyakta*). Once we come to the awareness of being the One who sees (the Self), everything is reabsorbed into the space of content, where the speed of propagation approaches and goes beyond the speed of light.

This mirrors the formula $E=mc^2$ postulated by Einstein.

The Self is a transcendental Reality, which, by Nature, goes beyond Laws that codify manifest matter, following the "Great Laws of the Spirit", that cannot be understood or demonstrated with the tools that positivist thought knows and applies but which underlie manifest reality and tangible effects.

The essence of mind is essentially pure, as Patanjali and the Sixth Patriarch of Zen Buddhism in China, Bodhidharma, teach us: all things are the manifestation of the Essence and Its Mind.

4- Knowing How and Knowing Why

The Self and the "I" are a single Reality, as Assagioli also teaches us through the dynamic process of his Psychosynthesis.

The Value of the Extraordinary in the Ordinary

A.H. Almaas, author and spiritual guide, defines the process of Self-realization as experiencing "The Pearl Beyond the Price", the journey of contacting one's authenticity beyond conditioning and personal history as a response or reaction to something.

It is not about being something for someone: it is all about embodying the sense of being freely oneself, "the freedom to be". It is the process of developing the Essence from impersonal to personal and bringing it into manifestation through experience.

Contemplative practices, intuition, and meditation as major ways to the transpersonal (Walsh & Vaughan), as well as rituals and shamanic practices, facilitate the discovery and development of the connection with the transpersonal as a profound reality of Being. Methodological pluralism is necessary to study all that is contemplated in context, contents, and process in the transpersonal realm.

The essence of this approach is the integration of a scientific-based research methodology conferring the ability to complete the study of human experiences (including non-ordinary states) beyond empirical analysis, through an inclusive attitude that shifts the focus of research from behavior to the meaning of that behavior and related experience. This becomes a journey into the profound reaches of the psyche that can reveal the ultimate meaning or the "Will to Meaning" (Viktor Frankl) and the universal network or "Morphogenetic Field" (Rupert Sheldrake) which unifies and connects the Whole as Unity into diversity.

In the Vedas, the concept of "Unity into diversity" and interconnectedness is described in the theory *Achintya-Bheda-Abheda Tattva*: the inconceivable Reality which is both differentiated and undifferentiated (Chaitanya Mahaprabhu 1486–1534).

For Walsh and Vaughan, meditation is considered the royal road to the Self, and this emphasis is also underlined in the field of Psychosynthesis. There are many meditative techniques deriving from millennial wisdom traditions, each of which represents in its way the art of transcending mental boundaries, realizing one's transpersonal potentials, and returning to ordinary reality, knowing how to use these potentials for evolutionary purposes.

Patanjali's *Yoga Sutras* are a milestone in the science of meditation, as the *"Way to Kaivalya"*, the "Liberation" from unconscious identifications with matter (*Maya*) through the realization of one's Essential Nature.

The common thread of every meditative technique is the assumption that the waking state represents one of the states of consciousness and therefore does not represent the full potential of the mind.

Meditation is a constant training in maintaining the flow of presence in the here and now with vigilance, moment to moment, a fundamental technique in transpersonal development of the "I". It can be defined as a series of practices that train attention to focus on a fixed point or seed, leading to awakening in consciousness and the emergence of the "I" in the field of awareness, freed from psychic contents. Such contents and related dynamics on the "I" generate modifications of the mental field represented by the Egg Diagram. In the *Yoga Sutras*, Patanjali defines these as *Vṛtti*, the mental waves.

The "I" realizes its True Nature when, through the technique of disidentification, it manages to suspend the attraction exercised by mental contents. Disidentification is an inner attitude that allows mental and emotional detachment from unconscious identification and the creation of a neutral intermediate space, reacquiring the ontological ability of Observing - Directing one's own inner realm.

Mental contents manifesting as recurring thoughts (*Vṛtti*) can be metaphorically described as passages of thought that, through repetition, become "cerebral pathways", generating modifications in the mental field defined as *"Cittā"* in the *Yoga Sutras*, and represented by the Egg Diagram in Psychosynthesis. These modifications and the associated

4- Knowing How and Knowing Why

specific mental arrangements which form beliefs lead to the use of the psychological functions even against the will of the "I" (as explained by Assagioli in the Laws of Psychodynamics, particularly in the eighth), creating real personalities within the person, the subpersonalities of which the subject is generally unaware.

At the point when, through disidentification, the "I" positions itself as the Observer and Director of its inner dynamics, it becomes aware of the incessant modification of the mental field to which it is unconsciously subjected, diverting its attention toward the satisfaction of needs related to subpersonalities. At this point and from this awareness, through an act of will, the subject can choose to inhibit the *Vṛtti*, realizing themselves as Self, achieving the non-dual state of Being or Yoga.

As defined by Patanjali and presented earlier in Chapter 3:

> "yogaś cittā vṛtti nirodhaḥ"
> - Samādhi Pāda v1.2

The connection with the Self suggested by Assagioli- represented in the Egg Diagram by the dotted vertical line joining the center with the apex is, to my perception, indicative of the "Bhakti Way" described in the Vedas, particularly in the *Bhagavad-Gītā* and the *Narada Bhakti Sutras*, the "*Bhakti Yoga*", the Yoga of Love.

It is through the constant practice of disidentification that the mind is aligned in the I-Self axis, becoming the instrument of the Self. According to Yoga psychology, mental processes can be voluntarily controlled and directed by the subject toward elevated ends for an inner ecology, resulting in clarity of vision and understanding of the relationship between micro and macro cosmos, until the core, the Essence that underlies and transcends everything, is reached.

The term meditation refers to a complex of self-regulatory practices that focus on training attention to a point and awakening awareness to gain voluntary control over mental processes, which cause the modification (*Vṛtti*) of the mental field represented by the Psychosynthesis Egg Diagram.

Yoga is training the mind in the service of the "I" in the realization of one's true Nature. Yoga creates a space empty of content (the field of consciousness of the "I"), a space where the modifications (*Vṛtti*) of the mental field (*Cittā*, or Egg Diagram), cease, facilitating the emergence of the state of emptiness (*nirodhaḥ*), the stillness of mind, the silence that is a true core competency that we so much need to know how to manage in coaching.

Generative silence is a space that is masterfully created over time and is achieved in Psychosynthesis through the technique of disidentification. Maintaining the neutral space in which active listening can emerge is a skill that requires vigilance, and mastery over the psychological functions through the purposeful use of will, to emerge from this process with the ability to choose where to direct attention in a focused way as content moves in and out of the field of consciousness.

We can grasp the energy of the client's speech and nonverbal communication as we are diligently listening to the silence existing between the words and how they are expressed, diligently maintaining Presence to what we are perceiving. In silence exists the energy that moves communication, indicative of the origin of words and nonverbal communication. In other words, it is in silence that we can perceive the energy of the psychological field from which the client is communicating, referring to the Egg Diagram to map this origin.

As a PLC we ask ourselves: "*Does that content come from the pre-personal unconscious? Personal? Superconscious? Collective at what level?*" We, therefore, use the Egg Diagram to ask the client to locate these contents, in one or another region of their psyche.

We bring into communication as feedback what we have heard as an energetic vibration quality, once it has been passed through the heart, where we cultivate it in silence, having perceived it in the client. During the interaction between two Selves, the quality that has passed through the coach's heart is returned, seeded with intention in the client's heart, so that it can sprout as a creative element in manifesting its Ideal Model, following the

4- Knowing How and Knowing Why

client's unique and valuable nucleic energy blueprint.

We bring Intuition into the field of the coaching relationship and ask for permission to eventually share it. We participate in the generation in the client of awareness of the transpersonal qualities of which they were previously ignorant by resonating with the same qualities in us- since at the transpersonal level, the qualities that emerge from the Source are universal Values. In this exchange of energy, the task of the PLC is to transmute the energy with which it has entered into resonance and return it freed of content to the client, stimulating them to choose whether or not to use it to enter into resonance with their Source, through the creation of their Ideal model.

It is in the space of silence that a fertile field is generated, in which energies of the Self flow through the coach to the client and vice versa. A partnership between two Selves on a transpersonal level. We are the ideal instrument to generate the transpersonal field in which this alchemical process takes place on a transcendental level if we are trained to maintain Presence to our Self, the Leader of the whole process who requires obedience. The word "to obey" from the Latin "ob" (in front) and "audire" (to listen) means to be in front of someone and listening to them. For us as Psychosynthesis Life Coaches, this means in front of the Self.

I "obey" in the sense that I unconditionally accept to remain in the neutral space of the "I" to benefit from the state of pure awareness and will without contents. I am the Leader of my inner realm and I place myself at the service of the client as an Ideal Model so that the client can mirror themselves through me, and enter into resonance with their Self. This process has, as an outcome, becoming the Leader of oneself and actualizing the energetic qualities of the Self in an ideal project.

Into the space of silence, we can finally hear the "Call of the Self" among the myriad of seductive inner voices that draw the subject to their call.

The "Call of Self" is masterfully described in the first book on modern Psychosynthesis Life Coaching created and edited in 2018 by Dorothy (Didi) Firman, Ed.D., and published by

COACHING THE ESSENCE

Synthesis Center Press (see references on p. 80). This work brought together thirty authors from around the world. I wrote two chapters in this book: "I'm a Psychosynthesis Coach" and "Psychosynthesis Coaching in Action: A case study- Alice". William Burr (Bill) wrote a chapter about "Psychosynthesis and the Martial Way".

Silence

"Humanity, as a whole, needs silence at this time as never before, it needs time in which to reflect, and the opportunity to sense the universal rhythm."

— Roberto Assagioli

For example, meditation, direct contact with nature, art, music, and many other ways of introspection can amplify the awareness of the deep connection with oneself, facilitating the "peak experiences" and the elevated states of consciousness also described by Assagioli. The American psychologist Abraham Maslow suggested that the reluctance to share these experiences seemed like a resistance, a defense mechanism of the ego. He coined the term "desacralisation" to describe this defensive mechanism of the ego against the emotional flux resulting from altered states of consciousness, contact with mystery, and awakening experiences in consciousness. He clarified that this defensive attitude toward "peak experiences" is correlated to the perception of then having to bear the responsibility for what was experienced, and the consequent need to support the emotional flow related to these experiences.

This may be one of the reasons why many people repress this state of consciousness and conform to the norm of the moment, needing to feel "normal" towards the system in which they are inserted, starting with themselves.

In this regard, I often mention to my clients and students the Greek metaphor of the "Bed of Procrustes", to stimulate a reflection on the state of "normality" in the framework within which they contextualize their own obstructing experiences. The metaphor has Greek origins and psychologically it is used to

4- Knowing How and Knowing Why

indicate a process of adaptation to a circumstance different from one's psychological nature up to the point of being physically painful. The subject finds themself forced to wear a mental model or a value system that is not their own, internally experiencing a difficult, conflicted, intolerable, and even tormenting condition.

When the values of transpersonal experiences are used by the not metabolized ego for the fulfillment of its ends, it is defined as "ego appropriation", "narcissism recruitment" or "spiritual materialism" (Trungpa Rinpoche, 2002).

Focusing exclusively on transpersonal research can fuel the tendency to devalue the experience of the present moment because we're looking for something even more special. This phenomenon is typical of "spiritual materialism", the tendency of the conditioned "I" to use spirituality to reinforce the ego.

From another, opposite, perspective, we can think of the value of the *"extraordinary in the ordinary"* and of the sacredness of every moment.

Any transpersonal realization is at risk of narcissistic recruitment and may be an obstacle to transpersonal development: one may come to believe that they have developed spirituality while, instead, they're merely increasing their own egocentrism through spiritual techniques.

Trungpa Rinpoche, in his book *Cutting Through Spiritual Materialism* (2002), explains the importance given by every spiritual practice to freeing oneself from the dynamics of the ego: this means distancing oneself from the continuous egoic desire to acquire a higher knowledge of which one can then boast. A similar attitude is also defined by Epstein as "Narcissistic Recruitment" in which one appropriates spiritual experiences to feed one's esteem, obtain approval from others, avoiding or trying to fill a deep sense of inner emptiness.

Two errors that can occur in spiritual emergencies are "Reductionism" and "Elevationism"; the first is an attitude that does not recognize the spiritual emergency and reduces it to pathology, and the second is to elevate a pathological process (such as schizophrenia) to a spiritual emergency. The limit is subtle and not easy to delineate, as there are phases in which the altered state coexists and resembles each other, the so-called dark night of the soul, of which Assagioli also speaks in his essay on *Self-Realisation and Psychological Disturbances* (published 1986).

If correctly evaluated, spiritual emergencies represent a decisive moment of evolutionary growth. Various factors can help in this process, including an ideal supportive relationship in which the person, welcomed in a space of non-judgment and deep understanding, feeling safe, can freely express themself, sharing their experience of the limitations which provoked the emergency.

Spiritual awakening is a tumultuous process and peak experiences can sometimes compromise the field of consciousness of the unprepared "I" (unmetabolized into the Self), but once transformed in the light of the Self and integrated into the disidentified "I" they produce a positive and evolutionary transformation of the personality. Spiritual crises always lead to an evolutionary development of the subject's conscience.

Spiritual emergencies (transpersonal crises) can occur spontaneously or be induced by various factors, such as excessive stress, illness, intense emotional experiences, accidents, birth, traumatic events, and drug use. All forms of transpersonal crisis can be seen as the externalization of unconscious and/or transpersonal dynamics of psychological forms that underlie the visible, a multidimensional dimension without boundaries.

"When the forces of growth overwhelm the forces of inertia, a developmental transition or crisis occurs."

— R. Walsh

Assagioli understood that such experiences can have a great evolutionary value and that they derive mainly from the superconscious. Spiritual emergencies can lead to the development of awareness of the "I" as Self, realizing that we already are a Self. In other words, the crises that come from material emerging from the superconscious in the field of consciousness of the "I" are generally signs of evolutionary growth for the subject if contextualized in a suitable relationship of psychological support.

4- Knowing How and Knowing Why

The material emerging from the pre-personal unconscious can lead to involutional crises, hindering the evolutionary growth of the subject and the development of awareness of one's ontological True Nature, if not contextualized and elaborated in an ideal field of psychological support.

Self-realization is an awakening into the consciousness of an area of experience (the superconscious) precluded to the many, in which the creative process of Synthesis leads to the harmonization of the many subpersonalities present in the psychic system represented by the Egg Diagram into an organic and functional whole, a motivating and catalyzing element endowed with elevated qualities. A nature that Abraham Maslow defined as higher-order and Stanislav Grof, in The Revolution of Consciousness as progressing along a spiral:

"What we are going towards is not just a simple regression or return to old ideas but a progress along a spiral, where some old elements turn out to be on a higher level as part of a creative synthesis between ancient wisdom and modern science."

- Stanislav Grof

The question now is how to free the mind from those chains that make the subject a prisoner of habits. This is a key topic in coaching. In the *Yoga Sutras* Patanjali gives a detailed codification of this fundamental passage from bondage due to enchainment with the material to the liberation from it, called *Kaivalya* or *Moksha*. In this process of Yoga the mental field becomes crystalline, gaining the ability to reconnect with the Self and draw on the latent transpersonal qualities, the Virtues (*Siddhi*), streaming from the transpersonal region of the psyche, the Superconscious.

When the egocentrism related to unconscious identification with subpersonalities and related dynamics begins to loosen its grip through disidentification, a transmutation of values takes place. The vicious grip of attachments to one's ingrained beliefs relaxes because of the change in the meaning of identity as it becomes no longer egocentric but reconnected to the Self; this is a critical and delicate step that puts us in touch with the wisdom deeply inherent in ourselves so that we can later express it in our daily lives.

COACHING THE ESSENCE

An unprepared field of consciousness of the "I" or one that has not accomplished sufficient personal psychosynthesis to metabolize transpersonal energies is subject to the dynamics described above of "ego appropriation", or "narcissistic recruitment". The result is "spiritual bypassing", accessing the spiritual world without going through a proper process of personal self-development- a process that allows one to position oneself at will in the psychic field as an Observer and Director, to truly be the Leader from the Self.

Abraham Maslow, in his unfinished and little-known "Plateau Experience" theory (1964), left significant research insights into experiences of the transcendental nature of Being and unitive states of consciousness or non-dual states. Settling, one step at a time moments, of enlightenment, insights, significant or impactful experiences throughout life, as well as moments of flow in which a sense of belonging is experienced as inner peace, is preparatory to the natural development of consciousness, experiencing in daily life the extraordinary in the ordinary.

"The result was a kind of unitive consciousness...the simultaneous perception of the sacred and the ordinary, or the miraculous and the ordinary, or the miraculous and the generally constant or easy-effortless sort of experience. Now I perceive through the aspect of eternity and it becomes mythic, poetic and symbolic about ordinary things... one always lives in a world of miracles."

— A. Maslow

References for this chapter:

Curtis, Andrew S. (2008). *Thinking about the Will in Coaching.* The Synthesis Center

Firman, Dorothy. *Strategies for the New Coach.* The Synthesis Center

Firman, Dorothy, Ed. (2018). *The Call of Self-Psychosynthesis Life Coaching: Taking Coaching into the Depths and Heights of Transpersonal Psychology.* Synthesis Center Press

Pelizzatti, Cristina (2013). *Transpersonal Psychology and The Human-Animal Connection*. Thesis Presentation, Naropa University USA.

Rogers, Carl (1978). *Carl Rogers on Personal Power: Inner Strength and its Revolutionary Impact*. Delta

Scharmer, Otto & Kaufer, Katrin (2013). *Leading from the Emerging Future*. Berrett-Koehler Publishers

Shaub, Richard & Shaub, Bonney Gulino (2015). *Transpersonal Development*. florencepress.com

Shaub, Richard & Shaub, Bonney Gulino (2015). *Dante's Path*, florencepress.com

Tart, Charles (1984). *Transpersonal Psychology*, Crisalide ed.

Vaughan, F. (2008). *Thinking about the Transpersonal*. Andrew S.Curtis for The Synthesis Center

Vaughan, F. (2008). *Transpersonal Context, Content and Process*

Williams, Patrick & Menendez, D. (2015). *Becoming a Professional Life Coach*. Norton & Company

COACHING THE ESSENCE

CHAPTER 5

PSYCHOSYNTHESIS COACHING
The Stages of the Process

In Psychosynthesis Life Coaching we frequently use a sequence that consists of five steps. Each step represents a specific coaching process.

1. Recognition, naming, and subsequent mapping in the Egg Diagram of main psychic contents.
2. Acceptance of the presence of these contents
3. Coordination of psychic contents by the "I"
4. Transformation of psychic contents, bringing to light the transpersonal quality present in their core
5. Synthesis: psychic contents now exist as enablers for the "I"

Through the new awareness gained in this process the client realizes the importance of the objective world. It is like a laboratory where they can experiment, learn how to challenge themself and train their skills, and to grow, not through exploitation but learning through experience how to grasp every nuance and appreciate it with gratitude, as every moment, every experience, is valuable and given to us as a precious evolutionary opportunity.

We can truly revolutionize our path by going through each experience in objective reality knowing how to choose which inner attitude to take in order to be proactive, going beyond moments of discouragement and perceived inability, and reconnecting with our deep spiritual nature.

By heading to the profound heights of our essential reality we can truly choose to live each experience soulfully, tapping into the highest potentials and actively participating in the evolution of our consciousness.

Being Who We Already Are

"When the demigods leave, the gods come."
- R. W. Emerson

The process referred to as *Ahaṁkāra* of creating the sense of separateness, forming the conditioned "I" as indicated in the involutional cascade of the Samkhya, distances and alienates us from our True Spiritual Nature, but the awareness of this connection is never completely lost. The motivating force rooted in the psyche that expresses itself at all levels of development in Maslow's scale of needs is indicated by the I's desire to return to the experience of its natural divinity, the meta-needs at the top of the pyramid, instinctively or deliberately following the "Call of Self" whispered among the hubbub of multiple self-images.

I call this primordial separation and sense of non-belonging, colored by an underlying nostalgia, the "primeval wound" which we all carry. It refers to the natural process that leads the subject to move from the transpersonal dimension to the objective and manifest one, linked to the personal dimension, composed of a multitude of self-images carrying basic needs. This process is described by Maslow in his five categories of human needs, which I see as dominated by "primeval wounds".

The "primeval wound" creates the sense of separateness and distortion of the I, defined in the Vedas as *Ahaṁkāra*. The "I" becomes encapsulated in the psyche, identified with the various changing self-images and becoming ignorant of its True Nature, linked to the dimension of doing- therefore to suffering.

In the *Yoga Sutras* Patanjali describes the purification process

5- Psychosynthesis Coaching

of the mental field, making the field of consciousness of the conditioned "I" / *Ahaṁkāra* clear as a diamond so that it can finally reflect the light of the Self, through the transformation of psychic contents and transmutation of related energies, rendering them at the service of the Self.

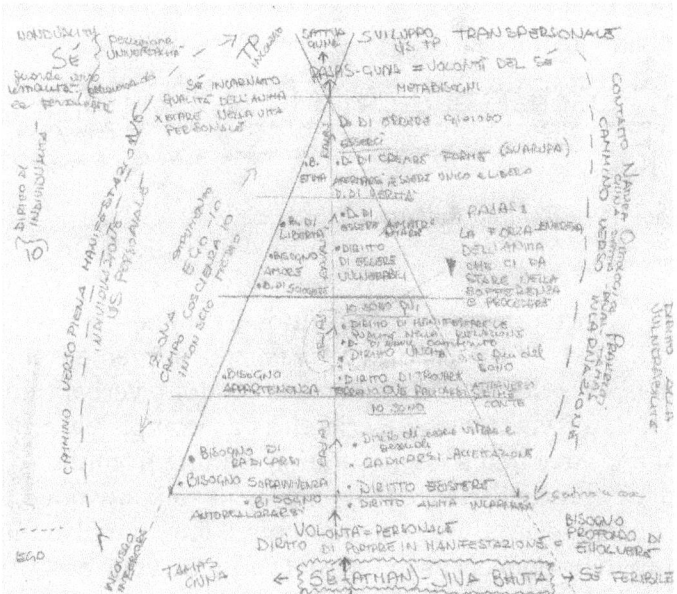

Graphic: C. Pelizzatti (2015)

The Self is positioned at the base of Maslow's pyramid as a motivating force pushing for the full realization of the five basic needs. We can contextualize this process as Personal Psychosynthesis, developing all the necessary tools mapped in the Star of the Psychological Functions, harmonizing them and making them available to the "I" for the next step up to the meta-needs and beyond- Transpersonal Psychosynthesis. This is the path of realization of one's True Nature: Being a Self that manifests and expresses Itself through the "I", Its reflection and counterpart, equal in quality and different in magnitude, with psychophysical tools suitable for one's evolution.

The Vedic Tradition teaches us that among the myriads existing in cosmic manifestation the human form is very, very rare to obtain, possessing as it does (as we do!) all the requirements and power for acquiring Self-realization and thus the evolution in consciousness which is our spiritual birthright and path.

"By doing the difficulty will be solved."

- Aurobindo

From Personal Leadership to Transpersonal Leadership

"The Self is Peace, that Self am I"

- Roberto Assagioli

The science of consciousness finds its highest expression in the Vedic texts of the *Bhāgavata Purana*, the supreme compendium of all knowledge. This is ancient Wisdom, verbal traditions thousands of years old, described as a "completely transcendental and liberated sound vibration coming from the spiritual world", a spiritual science that enables us to know not only the root cause of everything, the Supreme Being, but also the relationship that connects us to the root cause in a meaningful way.

A text dense with spiritual power, the *Bhāgavata Purana* is composed in the Sanskrit language. Also called simply the *Purana*, it is the authentic commentary on the Vedanta sutra by the author himself, Viasadeva. The wisdom of India is outlined in the *Vedas*, ancient Sanskrit texts that are part of the Revealed Tradition (*Shruti*), which touches on every area of human knowledge.

According to Vedic wisdom, we are a material manifestation of a state of consciousness, subject to the great Laws of Nature defined as *Prakṛti* and its energy bonds, the *Gunas: Sattva, Rajas, Tamas*. Releasing oneself from these very powerful external energies of the Supreme Being which condense matter into various forms is the basis of the choice, handed down by all sacred Traditions, to follow the evolutionary path toward the Source. The reconnection of all things with the Source allows the

5- Psychosynthesis Coaching

achievement of Liberation (*Kaivalya* or *Moksha*) from the bonds with the Guna and attainment of the state of Non-Duality or Synthesis with creation, creatures, and the Creator.

In Psychosynthesis this process consists of achieving the realization of being a Self in expression through an "I" immersed in a certain historical personality composed of multiple chronically conflicting parts, which has the ability, thanks to a reconnection with its Source, to harmonize and master the dynamics of evolution in consciousness. The result is Leadership at the transpersonal level or Self-Leadership.

Originally the Vedas were transmitted orally (Guruparam-para) and first written down over 5000 years ago by Srila Vyasadeva. After compiling the Vedas, Srila Vyasadeva codified their essence in the aphorisms known as the *Vedanta-Sutras*. The *Shrimad Bhāgavatam* (*Bhāgavata Purana*) is his commentary on these. It consists of approximately 14,500 stanzas divided into twelve sections.

"A person who mistakes a rope for a snake is overcome with fear, but his fears vanish as soon as he realizes that the so-called snake does not exist. Similarly, for those who fail to recognize You as the Supreme Soul of all souls, the illusory material existence presents itself in its full extent, while for one who knows You, it instantly disappears."

- Şrimad-Bhāgavatam C.X, cap. 14, v. 24

From the *Yoga Sutras* of Patanjali, Kaivalya Pāda:

4.34 *"Pure aware consciousness, empty of objective contents moved by an uninterrupted flow of the fundamental qualities of nature (guna), is the foundation of liberation, isolation in pure awareness, the power to see one's ontological form (svārupa) or power of vision that liberates."*

The question posed by Stephen Hawking *"What puts fire into the equations?"* finds a prospective answer in considering consciousness not as "something out there" but as the focus and engine of the manifest and measurable physical world; a deeply interconnected and correlated system. This concept is described

COACHING THE ESSENCE

by many schools of thought, including Rupert Sheldrake's Unified Field Theory and Heisenberg's principle of Non-locality or Uncertainty.

"As in the human body, so the cosmic body. As in the human mind, so in the cosmic mind. As in the microcosm, so the macrocosm. As in the atom, so the universe."

-The Upaniṣads

To ascend to heaven Dante, in the Divine Comedy, must immerse himself in the Lete and the Eunoè- to remember the good things done in life and forget the actions committed not in line with the Supreme Good. Psychosynthesis has a similar metaphor in that to ascend to heaven (the superconscious) one must lighten up: as defined by Assagioli, *"problems are not solved, they are forgotten"*.

This does not mean removing them, it is forgetting them that represents a catharsis. This takes place by shifting thought to something else that can counterbalance, scale back the dominant emotion and stop energetically feeding the recurring problem or idea. Something that is good, positive, joyful in context and in the larger frame of life, which we can by choice increase.

Psychosynthesis Life Coaching facilitates this cathartic process, which also coincides with the process of resilience at the transpersonal level that I mentioned earlier.

Not in the least, forgetting, in this sense, means that at the level of the Self we are untouched by any emotional movement. The "I" or personal self, unconsciously identified with psychic contents and forgetful of its Essence, is Its reflection, intent on moving exclusively along the personal dimension as if this were the only possible way that existed.

We need to get help from the soul, the Source, deeply wounded in its manifestation, the "I" encapsulated in the personality, subject to the dynamics of the unconscious system represented by the Egg Diagram in the space-time context. When we make the soul, even if "only" briefly perceived in ourselves or each other, the primary ally, we become familiar with it, can invoke it,

5- Psychosynthesis Coaching

learn to discern its "Calling "and choose to manifest it in actions in line with our Great Life Purpose, the Dharma (Universal Ethical Cosmic Order).

For my 50th birthday, I gave myself the first edition of the splendid book by Carl Jung that was coming out at that time.

From "The Finding of the Soul" *Liber Primus - The Red Book*- C. Jung:

> "My soul, where are you? I speak, I call you...are you there? I am back, I am here again... after long years of wandering I have returned to you. Do you want me to tell you all that I have seen, experienced, and absorbed in me? Or do you want to hear nothing of all the noise of life and the world? But one thing you must know: one thing I have learned, is that this life is to be lived. This life is the way, the long-sought way to that which is unknowable and which we call divine. There is no other way. Every other way is wrong... How long has this separation lasted?... What immense joy to see you again, O my soul for so long disowned! Life has brought me back to you. Let us say thanks to life because I have lived, for all the serene hours and the sad ones, for every joy, for every sorrow. My soul, my journey must continue with you. With you, I want to go and rise to my loneliness."

In leafing through this impressive text, I saw with delight so many representations from the Vedic Tradition among its drawings. Assagioli was also a passionate scholar and connoisseur of this thousand-year-old Wisdom Tradition, and his constant references to this context are a source of renewed motivation for me in pursuing my studies and profession.

Being a Psychosynthesis Life Coach ... *to be an Ideal Model of Self-Leadership, which my clients and students can draw on, to become truly, authentically themselves.*

This, in a nutshell, is the essence of our attitude and positioning as PLCs, the profession as the tool that becomes the catalyst for Leadership, first passing from the personal level and then

COACHING THE ESSENCE

rising to the profound depths of our essential energy core at the level of the Self. Without the process of Personal Leadership (Personal Psychosynthesis) Transpersonal Leadership (Transpersonal Psychosynthesis) remains idealized, unattainable in its ultimate meaning.

"If one knows the Self and recognizes oneself in It, what desire, what attachment can hold the person in the body? He who by awakening has found the Self, embodied in this composite abode, becomes the creator of everything, master of the world, is the world himself."

- Bṛhadāraṇyaka Upaniṣad 4.4.33

The Ideal Model for the Self

Elio Pelizzatti: "Autoritratto" (1962)

Do you love me? But how much do you love me? What do you think about me? But how much do you think of me?

5- Psychosynthesis Coaching

How much do we want to adhere to the changing, fading, enchanting images that we inhabit so comfortably?

How often does our thought insistently return to an idea, a phrase that has impacted our mind?

How often because of a thought, a heartfelt phrase, an elusive image that makes us feel "full of what we really needed" at a certain moment, do we revolutionize our life by making it an odyssey, to follow its persuasive and bewitching song, attracted by its allure that confounds the "Call of Self"?

Our Source, the Self, whispers to us amidst the myriad inner voices of superficial self-images, which enchantingly seduce us, leading us back again and again to themselves, through the hubbub of rethought thoughts adhering to the past. They are truly adept at flatteringly diverting our attention away from the ontological goal, interfering with and slowing down the evolutionary journey that has as its goal the realization of our authenticity and essentiality, hindering the reconnection with the Self that only a flexible and dynamic Ideal Model can guarantee us.

As sleeping souls, when unconsciously identified with a superficial self-image (belonging to the objective dimension), we experience life from a limited perspective that has its meaning and value, but which by its nature is destined to end upon awakening. Subpersonalities hinder awakening by binding us to a dream that sometimes ends as a nightmare. Awakening to the realization that what we experience is of vital importance for evolutionary purposes but that once experienced it must be let go in order to embark on another adventure is an opportunity to enact qualities that need to be developed, trained, or acquired while, with gratitude, casting off others which are no longer useful.

The PLC as a trainer of mindfulness, consciousness, and will, is prepared to accompany the client in this critical step of awakening, according to the client's level of consciousness development. The partnership that is established from the very first meeting must have a certain quota of mutual chemistry, in which trust and safety are present all along the journey. This is the foundation of a successful expedition in which a

COACHING THE ESSENCE

mountaineer about to climb a peak trusts in the expert hands of their professional guide, hiking together along the route to the summit, carrying their backpack on their shoulders.

Cris: Biancograt (Bernina Group, m. 4050, 1996)

To hear the "Call of Self" emerging among the multitude of voices is to realize that despite the fulfillment of the primary needs related to subpersonalities and the realization of their goals (which are then always our own), despite the fatigue in the journey to reach them, we feel like we have reached a mirage. Something essential, something more deeply satisfying is missing. Then we embark on another goal and one after another we always come to feel the same lack of something indefinable, elusive but powerful and overpowering.

What we're up against is that there is an actualizing tendency that exerts a attractive power over the "I". Whichever is the field we're attracted to makes the difference between evolving or remaining stationary in an evolutionary process which is in itself inevitable.

Each self-image possesses an activating power; each, as Assagioli describes it, represents an idea-force (Alfred Fouillée, 1893), a synthetic principle that energetically condenses spirit and matter, generating a state of consciousness resulting from

5- Psychosynthesis Coaching

the fusion, in an undifferentiated way, of thought and emotion, from which emotionally related action emerges.

This psychoenergetic vision provides useful tools for the management of the inner dynamics related to subpersonalities. These are skills we can practice the moment we are disidentified from the subpersonalities: at this point, by surpassing them, we can bring to light the transpersonal qualities present in their core, empathetically welcoming them into the "I", into the vast psychic universe, aware that we are moving beyond limiting beliefs, heading toward the great evolutionary journey whose goal is Love.

These are dynamics that would be objective and functional for the subject if they are well coordinated and serve the emergence of the Self. The point is that instead they ensnare and imprison the subject unaware of their presence and power in the fulfillment of primary personal needs of which each part is the bearer. They become the motive and purpose around which the "enchanted and seduced" subject, unconsciously identified, revolutionizes their life's purpose, objectifying themselves and thus devoting their existence to the realization of this, illusory, purpose.

Assagioli describes in detail the cause/effect relationships involved in this dynamism in his Ten Laws of Psychodynamics presented in his volume *The Act of Will* (1973).

At the same time, we need the superficial images so badly that we wear them as masks one over the other, burying the authentic face of who we essentially are because, in one way or another, they are functional as representations of that potential that lies latent deep within us.

Through these masks we have the impression we can "function normally", they help us feel that we can belong to a certain group context and, in their way, they help us to fill objective needs appropriately, too often at the expense of subjective needs.

Some masks become overwhelmingly preponderant or dominant, exercising a coercive "power over" the personal self, that, confused, (fused with them) represents them as if they were its true authentic self-image. The result is that the mask becomes

COACHING THE ESSENCE

the director and the main actor in what becomes a movie that has no accomplished plot and ultimately leaves the time that was spent, empty and unsatisfying.

A lot of effort to arrive at dissatisfaction.

Each self-image is made in the image and likeness of the Essence; it is potentially empowering if we learn to broaden and elevate its perspective, stepping out of its comfort zone, assuming the attitude of the nonjudgmental neutral observer. As PLC we listen with empathy to its need and learn how to direct it with loving firmness toward the essential goal: its development and subsequent integration into the "I". This transition can take place successfully once it is empathetically accepted in its primary need and positive intention.

By providing for its growth through the transformation and fulfillment of its primary need, once welcomed into the heart, we allow this image, and thus ourselves, to free ourselves/us from the dynamics associated with the past, to become useful qualitative energy in the present to create the ideal future that calls for its manifestation.

At that point we gain the ability to perceive the importance and value of its presence, as each image is a facet that points us to and represents a fundamental piece of the great intrinsic self-image, transcendent, implicit, and not directly perceivable but intuitable through its explicit counterpart, the "I" immersed in the personality: pure awareness, will, free of content.

Once the subject becomes aware that he or she is represented by multiple self-images each orbiting around a primary need, having at this point actualized them for evolutionary purposes through an inner ecological process, he or she can wear them as he or she chooses to achieve the desired and at the same time highest goal: Self-realization.

When the "I" realizes its True Nature, that of being a spark of the Self equal in quality yet at the same time different in quantity and power, It becomes instrumental to the Self; a Self that, while always remaining immobile, expresses and acts through the "I". The consequence of this "dynamic immobility" is a loosening of the ego-centered behavior of the self-images that thus become

5- Psychosynthesis Coaching

Its ideal agents toward achievement of the various life goals.

Each goal will thus be naturally aligned with the "Call of Self", actualizing and realizing more and more the "I" in its "True Nuclear Nature".

In other words, the "I" that identifies with only one superficial mask/self-image (belonging to the historical personality) and perceives and functions only from it, precludes itself of so many talents, limiting its possibilities of expressing itself authentically and fully, constrained by its self-imposed limitations, excluding itself from the higher potentials present in the inner multiplicity and, ultimately, access to the Self.

It experiences objective reality by functioning- employing the psychological functions- associated with only a single self-image, and the potential of this mask/role also becomes de-powering as it enchains the unconscious subject to the fulfillment of its egoic ends.

From this perspective, the ego or personal self, unconsciously identified with a self-image and related dynamics, becomes both "victim and executioner" of a game that inevitably leads to suffering, a game which is ultimately rooted in the belief that it is the object with which it identifies, forced to see only the reflected and distorted shadows of the real Truth, and dormant to its essential Reality.

"Darkness is but a garment of light. It is still light, but veiled; the darker it is, the more numerous the layers of the veil. Likewise, everything in life is one with its opposite, the extreme of each a veil for the other in varying degrees. If you feel hatred, remember that hatred. Is a thick layer that veils its opposite, love. And so it is the same with everything; everything is one. The union of the whole is individual, but also interdependent."

— Sefer ha-Zhoar, vol 1, f. 22v

COACHING THE ESSENCE

CHAPTER 6

DUKKHA: SUFFERING
A brief exploration

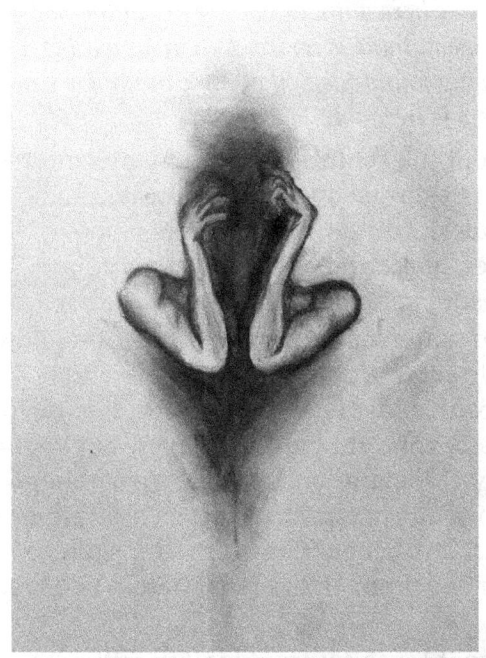

Graphic: Carmen Lenatti (2009)

"Sorrow. Its necessity, function and positive acceptance (understand its meaning)"

- Roberto Assagioli

COACHING THE ESSENCE

As underlined by the Millennial Wisdom Traditions, especially in the Vedas, *Dukkha* - suffering, can be overcome through the realization of one's True Nature. The teachings of Psychosynthesis also emphasize this point.

From the *Bṛhadāraṇyaka Upaniṣad* 8.1.74-75

"Om! In this city of Brahman, there is an abode, a small lotus flower. Within it is a small space. What is found in this small space is that which is to be sought, is that to whose understanding one must aspire."

"That does not grow old with old age and does not die if the body is killed. That is the true city of Brahman, which contains all desires. That is the Self, immune from evil, old age, death, pain, hunger, and thirst. Its desire is truth, what it conceives is Truth."

"Those who leave here without having found the Self and the desire for truth, for them, there is no freedom in all worlds. But those who leave here having found the Self and the desire for truth, for them in all worlds there is freedom."

Throughout the centuries and in many cultures the concept of suffering is expressed in different ways. Today's technology allows us quick, do-it-yourself insights: one goes on the Internet and types "suffering" and finds everything. This does not, however, ensure its understanding and elaboration.

I desire to understand where it starts from, how it acts, how we can go through it, overcome it, transcend it and synthesize it from a positive, evolutionary perspective devoid of dogma and then go beyond, toward ourselves, our root of authenticity veiled by the many enchanting appearances. Overcoming suffering from this perspective means training resilience at the transpersonal level, making it a primary skill in the Leadership process, starting from the personal level or Personal Psychosynthesis.

The moment I was confronted with Suffering, with a capital letter, I chose to face the heartbreak lucidly to understand what the meaning of suffering is, to learn how to react, to move forward by going beyond it, by going through it, to connect with meaning where no meaning can be found.

I learned to find the "Will to Meaning" that Viktor Frankl

6- Dukkha: Suffering

and Roberto Assagioli talk about in the darkness of pain, that "why" that once found, allowed me to endure suffering and find how to move beyond. This is a practice I do every day, every moment, when this suffering that accompanies me like a shadow seems to override the Light of my Self. At that point, I invoke my Self, ask for its strength, put myself back into its flow, and cling to its Light. Only then does the darkness lift, a new opportunity that I couldn't see before emerges from the fog of pain, and I seize it.

When I had everything I could wish for, life set before me my destiny. Together with the suffering of my beloved son Bianco, the Vedas and Psychosynthesis manifested themselves on my path and I welcomed them both, beacons in the total darkness of non-sense, where I began laboriously and painfully to find myself authentically.

I have since then embarked on the path of transformation, passing through and revisiting my life's experiences from another perspective: neutral, emotionally, and mentally detached. A higher sense, drawing on the potentials I have used, trained, and acquired along the way, especially through close contact with nature in its various manifestations.

I have learned so much from my beloved Valtellina mountains, which I have walked, climbed, skied, and experienced, as well as from the vast expanses of the rolling beaches of Normandy where I used to run as a child. Also from the majestic cold of the Great North that I crossed in my years of Sleddog practice together with my 'brothers': Siberian Huskies, as well as from the Art that I have breathed since childhood thanks to my father Elio (www. eliopelizzatti.it).

The many years spent in Paris with my grandmother told me about nonduality, living the reality in which multiplicity and multidimensionality found synthesis in the small details of luminous, nostalgic, and mysterious beauty that I visited and savored with so much love and passion together with her. From the years when, in the role of manager of an Alpine refuge, I worked to give shelter and nourish people from a material point of view I have learned to nourish human beings from another perspective through Psychosynthesis.

COACHING THE ESSENCE

From the moments of immense joy and those of immense pain as a mother, still today a very difficult "job" to sustain and manage at best; and from my own mother who of the will in every detail she's a Master, I have learned that I'm a Willer!

Without these lived life experiences, I would not have been able to face myself as myself, with myself, in my vicissitudes, paradoxically a human and at the same time spiritual being, driven by a mysterious force to always go beyond, traversing in the awareness of the moment the arduous paths that I walked one by one, step by step, stumbling, falling, always getting back up, more aware and stronger about myself, driven by the energy of my Self.

This is an arduous journey that I continue to travel, today no longer on the peaks of earthly mountains or racing for goals at the end of snowy tracks, or as a refugee in a material structure, but in the depths and heights of the soul as Psychosynthesis teaches and always flanked by the Vedas, foundations of my "Being Coach".

The mystery of life and the meaning we attribute to it is a matter with which we all come face to face, sooner or later, willingly or unwillingly. Caught up in a multitude of commitments, often without an awareness that shows the way forward, most people spend their lives being carried away by the current of the moment and die without having understood what it all was supposed to mean.

"...Slowly he dies who does not risk uncertainty, for the certainty of following a dream. Slowly he dies who does not find grace in himself, who destroys self-love, who does not let himself be helped. Slowly he dies and spends his days complaining about his misfortune, he does not ask questions about subjects he does not know. We avoid death in small doses, always remembering that being alive, requires far greater effort than simply breathing. Only ardent patience will lead to the attainment of splendid happiness."

- Pablo Neruda: "Ode to Life"

We must understand, first of all for ourselves, what is the

6- Dukkha: Suffering

meaning of living life, what is the meaning of being born and dying, passing through suffering. The brief earthly passage of my beloved son Bianco summarized jnana in vijnana (theoretical knowledge in awareness). His teaching and pattern of life was that of a Great Soul; his thoughts always turned to others, even in the most difficult times, his smile as pure as his name, that of an enlightened one. His teachings and words are those of a Great Sage. Luminous Soul, a beacon that lights the Way.

"My Light that illuminates the Way."

- Carmen Lenatti

"Serene, the Old Master Child
The blessed man, the candid father,
Has reunited with his Heaven.
Now is the light that watches over and sanctifies the world
Now is love in everyone's heart
'Be not afraid,' the voice resounds between heaven and earth, between mind and flesh.
'Be not afraid'."

- Lao Tzu

"He who knows the Supreme Brahman, in truth becomes that same Brahman. He goes beyond suffering, he goes beyond evil. Untied the knots of the heart, he becomes immortal."

- Māṇḍūkya Upaniṣad, 3.2

Realizing the Seed of Divine Intention until its Manifest Fulfillment

"He knows that he has an immense unrealized field to be made practically effective, and it is this sense of dissatisfaction that we must cultivate, striving to evoke the spiritual will that is burning in us and that we can summon and use as our accelerator."

- Roberto Assagioli

COACHING THE ESSENCE

So, when the "I" is under the hypnotic influence of unconscious contents, it has no access to its essential counterpart, adding suffering to suffering. The Self is not contacted because of distortions due to unconscious identification with subpersonalities and higher faculties are not accessible in their essence. Even should contact with the elevated regions of the psyche occur through various routes, transpersonal potentials may suffer a deviation of meaning due to the dominance of the main subpersonality aiming at the fulfillment of its ends, as previously indicated. This mechanism is called by transpersonal psychology "ego appropriation", "narcissism recruitment" or "spiritual materialism" (Trungpa Rinpoche, Epstein).

Photo: Biancograt (Bernina Group), C. Pelizzatti

On the path of Self-realization, when the "I" can distance itself from the attraction exerted by the various self-images through the technique of disidentification, it can use them at will by accessing from time to time the wide range of qualities and potentials that each part carries at its core. These contribute to consolidating the reconnection with the I-Self axis, thus the transpersonal amount of energy that the "I" can metabolize in the field of awareness.

At this point the "I" is sufficiently free from the dynamics of subpersonalities to be able to govern them as Director, through

6- Dukkha: Suffering

a power that finds synthesis in the heart: the Power of Love. From the heart and through the Power of Love flowing from the Self, suffering takes on its ultimate evolutionary meaning. The Power of Love is also definable as the "Will of Conscious Consciousness".

"Inner time does not admit past and future. Every moment is inscribed in the present. It is in the present instant when we turn to ourselves that this or that state of mind, this or that image emerges. Past and future do not belong to inwardness; they are only an outward way of framing the inner dynamics of consciousness."
   - Plutarch, 46 a.C.:

"Remember that it lies hidden within you what moves the threads of your existence and it is activated, it is life, it is a man if you can call it that."
   - op.cit. X, 38 Seneca: III a.C

From the archives of R. Assagioli:
"Each minute must be guarded,
Made worth the while somehow.
There is no other moment,
It always is just now.
Just now is the hour that's golden,
The moment to defend.
Just now has no beginning
Just now can never end."

The inner action described in Assagioli's writing as part of the three introductions to his son Ilario Assagioli's book, "From Pain to Peace" around 1951, the year of Ilario's departure, is aimed at *"affirming that pain and peace are the two extreme points of the trajectory that man travels in the course of his internal evolution, from the time he begins to acquire true self-awareness until he comes, willingly, to unite with universal Life, to fit harmoniously into cosmic rhythms."*

COACHING THE ESSENCE

The suffering that shakes us free from mental and moral laziness, from passive self-centered settling, that forces awakening, that arouses our latent energies and puts our "talents" into action is useful pain, as Assagioli points out:

> "To free man from excessive attachments to things and persons; to free him from the bondage in which his instincts, passions, and desires hold him; to prevent him from committing new errors and new faults... to discipline himself, to master the incomplete instinctive, emotional, and mental energies stirring within him, to order and organize them so that they become constructive and not destructive; to transform them, channel them, use them for fruitful and beneficial activities, for lofty and humanitarian ends... Grief induces and compels recollection, reflection, and meditation. It has the valuable and necessary task of calling us back from the outward-turning, scattered, dissipated, superficial, and materialistic life we too often lead. Grief shakes us, makes us "come back into ourselves", stops our harried rush; it makes us turn our gaze inward and upward... Then we begin to create silence within ourselves, to 'question', to 'pray' to 'invoke'. Then the conversation begins, the internal 'dialogue' with a Principle, a higher Reality, with our Soul, with God."

Paradoxically, considering suffering from the perspective of the Self, a catharsis occurs, from pain to joy, and Assagioli writes:

> "Pain has value if and insofar as it leads to its elimination, its overcoming. In other words, pain is not an end in itself, but a means of producing certain effects, of teaching certain lessons... When it has fulfilled these functions, we can and should say 'thank you' to it and then resolutely leave it behind. Indeed, the evaluation of pain should not make us suspicious and distrustful of joy. This has, like sorrow, high and necessary functions. First of all, it is 'dynamogenic': its first gift is to awaken and increase our energies, to activate even organic turnover, and to raise our vital tone. It can truly be regarded as an effective means of healing. Joy chases away the mists of depression, frees

6- Dukkha: Suffering

us from fear, and, above all, from unhealthy self-pity. Joy then is 'communicative': it pours out, and radiates on others benefiting them, and creating harmonious and fruitful relationships between us and them. Joy, therefore, far from being something to be scrupulous about, constitutes a real duty to others."

Joy is a duty to others starting with ourselves. Joy is ontological and calls for its expression through every possible path. In the Vedas, the living Being or spiritual entity, the *Jiva, Atman,* or *Purusha* depending on the context in which it is described, consists of Awareness, Immortality, Bliss - *Sat, Cit, Ananda*. In Psychosynthesis, the reflected Self is pure awareness and will, without content.

By penetrating and traversing the experiences of manifest life with an attitude aimed at Essential Joy, with an attitude of transpersonal inner resource through positioning in the Self as a "Guide-Coach" starting with ourselves, we can transform the meaning of suffering into a powerful evolutionary tool and help others to do the same, while simultaneously helping ourselves as well.

The PLC process is fundamentally a partnership between two Selves and showing our authenticity also means being able to show, if and when appropriate, our vulnerability and thus simultaneously our weakness, because we are human beings. The human factor is the most valuable tool we place at the service of our clients and it is the greatest goal we strive for, to be humanly and honestly ourselves as a transformational instrument for the client when we can manage our inner dynamics so that they do not interfere in the client's process.

Accepting our weaknesses in certain situations as a powerful potential is not easy and requires a lot of training. With "divergent" thinking, as I like to call it, I then try to look at my weakness as an inner strength, a great potential that is always in training, since to contain my weakness related to the suffering of my self-image as a mother it is required of me every day, every moment, to predispose myself to seek an ultimate meaning beyond the rational mind, that otherwise finds no peace.

COACHING THE ESSENCE

Through my weakness I can face my vulnerability, which allows me to be authentically myself, showing myself as I am, without masks, without makeup, in the nakedness of my being-which has nothing to do with physical nakedness of course! To be authentically myself, a perfectly imperfect human being, in search of perfection through the unveiling of Meaning beyond appearances, with Love as the ontological Force to draw on to help the living beings I meet on my path draw on their loving Source of Power.

"Love is a choice and a Verb. Love is a choice, not simply or always a rational choice, but rather the willingness to be present to others fully without pretense."

- Patrick Williams

"Love is the only way to welcome another human being in the most intimate nucleus of his personality."

- Viktor Frankl

This is my experience and my way, which since Bianco's departure has taken on the characteristics of helping people to make the soul the natural instrument in the becoming of life with its varied experiences, through Counseling and Coaching in Psychosynthesis, Ecopsychology, and Indovedic Psychology as the Science of Self-realization.

The Four Noble Truths are the basis of Buddhist teaching regarding Suffering:

"There is suffering"
"There is the origin of suffering"
"There is the cessation of suffering"
"There is a way to the cessation of suffering"

In the Pali language, derived from Sanskrit and used by the Buddhist canon, suffering is called *Dukkha*: "pain"- implying an incomplete, incongruous, unsatisfactory situation. The term *Dukkha* is composed of "Duh" and "Kha". "Duh" is a negative

6- Dukkha: Suffering

prefix and "Kha" means emptiness, thus a meaningless void.

Very briefly, the First Noble Truth deals with the fact that suffering "exists".

The Second Noble Truth teaches that greed is the main cause of suffering. Attachment to desire, not so much desire itself, is the matrix of suffering.

The Third Noble Truth defines how to emancipate oneself from pain by realizing the state of inner stillness called "*Nirodhaḥ*" in the Vedas.

The Fourth Noble Truth emphasizes the path to be taken to realize the cessation of suffering.

From the Gnostic Gospels of Jesus, taken from the "Nag Hammadi Library" circa 2nd century CE:

The suffering of Jesus and all human beings is treated in the "Carola of the Cross". He clarifies the meaning of suffering thus:

"If you know how to suffer
You will be capable of non-suffering.
Learn to suffer
And you will be capable of non-suffering."

From the "Inferno-Canto I" of Dante's "Divine Comedy": (1321-1472)

"In the middle of the walk of our life
I found myself in a dark forest,
for the straight path was lost."

A journey within suffering, to go beyond it, which Dante also undertakes in his "Divine Comedy". In this he is accompanied by the wise guidance of Virgil in undertaking a moral, value-driven, fully human journey through deep psychological regions to reach the peaks and meet Beatrice, representing spiritual Love, and together being able to "Mirar", to see, from that perspective, the absolute Beyond, the transpersonal realm.

This is a splendid metaphor for the inner transformational process that begins precisely in "the middle of the journey of our life", at the moment when the crisis leaves no alternative but to face it, for the Self calls in many ways. Having lost the "straight path", the "dark forest" appears in its difficulty, even in describing it. The traveler who realizes that he or she is in that existential state in which darkness, the more animalistic and instinctive component, prevails, they are trapped in a vicious circle related to the fear-attack-block or escape dynamics caused by the wilderness of personal life where dangers are always lurking. In this state they see only two paths: to flee or freeze.

From this psychological state of crisis related to existential change, thought can trap the person in self-reinforcing mechanisms; they become lost in this vicious cycle of thought that looks to the past for ways to move forward, generating a future bereft of spiritual awareness destined to only find them again cast into darkness.

From the *Bhagavad-Gītā*:

"Even if you were considered the worst of sinners, once you board the vessel of transcendental knowledge you will be able to overcome the ocean of suffering."

- Bhagavad-Gītā 4,36

"He who is never the cause of difficulty for others and by others is never troubled, who is equanimous in joy and sorrow, in fear and anxiety, is very dear to Me."

- Bhagavad-Gītā 12,15

"Nature is considered to be the cause of every material cause and effect, while the living being is the cause of the pleasures and sufferings he encounters in this world."

- Bhagavad-Gītā 13,21

CHAPTER 7

THE SCIENCE OF CONSCIOUSNESS

Involution and Evolution of the Psyche: the Cascade of Samkhya

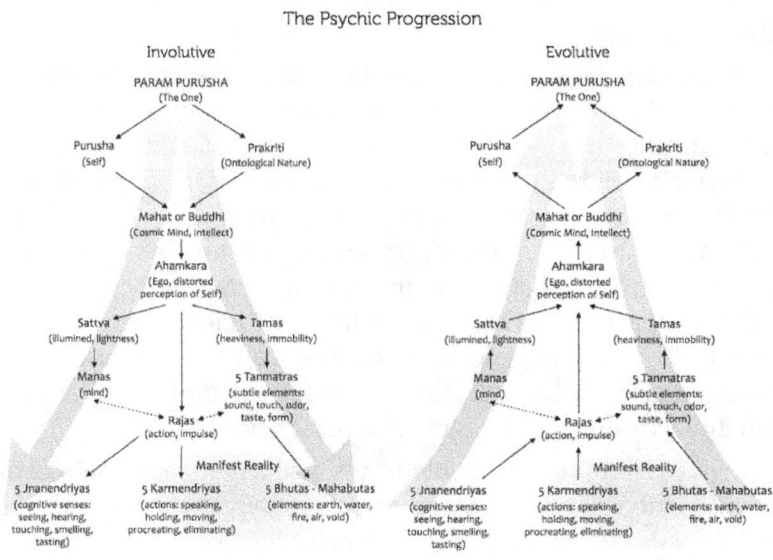

Graphic: W. Burr

Founded by the great sage Maharishi (Rishi) Kapila, the *Sāmkhya* is one of the oldest and most important schools of spiritual science. The *Sāmkyakārikā* compiled by Ishvara Krishna is the reference in this context. The central theme of the *Sāmkyakārikā* is *Dukkha*, Suffering, and the way to alleviate it. For an extended and thorough understanding of both subjects the *Sāmkyakārikā* is studied along with Patanjali's *Yoga Sutras*, providing a systematic enumeration and rational exploration of the principles that bring consciousness into manifestation.

Dukkha is intrinsically related to *Maya*, the manifest and impermanent nature, the effect of the underlying transcendental reality, thus real in its manifestation subject to the momentarily manifest dissolution or energy of an ontological, unmanifest energy reality present at its core and from which it originates.

The perception of the incessant change, appearance and dissolution of tangible forms (including the human form) subjects a spiritually unevolved consciousness to the emotional experience of deep fear related to a sense of loss. According to this current of thought this fear finds its root in *Avidyā*, the lack of spiritual awareness, resulting in an unclear, distorted view of reality due to unconscious identification with content with which the subject identifies, creating a sense of impermanent identity.

In the *Sāmkyakārikā* the psychological mechanism that determines the identification of consciousness with psychological contents and the manifestation of the sense of identity separate from one's original Essence, the conditioned "I" or psychosynthetic personal self, generally better known as ego, is studied with detail and scientific rigor. The ego from this perspective is the result of unconscious mechanisms to which the subject adheres due to ignorance about its ontological nature. Such a "product" is referred to as *Ahaṁkāra*, reflex and conditioned consciousness of the self, the "I" under the domain of subpersonalities from a Psychosynthesis perspective.

Two essential components in the science of *Sāmkyakārikā* are *Purusha*- the Self or Spirit, and *Prakṛti*, manifest ontological energy or matter consisting of three nuclear elements or influences of material nature, the Gunas: *Sattva, Tamas, Raja*.

Sattva is Purity, luminosity, immortality, pure consciousness; *Tamas* is heaviness, solidity, darkness, ignorance; *Raja* is movement, dynamic energy, anger.

From the interaction of the Gunas and their amalgamation emerge innumerable forms of manifestation and psychological types.

7- The Science of Consciousness

"The embodied soul, master of the body city, does not generate any activity, induce others to act, or create the fruits of action. All this is the work of the influences of material nature."

- Bhagavad-Gītā 5, XIV

The interaction between *Puruṣa* and *Prakṛti*, between Spirit and Matter, which begins the moment the Universal Self "casts" Its gaze upon them, sets in motion the combination of these three constituent elements of ontological Nature in a differential manner: the result is the manifestation of a specific forma mentis in a specific bio-psychic form.

Ahaṁkāra is the first form of the split personality, the "primeval wound" as I define it, indicative of the division that occurs immediately after the union between the *Puruṣa* / Spirit and *Prakṛti* / Matter, a wound which we all bear.

As a result, the field of consciousness of the "I" becomes isolated and narrowed, veiling awareness of its Essential Nature due to incessant identification with psychic contents, within the overall mental system called the *Cittā*, represented by the Egg Diagram of Psychosynthesis. The *Cittā* is composed of a multitude of energetic contents called *Samskaras*, which, agglomerating by equal energetic valence, give an instance to symbolic self-images exerting a strong attraction on the living being, the *Jiva*, (the psychosynthetic "I"), equal in quality and different in quantity from its source, the Self-*Puruṣa*.

Because of the incessant unconscious identification, the "I", pure awareness and will, becomes *Ahaṁkāra* / conditioned "I" and identified with the myriad contents (*Vṛtti*) flowing into the mental field and modifying it. The awareness of one's spiritual ontological origin is veiled, to the point of being sometimes completely obscured due to contact with the material emerging from the unconscious in the field of awareness. The "I" disconnects from its Source, thinking to be the proponent of every action and beneficiary of the result related to the action that is performed under the influence of the Gunas. The agent "I" is acted upon unconsciously, objectifying itself.

From this conditioned positioning, every action is subject to the Great Laws of Karma, whereby every action is correlated with an equal and opposite reaction, that is, one that returns to the sender and binds the subject to an endless cycle of birth and death, the *Saṃsāra*, and consequently to suffering, *Dukkha*.

The action that follows the profound and elevated "Call of Self" emerges at the point when the "I" dis-identifies from mental contents and observes them from a different and elevated perspective, directs them at will and follows the Purpose of the Self that calls for manifestation. At this point, the action that emerges is in line with one's Dharma or Life Purpose according to the Great Universal Laws, the Ethical Cosmic Order.

This is the quintessential action or Yoga of Action, which in Psychosynthesis is translated as acting by grounding the Self into manifestation in everyday life through a personality well harmonized around a coordinating center: the "I" that has realized its True Nature, that of Always and Forever Being a Self.

The Ideal Model is a subpersonality that we create to manifest Self-animated action through awareness of one's ontological Nature and simultaneously chronic inner dynamics, which must be managed with all our abilities.

Avidyā is considered the "Great Ignorance", the first of the five great conditionings Maharishi Patanjali describes in his *Yoga Sutras* (s.III below), which binds the living being, the *Jiva* (the psychosynthetic "I" encapsulated in a bio-psychic form), to suffering.

According to the *Yoga Sutras*, there are five major obstacles to spiritual realization or five afflictions called *Pancha-klesha*. These represent the motivating factors of human action, an action that produces, as mentioned earlier, Karma and thus *Dukkha*, suffering in the endless cycle of *Saṃsāra*.

"Because of this forgetfulness, the individual being, which is spiritual in nature, accepts the influence of material energy as its field of action and mistakenly attributes to itself the activities it performs under these influences."

- Bhāgavad Purana, III.26.6

"Avidyāsmitaragadveshabhiniveshah klesha"

-Patanjali, s.III Sadhana Pada

7- The Science of Consciousness

The Pancha-kleshas are:

Avidyā (Cosmic Ignorance)

Asmita (Attachment- Selfishness)

Raga (Egoic Desire, Greed)

Dwesha (Aversion-Repulsion)

Abhinivesha (Fear of death)

Avidyā: Essential ignorance about one's True ontological Nature. The subject becomes confused or fused, therefore identifying with psychic contents, thinking they are those contents, clinging to them greedily and adopting a sense of identity tied to transitory reality. In this state they exchange the eternal for the non-eternal, good for evil, being for non-being, life for non-life, to the point of losing awareness of being a Self which is doing a journey in a manifest form, so as to learn how to return to the Source. The subject has become the object, subjugated to the senses and psychological contents, in the space-time trajectory of the incessant cycle of birth and death.

The consequence of this unconscious association with contents is called *Asmitah*: the identification of the Self with the historical self, which Jung defines as "the total sum of the psychic contents with which the subject identifies" and which in Sanskrit is *Ahaṁkāra*- the distorted reflection of the self, the "I" unconsciously identified with the contents.

From this perspective, we can understand the enormous amount of energy consumed in this incessant process and the struggle necessary to identify the contents and related dynamics because of the unconscious identification that practically carries the subject against the current oriented toward its Source. Like an object on the surface of the river follows the current of the river, the subject is following the flow of the current of events, being unaware of unconscious identifications with them, having no power to change, and remaining in the path carried by more powerful energies, tossed about by the obstacles they encounter, somehow trying to survive their own life.

The senses or psychological functions are trapped in the

identification of the moment, and the conditioned subject perceives objective reality from a perspective functionally limited to the fulfillment of the need each subpersonality carries for its survival.

Spiritual realization is defined in the Vedas as going against the energetic current of manifestation: *Maya*, the external energy of the Creator. The ascent into the cascade of *Sāmkyakārikā* is defined as the evolution of the psyche and represents the path for the subject to return to the Source, first going "into the current by crossing it" or involuting to experience it, and then choosing to change direction and direct the course "against the current". This is related to the Self-realization process, the natural tendency to return to the Source. In Psychosynthesis, this upward direction is motivated by the Self at every level.

"*Motto of Ψ*
The only way out is the way up"

-Roberto Assagioli

Going Through and Beyond is the process that underlies the context of Psychosynthesis as a Transpersonal psychology. It involves going through obstacles to learn how to train one's abilities, putting innate talents into action, acquiring others, balancing one's energies, and generating ecological psychological energy to be injected into the context in which the subject interacts. Tapping into the Source to manifest one's authenticity every moment, since every moment matters.

Photo: Cris (Cambridge, MD)

7- The Science of Consciousness

But before we can go against the current of *Maya*, we have to go into it all the way, go through it, learn to bring into play our essential qualities and the abilities that we already possess, acquire others, and train innate resilience, the innate ability to direct the course of our path toward our destiny.

By traversing and going Beyond the dynamics of the manifest personal dimension, toward the unmanifest transpersonal destination, the "goal beyond goal", we experience our full humanity; this is the path that has been waiting for us forever, to then return to the dimension of the here and now, not only strengthened but grown in awareness and rooted in our Essence.

This is the process of Self-Leadership that underlies resilience as the ability to traverse obstacles by training one's highest potentials through tapping into the dimension of Being and essential values, growing in awareness and manifesting much higher energies in ecological and sustainable action. The psychosynthetic approach, and millennia earlier the Vedic Wisdom, point to this process through detailed, evidence-based methodology and direct experience, codifying the science of spirit as a solid approach to Leadership from the Self.

The mind, once conditioned by unconscious identifications with sense objects, produces a continuous chain of thoughts that follow one another incessantly, hindering any attempt at meaningful concentration. *Asmita*, or the subject's identification with psychic contents, confuses the observer's Real identity with what is seen (the object), becoming from that perspective the object itself (objectifying itself).

Raga and *Dvesha*: attraction and repulsion, represent the dynamic duality that characterizes the polarity due to the subject's unconscious identification with the observed objects.

Abhinivesha is the attachment to transitory forms, including self-images, resulting in fear of their loss, and ultimately fear of death. From this conditioning, the subject, fully identified and therefore subject to the content to which they adhere, has no access to awareness of their ontological Essential Nature. They bind their own identity to a self-image that not only masks their awareness but also binds them to the dynamics described

COACHING THE ESSENCE

by Assagioli in the Ten Laws of Psychodynamics. The fear underlying the state of being resulting from this conditioning can only be overcome by Self-realization.

The psychology of Yoga teaches that serenity cannot be achieved unless the mental field is established in the Self. Interference (*Vṛtti*) or modification of the mental field shown in the Egg Diagram agitates the mind of the identified subject who fails to maintain a presence on their internal center of synthesis, the "I". They remain, as it were, entangled in the incessant flow of content and subpersonalities, impairing concentration on the Self, and consequently impeding connection with their intuitive function.

Psychological functions, therefore, are under the dynamics of the subpersonality that dominates the subject's field of consciousness at any given time. As defined in the *Bhagavad-Gītā*, the mind can be the subject's best ally or worst enemy.

"Man must use his mind to liberate himself, not to degrade himself. The mind is the friend of the conditioned soul, but it can also be its enemy."

- Bhagavad-Gītā 5, VI

"For the one who has mastered it, the mind is the best friend, but for the one who has failed to do so, the mind will remain the worst enemy."

- Bhagavad-Gītā 6, VI

The mind can re-emerge to its original state as an instrument of the Self, becoming clear and transparent again, through the discipline of Yoga or Self-realization. When the mind returns to being like a clear crystal, the light of the Self filters through the psychic contents, illuminating the "I". By maintaining a presence in the Self, the subject becomes aware of its intimate and unbroken relationship with its Source, positively transforming its experiences in contact with manifest reality as an opportunity for learning and growth in consciousness.

At this point subpersonalities undergo an evolutionary

7- The Science of Consciousness

transformation and become the best allies of the "I", thanks to contact with spiritual energies that can now flow clearly and without distortion into the field of consciousness, shown in the middle unconscious of the Egg Diagram, our mind-field.

"Visible nature has splendor, action, and stability and consists of the encounter of the sensory faculties and sense organs, with the elements. That which is seen has for its purpose the experience, pleasure, and liberation of the jiva."

— Patanjali, s.XVIII Sadhana Pada

The following is a map of the involution of the psyche as described in the *Sāmkyakārikā*:

Involutive Cascade of the Psyche

PARAM PURUSHA (The One)

- **Purusha** (Self)
- **Prakriti** (Ontological Nature)

Mahat or Buddhi (Cosmic Mind, Intellect)

Ahamkara (Ego, distorted perception of Self)

- **Sattva** (illumined, lightness)
- **Tamas** (heaviness, immobility)

- **Manas** (mind)
- **5 Tanmatras** (subtle elements: sound, touch, odor, taste, form)

Rajas (action, impulse)

Manifest Reality

- **5 Jnanendriyas** (cognitive senses: seeing, hearing, touching, smelling, tasting)
- **5 Karmendriyas** (actions: speaking, holding, moving, procreating, eliminating)
- **5 Bhutas - Mahabutas** (elements: earth, water, fire, air, void)

Graphic: W. Burr

COACHING THE ESSENCE

During the process of "falling" that cascades to incarnation in a certain bio-psychic form, the living being (*Jiva*) becomes *Jiva-bhuta*, a being encapsulated in a specific form, ignorant of its spiritual origin, with a distorted sense of identity with which it unconsciously associates itself (*Ahaṁkāra*). In the process it binds to the five conditionings described above, subject to the incessant change of matter that is transitory by nature. It thus partakes of the experience of the fear of death, being convinced that it is only and essentially the transitory form that covers it (the object), rather than the subject that experiences manifest reality to awaken and evolve.

In this involutive course, consciousness moves from the non-manifest state to manifestation. Consciousness remains untouched during this change; what changes is the subject's state of awareness of its own identity, according to the contents it experiences by identifying with them, as Assagioli confirms in the eighth Law of Psychodynamics:

"All the various functions, and their many combinations in complexes and sub-personalities, set in motion the realization of their purposes <u>outside our consciousness,</u> and independent of, and even against, our will."

- Roberto Assagioli

According to the perspective of Vedic science, matter - Maya, to which the psyche also belongs, is informed by substance, the *Purusha*-Self, every moment. Thanks to the plasticity of the psychic or mental field (*Cittā*, the Egg Diagram in Psychosynthesis), the subject, or more precisely the psyche encapsulated in the subtle matter, can mold itself and take on the form of the object it experiences. Thanks to its instruments, the psychological functions shown in the psychosynthetic Star Map, the experience of the object becomes detailed and complete.

The problem arises when the subject does not distance themself appropriately from the observed object and remains unconsciously identified with it, solidifying, through constant repetition, their roots in what they have observed. As awareness narrows to this perspective, the "game" is over. The subject's

7- The Science of Consciousness

identity becomes rooted in the image that allows them to "function" (in the sense of using their psychological functions) best and habitually in certain circumstances, a mode that allows the individual to feel experienced and able to live their life in a "normal", contextualized way.

In synthesis, each psychological content that is associated with equal energetic valence, corresponding to a specific forma mentis and emotion, takes on the appearance of the best ally for the subject at a given moment and becomes an inner agent of synthesis. While the subject has access to specialized psychological functions as codified by Assagioli in the Ten Laws of Psychodynamics, a subpersonality is formed that interferes in the realization of one's True Nature, or in the path of ascending the evolutionary cascade, blocking the subject at a certain level of psychological development, regardless of chronological age.

Such psychic conglomerates are referred to as Samskaras in the Vedas, powerful energy containers that we unconsciously carry around in the psychic field, energies that need to be transformed for evolutionary purposes, otherwise, they still find a way to manifest themselves, and not always for evolutionary purposes. The *Samskaras* are immense energy resources that we do not access, similar to having a large capital banked without knowing it, as Assagioli points out in one of his "Assagiolini" (handwritten notes):

"Ignored latent energies. It's as if one had a large deposit available in his bank and didn't know it!! It's an unlimited deposit!! Develop"

Each subpersonality is motivated by primary needs, and the satisfaction of these needs becomes the objective of each goal. A client always comes into session from a subpersonality with a goal brought by whatever self-image dominates the "I"'s field of consciousness in the moment, calling the "I" to the realization of its (the subpersonality's) goal.

The "Call of Self" is filtered by the subpersonalities and becomes an inner voice silenced by the din of the continuous inner hubbub that pushes the unconscious subject in every direction, except the one they desire and essentially need. The subject, being stuck in the incessant chain of primary needs, forgets the real need to be satisfied: the evolutionary one, and confuses the "Call of Self" with the persuasive and bewitching call of one or another subpersonality. This is the mode from which the conditioned "I" operates, in ignorance of its Ontological Nature.

The disidentified "I" is always moved by future, evolutionary ends, tending to return to the Source, through manifestation of conscious acts motivated by purposes in line with the power of "syntropic" energy (Assagioli), the *Dharma*. Bearing in mind the Laws of Psychodynamics (Assagioli), the power of the ideal image (Ideal Model) defines the vision of the goal to be pursued, holding firm the Presence at the Center (I-Self) in the movement toward the great goal: Self-realization.

This perpetuation of incessant needs to be satisfied related to the multiplicity of our inner world or "multiple" spirit, as Assagioli defines it, is due to the unconscious identification with whatever content is present in the field of consciousness at the moment, and hinders the evolutionary process of the subject. The more the superficial self-image exerts its power over the "I", the more the subject is under its control, draining spiritual energy toward the dimension of doing, instead of using it to rise back to its Source, the dimension of Being.

The realization of inner multiplicity as a quality of Oneness, thus as an immense resource of energy, is a focus in the PLC process. Being and becoming more and more oneself while achieving the desired outcome is the context of the transformational, transpersonal process with which we coach our clients. Therefore, in PLC we recognize that every event that the embodied being encounters along the life journey represents a huge opportunity for learning and training awareness, learning to distinguish the "Call of Self" among the many inner voices, thus building a solid foundation in the process of Personal Leadership or Personal Psychosynthesis.

At this point, the subject can choose at will to answer this "Calling", reversing their direction and regaining the ascending path (the meta-needs in Maslow's Pyramid) moving upward

7- The Science of Consciousness

and outward beyond their inner dynamics, finally reconnecting with their Source, as shown in the *Sāmkyakārikā* cascade and achieving Liberation from the viscous grip of the *guna*, as described by Patanjali in his *Kaivalya-pāda*, VI, 31, 32,33,34:

"When all the veils covering the true have been removed, knowledge becomes infinite, very little remains to be known."

"From this attainment, the transformation of the incessant flow of the fundamental qualities of nature begins to end, having fulfilled their mission for the realization of consciousness."

"The subject can now observe that the flow is a series of events appearing moment by moment, in which one form transforms into another."

"For the Purusha, pure content-empty awareness, the purpose of the activities of the fundamental qualities of nature in their flow is recognized in the moment of their interaction; by isolating oneself in pure awareness one is rooted in one's true nature, the power of pure vision. And that is all."

The "Will to Meaning" (V. Frankl) is the key to reversing the involutional process and ascending, to reconnecting with one's Source. Assagioli emphasizes, as do the Vedas, that cladding ourselves in a the human form is an opportunity that ultimately allows us to have the ability to choose how to act, to respond instead of react, once awareness of our Essential Nature emerges. At that point we can use personal will for evolutionary purposes, in line with the Transpersonal Will of the Self or Transpersonal Leadership.

This is also the process of Transpersonal Psychosynthesis or Self-realization. The evolution of the psyche as described in the *Sāmkyakārikā* transcends manifest experience by activating one's psychological potentials and functions to find the underlying meaning and the positive intention concealed therein, and then going further, toward the Essence. The larger goal of this process of evolution in consciousness is the realization of one's Spiritual Nature.

The motivational drive to return to the Source is the subject's deep desire to return "Home" in the Self-*Purusha* and at the same time to heal the "primeval wound" caused by the separation from the initial state of quiescence between *Purusha* (soul, Self, consciousness) and *Prakṛti* (ontological Nature).

As mentioned above, by "primeval wound" I mean the separation of an infinitesimal fraction of the Transpersonal Self from the higher Source, the Universal Self, which in turn embodies and experiences Its limited form through the personal self or "I". Once encapsulated in the psyche, subtle matter, the incarnated subject has potentially the ability to identify with the senses to experience and evolve through their interaction, and then dis-identify from them, recognizing them as other than themselves.

Through the process of Yoga or reconnection of the "I" with the Self through regained awareness, a transformation, purification, and sublimation of unconscious contents takes place. These become resources available to the "I", empowering it once chosen, with awareness, in their evolutionary functionality.

Only when the mind is focused and stable in the Self does Yoga take place, as the conjunction between the "I" and the Self: this is the state of Presence or non-duality that we want to achieve and maintain as PLC.

The *Vṛtti* incessantly agitate the mental field and prevent concentration, thus also the realization of the Self (the state of *Samadhi*). Patanjali explains in the *Yoga Sutras* how to transform the subtle causes of conditioning that bind us to the satisfaction of basic needs, slowing down the evolutionary process. Starting from what is manifest, by a backward process, we go to the subtle causes underlying the manifest, (from *Vyakta*- the manifest, to *Avyakta*- the substratum). This process also applies to the evolution from name- *Nama*, to form- *Rūpa*, then to Essence- *Svarūpa*.

Assagioli refers to this process as the technique of "Fractional Analysis", which is useful for working with unconscious content: from name, to form, to essence, starting from recognizing that they are there, naming them, and one small piece at a time, fractioning them precisely, just enough that the client can handle them.

7- The Science of Consciousness

We begin the exploration of contents to bring out their intrinsic quality and the positive intention related to their existence and presence, starting from the effect exerted on the subject. At this point clients become aware of both the presence of the contents and the effect of the dynamics of the contents on their personality and they can begin the process of acceptance.

Acceptance is a step that is not instantaneous; it is not about understanding but about comprehension, putting together, connecting reason, rational mind, and emotion by passing them through the heart where a different, empathic feeling emerges that comes from another dimension, the Self.

From here we move toward the underlying energy nucleus, and this core, brought into the light of spiritual awareness, becomes energy available to the subject, previously trapped in dynamics related to the subpersonality dominating the field of consciousness at the moment.

We therefore need to bring to the light of the Self, by a specific process, the unconscious contents that hinder both the attainment of the goal and the subject's self-awareness, so that they can be processed, one step at a time, and released, in essence, as a transpersonal value, then transformed into resources by their nuclear quality.

Being Manifest Consciousness

"In the Self are all powers. The Self is infinite Power."
- Roberto Assagioli

In 2013 I had the honor of personally meeting Prof. Vittorio Marchi, an expert in quantum physics, and organizing a seminar with him for an advanced training course that I was completing in psychoenergetics counseling. Here's a quote he provided during that occasion:

"What we see is the image in a 'mobile intelligent substance' which moves everywhere and yet remains always in itself. A substance that in its various aspects ceaselessly transmutes throughout the entire field of its visible and invisible mass, obscure and otherwise, and that, though located everywhere, resides at the same time in all points of Its Universal Organism. It is elusive to the analysis of scientific instruments and is revelatory instead to the cardio-neuro-cerebral system. One can only experience it deep within one's 'thinking essence' using the inner technology with which the human body is virtually equipped. It has no weight, in the sense that it does not feel centripetal or spherical gravity; it has no inertia, in the sense that it does not 'feel' strong nuclear force; it cannot be seen, in the sense that it does not interact with electromagnetism. It directs and governs cosmic evolution. It causes alchemy. It transforms nuclear matter. It governs the nuclear fusion of stars. It is masked by electromagnetic light. It cannot be seen but only felt in the form of emotion. It is the connecting link between the invisible and visible worlds. At the psychophysical level, we are involved in a biochemical network that is guided by an Intelligence Field that knows no limits, shared by all in the great psychosomatic network of 'cosmic grids'. This underscores the intimate interconnection between all systems of the human and universal organism, disrupting all principles of the traditional paradigm. What if we are a Unity interconnected with the Whole? We become what we think; life is a search for inwardness, through experience that is transformed into knowledge. If we ask what is the Quid that synchronously and creatively holds the universe together, the answer is Love. Love is that which animates and keeps Everything alive, as its very etymology 'A-MORS' which means 'Non-Death', the absence of death, hence life."

"Spirit and Matter, seemingly and relatively "enemies", can and must unite harmoniously in a dynamic synthesis, in the unity of life."

- Roberto Assagioli

7- The Science of Consciousness

Psychoenergetics Sampler

"Energy is substance and the substance of the dynamic divine Will"
— Roberto Assagioli

Consciousness acts in the psychic space of the relationship as a third element: <u>an Egg Diagram that unites that of the coach and that of the coachee</u>, whose purpose is to be a mirroring and reflective space. Consciousness is a-spatial, a-temporal, dissolving linear time related to the perception of the senses and the functioning of the rational mind. Space is condensed into a point at the center of the Egg Diagram, the "I", immersed in the field of consciousness, essentially composed of crystalline awareness, with evolutionary purpose and intention.

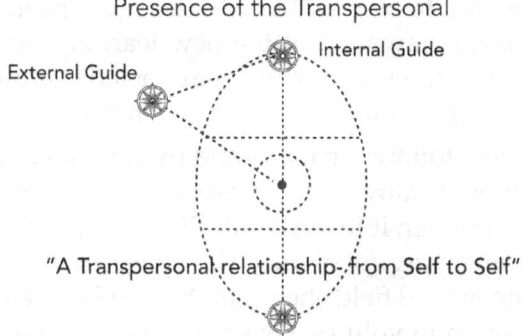

Graphic: Synthesis Coaching Associates

It is through identification with sensed objects through our organs of sensing as well as our physical bodies related to psychological functions that evolution can take place when identification is chosen at will. Time in a circular (curved) space moves in spirals, creating cycles. Time is a variable that must be condensed until it coincides with a *"locus"*, a state of consciousness which can be viewed metaphorically as a room to be furnished: the "I".

What do I put in this place?

The anchoring into the "I" of contents which enter the space to be furnished is fostered by repeated action, acting as if one were already that model which one chooses to wear. The efficacy of "Acting as If", a typical Ideal Model technique, is explained in neuroscience as the neuropsychological basis of learning: two interconnected neurons activated repeatedly reinforce their connection, creating a memory that lasts over time ("Hebb's Rule"). In the 6th Law of Psychodynamics described in his treatise *The Act of Will*, Assagioli explains:

> *"Repetition of actions intensifies the need for further repetitions and makes their execution easier and better until they are performed unconsciously."*

In the final stage of the coaching process, where the grounding of the new awareness takes place, the next steps are planned with the intention of acting upon the learning that has emerged during the session, to be then manifested into repeated actions. The coachee is now aware that the new learning can truly become an unconscious skill once they have acted responsibly, one step at a time, with continuity and perseverance.

Consciousness follows an order and rhythm not belonging to linear space-time. It moves in space-time when identified with a psychic object (when it furnishes itself with a psychic content) to expand, amplifying (evolving) the space of consciousness, throughout the mental field shown in the Egg Diagram. Moving with spiral motion in volutes, consciousness needs a slow pace to be understood- metabolized in the "I" as an empowering element.

In the slowness of movement spiritual energy slows down its vibration and can take on the specific form it chooses to embody, as it needs it for the evolutionary experience. Learning to perceive this spiraling movement everywhere, in the micro and macro, helps us in making the choice to change the incessant rhythm we are in and build new habits, choosing to be in the rhythm of life, resonating with the cosmic rhythm, beginning to follow the rhythm of our heartbeat.

This requires the ability to manage silence skillfully, obediently maintaining a presence to the central core, the Self, remaining

7- The Science of Consciousness

in the slowness of form, slowing down the energetic vibration to let the underlying substrate emerge. Awareness of the change in energetic speed has as its purpose the creation of a specific form in the image and likeness of the Source, to be clothed as the best expression of authenticity at the moment, the Ideal Model for manifesting the Self.

Every form is an expression of the energy that created it. Insight into its energetic aspect, beyond form, requires a high level of skill and openness of mind in considering the Self as a magnet, embedded in an ever-widening magnetic field. Consciousness follows attention: the "I" is a related transpersonal energy source, which has no form and can take on all forms with which it chooses to clothe itself, thereby experiencing every possible level of consciousness.

Consciousness from the psychoenergetic perspective is a "magnetic" field in constant interaction with other "magnetic" fields: depending on the polarization of the "I" there can be resonance or dissonance.

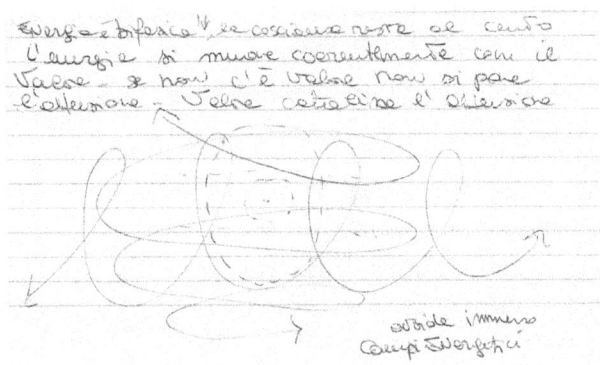

C. Pelizzatti- Note (2013)

In the PLC process, the coach's attention is focused on the energy of the psychic field within the Egg Diagram in which the partnership takes place. The coach's task in this leadership role is to remain centered in the heart, standing in the rhythm of the heartbeat as an indicator of the frequency vibratory field of the partnership- the third Egg Diagram shown in the sketch. At this point, through the feeling of the heart, through the rhythm of the heartbeat, it is possible to tune into the energy of the coaching field, facilitating the emergence of that which wants to manifest itself clearly and bring that feeling into higher and higher cycles, related to the cosmic rhythm.

Ideal Model Visualization Exercise

"...I clearly visualize my goal. I take the feeling related to it into my heart and from there into the heart of the Universe where I root myself.

I affirm: I am part of it!

I take my goal as far as I can go then I go Beyond, through connection to higher and higher rhythms, entering into the Rhythm of One Life, and from that positioning I resolutely let go of what is no longer needed, to create the space of emptiness, generator of transpersonal opportunities.

I let go, I create space, and the emptiness fills the space through creativity, that can reveal the underlying Purpose, my Purpose, my Value, in my Space.

I connect the intention related to my goal with the emerging energetic vibration and emotional charge and direct it toward increasingly larger, positive, evolutionary goals. In synthesis, I orient the energy of my goal toward ultimate goals in line with Dharma, the Ethical Cosmic Order.

Consciousness remains at the center of my psychic system, the mover of energy in concordance with my intrinsic value, now the catalyst of attention on creating a tool that allows me to act as if my goal were already realized.

At this point, I create an Ideal Model that allows me to achieve my goal by following the rhythm underlying unmanifest reality, a form that is informed by Substance and in the constant transformation toward Synthesis.

My Ideal Model for the Self.

7- The Science of Consciousness

A very relevant map that I use a lot with my clients is the Seven-Year Rhythm of Consciousness or Recapitulation scheme, which follows the Great Universal Laws. This trains awareness of the seven-year cycles associated with the Synthesis process:

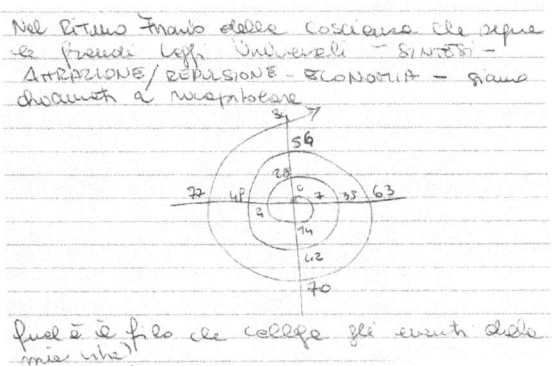

C. Pelizzatti- Note (2012)

This is a model that helps connect life events from the moment of birth in 7-year cycles, marking the significant events at that juncture, restoring the integrity of the energy field and recovering energies blocked in the past for various reasons, including damage caused by encounters with entropic energy fields that hinder the syntropic process toward ever greater Synthesis.

In moving toward the future an energy release occurs and the renewed energies are now available for evolutionary purposes, to be manifested through actions acted by the disidentified "I". The client emerges with more awareness of their own common denominator of life, meaning and willing to respond from now on, to hold Purpose in the chosen direction, with inner freedom from the dominance of the magnetic dynamics of force-ideas related to surface self-images. Their Ideal Model is intentionally related to the direction of evolution, acting in line with the "Ideal Idea", as if they were already the Self in manifestation.

Where do I orbit?

COACHING THE ESSENCE

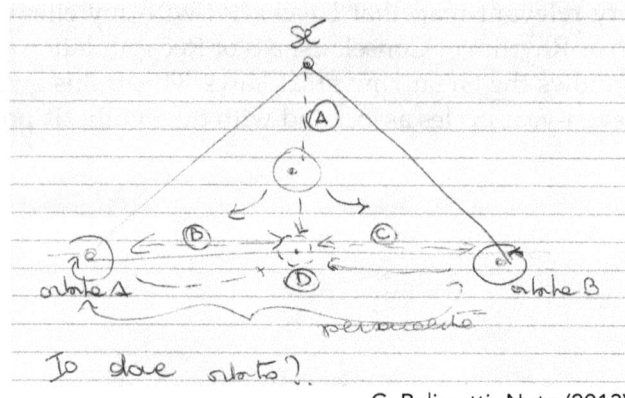

C. Pelizzatti- Note (2013)

When the "I" disidentifies, it orbits around the Self and the Self swings like a pendulum in the personality, within the framework of the poles that define the midpoint or compromise shown in point D. Through the I-crossing, the personal self, (which is to be crossed, not bypassed), the poles are magnetized or polarized of its energy, attracted toward synthesis in the horizontal, personal dimension, A.

When the "I" is anchored in the Self, it remains in the space of the creative void, full of transpersonal energy, free from polar dynamics related to the personal dimension. If it is not anchored in the Self, it is attracted toward the magnetism of idea-strengths and orbits in their direction, toward their B-C field of action..

Don't Lose Sight of Your Own Spiritual Identity

Where does the time go? Time does not go. Time Is.

When the "Call of Self" is stronger than the limiting voices related to past-related subpersonalities, the individual feels that they need support and guidance that can help on the uncertain path, as they realize that going further alone is no longer possible or even sustainable. At that point, the crisis can become an evolutionary opportunity if the person, realizing that they need help, is joined by the ideal support as they climb the slope of their awareness, taking into account that the responsibility of

7- The Science of Consciousness

emerging reinforced and grown up depends on themselves.

The presence of an experienced guide who takes into account the context and content of the traveler who is going through a crisis is the best resource to be found. As PLC we are aware that all the indispensable resources have always and will forever remain present within the person's higher unconscious, believing with confidence in the existence of a part of the individual that maintains clarity and wisdom and capacity for choice, even if at the moment this is a potential that is not fully accessible.

As professional helpers we stand by the person who is going through a difficult time in their life with determination and love, remaining by their side with trust and non-judgmental empathic presence, and able to maintain, if necessary, the space of generative silence.

The human factor, the greatest and most precious of potentials that can be found, metaphorically becomes the lifeline to rely on at the moment when strength fails and grief prevails, as even in the *Bhagavad-Gītā* the hero Arjuna confirms when he faces the existential crisis with his mind burdened by grief:

"Now I am confused about my duty and have lost my composure because of petty weakness. In this condition, I ask You to tell me clearly what is best for me. I am now Your disciple and a submissive soul to You. Instruct me, please."

- Bhagavad-Gītā 7, II

At that moment, Krishna turns smilingly to the unhappy Arjuna, defining the science of Spiritual Realization that finds synthesis in the *Bhagavad-Gītā*.

A loving smile and an empathetic presence form the ideal context to begin together on the path that leads to the most precious, essential, valuable "Knowledge", that endures when all else fails, and leads to longed-for Peace and Harmony.

The royal road to understanding suffering in the Vedas passes through Spiritual Realization. In the *Rig-Veda*:

"What I am I do not know. I wander lonely, oppressed by the mind.

COACHING THE ESSENCE

When the Primogeny of Truth came to me I was able to participate in that very Word."

- Rig-Veda I.164,37

In coaching, we do not deal with depressive states, but we can certainly deal with crises of meaning. As coaching deals with change, it is an ideal support to regain the ability to act in concordance with one's Essence, to train one's awareness of one's potentials, through the support of expert guidance through one's inner territory. The coach is the expert with tools and techniques that can be used for each psychological region and level of psychological development of the client, as defined broadly by Psychosynthesis.

A Kind Love That Motivates and Moves

"Wisdom implies Wisdom. It not only knows but understands: it understands by intuition, indeed by identification, by soul-melting: it is the intelligence of Love, Loving Understanding, Love of Wisdom."

- Roberto Assagioli

Unity is not a starting point, it is not a gift, it is an achievement, the highest reward of long work. That is what coaching is.

The International Coaching Federation (ICF) has provided a clear definition of coaching and this definition clarifies to potential clients what coaching is and what we do as coaches along the process defined by the ICF Core Competencies toward achieving their goal.

Achieving and maintaining neutrality, fairness and objectivity is the result of an ongoing process of constant training and commitment to excellence, to improve our coaching skills at various stages of our journey, building step by step a solid coaching identity and the ability to proudly provide an excellent service to the clients we work with.

The power of "Kindness" in the path of unveiling the Self as a great result in achieving the goal brought into the session, is

7- The Science of Consciousness

related to the Leadership process at the heart of Psychosynthesis.

We can define kindness as an act that humanly unites people. Kindness by definition is, among others, an act, expression, mode, exercise of virtue, the elevation of feelings, and a set of attitudes.

Let's start by naming the attitudes that define kindness for us, creating our vocabulary to define kindness personally and thus be able to use it with consideration and as an essential tool in coaching.

What generates kindness in us? When and with whom are we kind? Are we kind to ourselves? If yes, how and when? If we are not kind to ourselves, we can hardly be kind to others. And we are very diligent and have been well taught that first we have to look outward, indeed, we have to be primarily altruistic to call ourselves kind. And perhaps we have shut ourselves off from the deep feeling that is calling for expression: our Self, which wants to be contacted to manifest one of Its essential qualities, kindness.

This pure energy that pervades us, that pervades all life, creatures, and creation, is, by definition, kind. It is so because it is "conscious and aware", not conditioned by any psychic content, memory, history, trauma, judgment, teaching, or dogma.

Gratitude, empathic listening, presence, non-judgment, unconditional acceptance, and love are some examples of the qualities that spontaneously emerge when we are in touch with our Inner Source of kindness, the Self. Kindness is an ethical coaching attitude since it is ontological. We can create an Ideal Model of kindness that becomes a bridge for the "I" to reconnect with the Self. So, consider kindness as an ideal attitude.

I choose to act as if I am already truly kind, starting with myself, even though such an attitude sometimes requires great effort!

"Random acts of kindness are the best form of rebellion."

— Cit.

The power of kindness is felt by experiencing its effects on us. Thus, we learn that kindness is an inner attitude of Presence to the Self, our center of pure awareness and will without content, our inner Source that defines us as human beings in the true sense of the word. Maintaining Presence to the I-Self enables us to act kindly on "autopilot" starting with the first step: being kind to ourselves, savoring the effects of this nuclear "Quality of Being".

Kindness is an attitude of Being that allows us to be in constant contact with ourselves, from our Self, and simultaneously with others. When we operate from the Self, kindness flows naturally toward every creature and creation, resonating with the Creator. Kindness starts with the awareness that we are all in connection and relationship.

Every act we manifest from the Self returns to us in equal measure, according to time, place, and circumstance that are not in our control.

If I am inherently a kind person, I do not act expecting kindness in return, perhaps from the same person to whom I have given, through a gesture, the opportunity to benefit from the gift of kindness. Perhaps I have received nothing in return or an unkind response. Then it is a good time to use my awareness that anyway, even if I have not received what I expected, I have given high quality to the other person and this will go to work at a deep level, like having left a seed in ideal soil. Something will emerge anyway, and we will have truly gifted an act of kindness; offering a seed of kindness where it is deposited and sometimes even buried under a deep layer, metaphorically speaking.

Kindness is a continuous process of chosen contact, moment by moment, with our inner Source, the Self. Thus kindness becomes a way of living our life. Let each of us become "Ambassadors of Kindness", starting with our self-images. The power of kindness comes from the experiential fact that kindness is a quality of Being.

"However small, no act of kindness is wasted."

- Aesop

7- The Science of Consciousness

"This is my simple religion. There is no need for temples; there is no need for complicated philosophies. Our mind, our own heart is our temple; philosophy is kindness."

- Dalai Lama

"Kindness" and "Gratitude" are closely related. In coaching, gratitude is a powerful antidote. A question such as, "Is there something here you can be grateful for?" stimulates reflection to go beyond one's beliefs, beyond one's comfort zone, directing attention to what there may be inherently positive in something that superficially may have a negative connotation.

The coach's attitude of expressing sincere, natural gratitude to the coachee for their willingness to put themself out there, to show their vulnerability, for their commitment during coaching to explore more about themself, is a competency that the ICF particularly emphasizes in Core Competency No. 8: "Facilitate Client Growth".

In the moment the coach acknowledges and verbally expresses to the client their sincere appreciation for the growth the client has shown throughout the coaching program, during each session and in the entirety of the sessions, celebrates in synthesis the client's Will and thus the client in their Essence.

Psychosynthesis repeatedly emphasizes the concept of "I" as Volitional Being, "I Will". In practice, with our attitude of gratitude implied by kindness, we not only facilitate the client's personal growth but in particular stimulate their evolution in consciousness through the enactment of their abilities in the three levels: pre-personal, personal, and transpersonal, by training self-awareness, self-confidence, assertiveness, stress tolerance and the development of more constructive and kind attitudes. Gratitude is an attitude to be recognized, accepted, nurtured, developed, exercised, and collected.

Useful questions to train gratitude may be:

- *What do I feel gratitude for in general?*
- *Why do I make myself available to feel gratitude here?*

- *Why does gratitude draw my attention here?*
- *What part of me hinders gratitude here?*
- *How can I express gratitude in this situation?*
- *What need do I fulfill here by expressing gratitude?*
- *How do I feel in this situation without gratitude?*

Gratitude takes time to process "indigestible" events. The first step in stimulating this transpersonal quality is to accept gratitude for itself: a valuable element to be brought at will into the space of the content-empty "I". Once accepted as a valuable presence, sown in the field of consciousness, it must be nurtured through the Force of Love.

Useful questions to be asked along its development are, for example:

- *What have I gathered in my life from a perspective of gratitude?*
- *On what belief system is my gratitude based?*
- *What does the substrate of my field of consciousness contain that allows gratitude to grow?*
- *What do I need to let go of to create a new space for the seed of gratitude that is sprouting in me?*
- *What is emerging in my life today from this seed of gratitude?*
- *What is the seed that I have always carried that through gratitude can now emerge?*
- *What affirmation emerges to be used as an antidote for gratitude?*

Gratitude is also related to respect: for the coachee as a valuable human being and for the coach as a valuable human being; together working toward a valuable goal at every level (pre-personal, personal, transpersonal, collective, universal).

"Gratitude", "Kindness", and "Respect" are indispensable values of Being.

My gratitude flows together with these and other transpersonal values as I trust that there is a Supreme Intelligence, composed of Love and Power (Will) and I am a part of it.

The Phases of IDA

The stages of Identification-Disidentification-Self Identification (IDA) in Psychosynthesis lead to the ability to manage inner dynamics and obtain a certain fulfillment and satisfaction in the various spheres of life. These stages, or flow of stages, allow us to position ourselves at the center of consciousness as "Observers" of the multiplicity that inhabits our psyche and from there choose how to act from the role of "Director". They correspond to the attainment of Personal Leadership or Personal Psychosynthesis, the state of being in which the disidentified "I" (Observer-Director) achieves the ability to use the multiplicity of subpersonalities as resources by choice, empowering itself.

The person achieves sufficient functioning to cope with daily life in various areas with success and fulfillment. The sense of self-worth is solidified and relationships with the outside world are managed with harmony.

The sequence of the IDA process is characterized by the unfolding of the client's awareness of being a Willer or Being Will, through the three steps of Identification - Disidentification - Self-identification.

We need to recognize that most of the time, as Assagioli stated, we use the name of the "I" in vain as we pass from time to time through identification with one or another subpersonality, which always wish to satisfy their needs by shrinking the "I". We need to listen with kindness to their underlying need; then we welcome it into the heart and let the heart take care of what is needed so that transformation can take place through the power of Love. The most precious gift is to heal the primary wounds through their loving acceptance. This satisfies the basic need that subpersonalities bear and around which they have formed, which had the original objective of protecting or fulfilling the individual.

At this point, the next step of Transpersonal Psychosynthesis is possible and corresponds to the awakening of the awareness that one is already a Self, able to direct one's inner dynamics from another and elevated perspective, the Witness. By placing the Self at the center of the "I" in a vertical direction or vice versa by bringing the "I" into the Self, the transpersonal qualities will flow into the personality that is now ready to receive them and put them into action for evolutionary purposes. This process of flow of Being, or Being flow, corresponds to Self-Leadership or Transpersonal Leadership since it is from the Self that leadership proceeds.

As PLCs, we can manage these two directions of Being (personal and transpersonal) and accompany our clients into the dimension of well-Being that has as its goal being with one's Self, for the Good - Common Well-Being.

Through coaching we essentially provide an intellectual service, inspiring clients in a creative partnership to imagine their Selves in the future and unlock their highest potentials in the here and now, coaching the access to Intuition to manifest one's authenticity in daily activities, in the various spheres of life.

This is a Leadership process from the Self that is grounded in one's heart. Coaching is a lever to inspire the grounding of intentions and values in conscious actions, in a process of "Entelechy", the full attainment and manifestation of one's Purpose in alignment with one's Essence; a journey of Self-realization that results in the manifestation of one's Authenticity in action through an image as idea-strength: the Ideal Model for the Self.

Psychosynthesis provides a unique context as well as phenomenal tools for understanding and managing the complex dynamics occurring within the different regions of the human mind. In particular, it emphasizes, through the Ten Psychological Laws, how the psychic function of Imagination is the most affected, in turn affecting the other psychological functions represented by the Star Map. This leads to a detailed understanding of how self-images/subpersonalities affect the subject's level of awareness in decision-making.

Paradoxically, We Are Already a Self

The unfolding of superficial self-images toward the emergence of a deeper, more authentic one during the coaching process, is

7- The Science of Consciousness

crucial as emphasized by the ICF: the client's WHO among the WHAT of its contents, is the larger goal within each objective.

The approach of psychosynthesis points toward the emergence of the Self through Its reflection, the "I", the WHO among the WHATs- the subpersonalities, the so-called sub-agents with peculiar mental patterns, beliefs, and desires. All this is to arrive at a design of the Ideal Model for our Self, applicable in daily life.

Both the Ideal Model and the Self are central concepts in Psychosynthesis or, to use Assagioli's words, experiential FACTS.

Briefly underlining again what Psychosynthesis is and what it is about, it is a transpersonal, dynamic, and positive psychology, methodology, and evidence-based psychological practice. It was founded by Italian psychiatrist Roberto Assagioli almost a century ago as an evolution of Psychoanalysis, finding its roots in Existential-Humanistic Psychology. In the years 1906-1909 Assagioli published articles in the *Journal of Applied Psychology*. In 1909, in an article entitled "The Psychology of Ideas, Force and Psychagogy" he provided the theoretical and practical framework of what he called "Psychagogy" which became "Psychosynthesis" in 1926.

Since then, Psychosynthesis has defined the 4th force of psychology as Transpersonal Psychology, outlining its foundations and presenting a rigorous methodology aimed at Self-realization through a dynamic synthesis of the multiple human dimensions: physical, emotional, and mental, into the unity of the Self, our deepest Source of wisdom and power.

Psychosynthesis could be described as an educational process of reunification between the personality and its Source. A maieutics of the soul, a process centered on a continuous synthesis of the human personality to bring out the soul and manifest its energies into coherent actions.

It was in the period from 1957 to 1965 that Psychosynthesis began to flourish internationally and became codified as a scientific methodology in the books *Psychosynthesis, A Collection of Basic Writings* and *Principles and Methods of Therapeutic Psychosynthesis*.

COACHING THE ESSENCE

In 1973 Assagioli published *The Act of Will*, which, with its clear and methodical presentation of the process of setting and achieving goals, can be considered a comprehensive coaching manual. In this text, Assagioli outlines a positive approach that emphasizes the development of self-awareness as a motivating factor. He says that to experience the will, "*we must have a positive sense of life*". This quote defines the central position of Psychosynthesis within the framework of Positive Psychology for over a century.

In *The Act of Will* Assagioli describes the Ten Laws of Psychodynamics: imagery and the power of Imagination are present from the first through the sixth.

CHAPTER 8

KEY CONCEPTS
Synthesis of Maps and Concepts of Psychosynthesis

"Spirit is by its very nature above all dualism, all conflict, It is Unity; where It is present and operating, It renews, coordinates, harmonizes, unifies. Let us, therefore, rely on faith in the action of the Spirit, open to It the doors of our souls, aspire to unite, to merge with Him as much as possible, so that we may consciously and effectively become what we are in essence, that is, one Being, one Life. Thus we will move from multiplicity, from dispersion, from the wearisome travail of conflicting forces to peace, harmony, the fruitful cooperation of all our energies, to joyful PSYCHOSYNTHESIS"

— Roberto Assagioli

The 10 Laws of Psychodynamics

In *The Act of Will*, a coaching manual par excellence written in English and published in 1973, Assagioli postulates the Ten Psychological Laws. Knowing these and using them wisely in the coaching process leads to an understanding of the interconnected inner dynamics related to the various self-images and their action on the subject, facilitating the emergence of the client's "Who" among the "What" of contents in their mental field.

The 10 Laws are-

1. Images, mental pictures, and ideas tend to produce the physical conditions and external acts that correspond to them.

2. Attitudes, movements, and actions tend to evoke and intensify the ideas, images, emotions, and feelings that correspond to them.
3. Ideas and images tend to evoke emotions and feelings corresponding to them.
4. Emotions and impressions tend to awaken and intensify the ideas and images that correspond to or are associated with them.
5. Attention, interest, affirmation and repetition reinforce the ideas and images on which they are centered.
6. Repetition of actions intensifies the need for further reiteration and makes their execution easy and better, even to the point of being performed unconsciously.
7. Ideas, images, emotions, feelings and desires combine and group together, forming "psychological complexes [sub-personalities]".
8. Psychological complexes find and use without our awareness, independently, or even against our will - the means to achieve their goals.
9. Psychic energies that remain unexpressed and are not discharged into action accumulate, operate and transform in the unconscious and can produce physical effects.
10. Energies can express themselves:
    1. Directly (outburst-catharsis)
    2. Indirectly, through symbolic action
    3. By a process of transmutation

Assagioli conceives Psychosynthesis as an integral and holistic view of the human being, incorporating a methodology based on the principle of organizing the personality around a unifying center, the "I", a reflection of the Self into the personality.

The "I" is the experiential subject immersed in the field of consciousness, at the center of the unconscious regions of the mental field represented by the Egg Diagram Map, and is constantly impacted by contents, with which it unconsciously identifies. Some of these contents are known as sub-personalities.

8- Psychosynthesis Concepts and Maps

Assagioli's first insights into subpersonalities date back to the early 1900s.

Because of unconscious identifications with these superficial and transitory images, related to the personal dimension of doing, the "I" is imprisoned in their dynamics, assuming from time to time a partial and fleeting self-identity through which it functions, thus perceiving external reality in a filtered and changing way.

The main goal of Psychosynthesis is the unfolding of the inner process of rediscovering one's ontological Reality as a Self, removing the veils of the superficial contents and images of which the personality is composed.

There is no duality between the "I" and the Self, but different levels of awareness depend on the unconscious identification of the "I" with subpersonalities. These filter and distort self-awareness, using our psychological functions to satisfy their primary needs.

The Self is not an outcome. The outcome of the process of Self-realization gravitates around the "I".

The awareness of the "I" that evolves during the process of Self-realization transforms the impermanent self-images with which the subject incessantly identifies. The outcome of this process is the realization of being not qualitatively different from the Source: the conscious awareness of essential Oneness with the Self, awakening to the unitive, non-dual state of Being, and synthesis between I-Self.

The Self is immanent through the "I" and simultaneously transcendent, being a transcendental Reality. It does not belong to the space-time paradigm. The "I" connects to the space-time paradigm when unconsciously identified with subpersonalities. The Self belongs to the transcendental dimension, whose ultimate Source is the Universal Self, in the Vedas referred to as God, the Supreme Person.

Metaphorically, the image that reminds me of this context is that of a person comfortably seated near a body of water. Their image is reflected in it and the breeze in the air, blowing over the surface of the water generates ripples on the placid surface.

The person as Observer sees their reflection in motion, distorted by the ripples, even though the Source from which the reflected image originates remains essentially still.

The Observer can observe themself in movement and can choose through non-action to act, the moment they are aware that movement is taking place in the momentary appearance of the movement of water, moved by contact with air. Or they may identify with their reflection, to the point of losing awareness of being its Source. They become ignorant of their original neutral position.

The reflected image cannot see; it experiences movement only from the perspective of the person from whom it is observed and from whom it originates; it is a psychic object through which the subject experiences itself through the undulatory movement of water. The image is, and remains, a reflection of the Source from which it emerges, only real in its impermanence, and not actually real since it is evanescent.

Next to the person, another figure is Present. This is the Silent Witness.

That which is Real persists. That which is not Real is impermanent. Assagioli states in one of his handwritten notes (Assagiolino):

"Distinguish well always between the reality, existence, activity of the 'I' and the 'consciousness' of the 'I'"

Assagioli's definition of the "I" includes Will. The relationship between the "I" and Will is so intimate that the experiential discovery of Will culminates in the realization of "Being Will" or Self-realization. Assagioli considered it essential to make contact with the higher realm of the psyche from which the Self directly emanates transpersonal energies throughout the various psychic regions as a necessary prerequisite for the evolution of consciousness and outlined two necessary and fundamental stages:

The first stage is the journey toward Personal Psychosynthesis: the integration and harmonization of various psychological functions around a center of synthesis: the personal self or "I".

8- Psychosynthesis Concepts and Maps

The goal of this stage is the creation of a solid personality, based on a dynamic balance between multiple psychic components, the "subpersonalities", each representing a specific mindset, self-image, and way of "functioning" or using psychological functions to satisfy a specific need or desire. This dynamic balance allows the individual to remain at the center of events, able to observe them from a different and central perspective, the neutral positioning of the Observer, through disidentification: the most impactful technique available in Psychosynthesis.

It is through the ontological function "Will", whose primary role is to manage and modulate the other psychological functions- Thought, Impulse-Desire, Sensation, Emotion, and Imagination- that the function with which to resonate with the Self, Intuition, becomes available to the "I".

This process provides the foundation for a more solid personality that gravitates around the "deconditioned 'I'". At this point the individual has the grounding and awareness necessary for the second stage of Transpersonal Psychosynthesis, the process of accessing the higher dimensions of the psyche where the qualities and potentials of the Self reside. From the superconscious, where one can position oneself in an elevated dimension, one becomes Witness of the dynamics at the level of the personality. By maintaining this positioning, it is possible to bring the higher qualities into manifestation through the "I", infused in a personality and mindset built around a realistic and moldable Ideal Model, a synthetic and non-static, evolving model that acts as a bridge for maintaining the realignment of the I-Self axis.

The Egg Diagram: the Psychic Cell

Although Psychosynthesis employs many diagrams and exercises, the two primary maps are the Egg Diagram and the Star Diagram of the Psychological Functions.

The Egg Diagram is an archetypal representation of our psyche- *Hiraṇyagarbha*, the Cosmic Egg, the mental field, divided into four regions.

COACHING THE ESSENCE

The Pre-personal or Lower Unconscious, our psychic library of the past, houses intense experiences of meaning, long-term memories, elementary psychological activities that direct the life of the body, fundamental drives and primitive drives, and many complexes full of intense emotions.

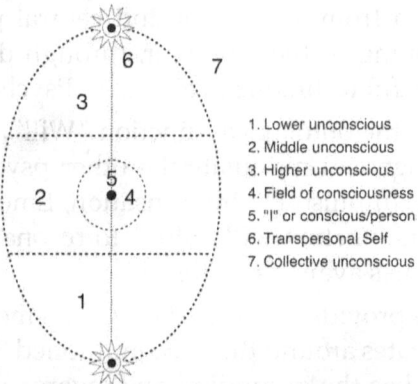

1. Lower unconscious
2. Middle unconscious
3. Higher unconscious
4. Field of consciousness
5. "I" or conscious/person
6. Transpersonal Self
7. Collective unconscious

Graphic: Synthesis Coaching Associates

The Middle Unconscious is the psychic region where memory access is fastest, in the short term. The circle represents our field of consciousness, of awareness in the present moment. At the center of our consciousness resides the personal self or "I", by definition a center of pure awareness and will, uncolored by psychic contents, a reflection of the Transpersonal Self into the personality.

The Higher Unconscious or Superconscious is one of the innovations of Psychosynthesis in the field of psychology. Classical psychology recognized the lower and middle regions, the unconscious drives of Freud, and many other thinkers. What Assagioli intuited and continued to demonstrate logically and experientially is that there is a higher region to reach, where the transpersonal qualities of the Self are present. In the timeline represented by the Egg Diagram, this region is the future.

The star at the top of the Egg Diagram represents another innovative and fundamental concept of Psychosynthesis, the Transpersonal Self, which is present throughout the psyche but its energies are more clearly available and radiating in the Higher Unconscious. In the lower regions of the psyche, the Self

8- Psychosynthesis Concepts and Maps

remains veiled and generally less and less accessible.

The outline of the Egg Diagram is dashed, emphasizing the permeability that allows osmosis between the field of consciousness and the unconscious, of the incessant flows of content generated and filtered by contact with the external world through the psychological functions and organs of action of the "I", when identified with respective subpersonalities.

Our entire psychic world is immersed in the Collective Unconscious, which is also divided into the four macro-regions just described.

In his text "Psychosynthesis", Assagioli emphasizes that we should not consider the conscious and the unconscious as two completely separate entities. The unconscious is a collective name: it does not constitute a single psychic entity. The unconscious is a word for the whole, the total of autonomous psychic activities taking place within us. Assagioli's text defined the plasticity of the unconscious, the structure of the unconscious and its relationship to the conscious, and the distinction between the part of the unconscious that is amorphous and undifferentiated and that which is organized into psychic structures of varying origin and complexity. This work is reflected in today's field of neuroscience and the neuroplasticity of the brain.

The second major map in Psychosynthesis is the Star Diagram or Star of the Psychological Functions.

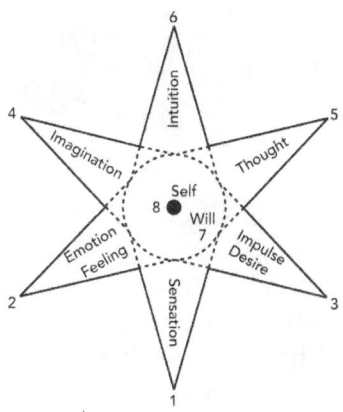

Star Diagram (R. Assagioli)

COACHING THE ESSENCE

A psychological function is a specific psychic activity with the ability to establish a connection between experiential fact and a brain function, associated with the synthesis of brain functioning during the subjective experience. Psychological functions are instruments through which the "I" functions at different levels, experiencing objective reality, and at the same time potential vehicles for self-expression in the world.

Eventually, each function is placed in its psychic field and, except for the functions of Will and Intuition, the sum of the fields of psychological functions generates the psychic structure represented by the Egg Diagram, according to Psychosynthesis neuroscientist Pier Maria Bonacina (1998).

What is a Subpersonality?

Elio Pelizzatti: "Giochi di ruoli" (2005)

In synthesis, Subpersonalities are superficial self-images, different self-representations, and/or group self-images within ourselves. Assagioli has defined them since the early 1900s in his innumerable writings as well as his "Assagiolini", his handwritten notes.

8- Psychosynthesis Concepts and Maps

These self-images are impermanent: conglomerations of habits, conditioning, beliefs, idea-strengths, roles, complexes, and other psychological contents relating to the world in which we are embedded and the way through which we perceive ourselves and our surroundings, moment by moment. There is no coordinating center where synthesis takes place; in a subpersonality, this center is a need, a drive that struggles to assert itself and fulfill itself.

It is toward this center with its own particular needs that various aspects of the personality are attracted and synthesized, creating what can be considered a "body/presence" in its own right with its ends and means of expression, beliefs, and behaviors. It is a mindset that becomes solidified as neural pathways in the brain become highways, recurring patterns of thought that emerge as a frequent inner dialogue and specifically related behavior.

It is considered a dominant or most mature (since it is the most attended and nurtured) subpersonality when the personality solidifies around a particular mindset and beliefs, becoming a partial internal unifying center, an element that defines the personality and around which orbits the "I".

At that point, the "I" loses awareness of its essential Reality. It becomes an ego or historical self, attaching itself to impermanent reality, inevitably binding itself to suffering. The personality revolves around this center and the Self becomes almost totally obscured, its energetic qualities being used in a distorted way by subpersonalities to satisfy their own needs, as confirmed in Assagioli's Eighth Law of Psychodynamics.

From a neuroscience perspective, clients come to coaching with a goal related to a belief and an expectation. A belief can be thought of as a mental model. Mental patterns are introjected along the path of life by gathering only partial information, imitations, significant events, and repetitions. Mental patterns are created in the brain, and the brain's main way of functioning is through recurrent patterns. Once a schema is established it is formalized with a mental model, which in return generates expectations. It is very interesting to consider subpersonalities and related dynamics from this perspective.

COACHING THE ESSENCE

Ideal Model or Idealized?

Graphic: Carmen Lenatti (2010)

During the coaching process we are participating in the client's unfolding of the Self as they achieve their goal. At the end of the session, the client's self-image will be different from the one they brought in. We begin the coaching process co-creating a future self-image, building and moving step by step toward this future, adjusting the trajectory and details along the way. Upon arrival, at the end of the session, the future Self that the client had imagined at the beginning is now in the past. It has changed in the process, as together we moved forward toward the outcome, having been reinvented and recreated along the way.

In the here and now, at the end of the session, the imagined future self was reshaped and realigned with the purpose, meaning, and values of the client's Essence. It has become an Ideal Model for the Self or a more authentic representation of the client's "Who" at the moment so that their Essence could become manifest.

This process revolves around the "I", which is initially influenced and conditioned by psychic content and subpersonality. "I" awareness evolves along a timeline, from the past, in the

8- Psychosynthesis Concepts and Maps

present, into the future unfolding its deepest and most authentic image, encapsulated in the multiplicity of transient and idealized self-images.

The future in the context of Psychosynthesis Life Coaching is a process of unveiling the core image, forming an ideal bridge to reconnect with the Self on the path to be taken toward achieving the desired goal. There is a timeline and a space to travel to get to the center. The outcome of the process of "Self-realization" while attaining a goal is the awakening of the "I" to the realization of Being already a Self, reflected and immersed in a certain personality and acted upon by a multiplicity of subpersonalities that are in chronic conflict with which it unconsciously identifies and is acted upon.

To disempower a subpersonality is to transform it into the "I"'s best available ally, to achieve the truly desired goal, as the intrinsic positive and valuable quality previously hidden by need and related dynamics now emerges disengaged from those dynamics that brought the "I" into the orbit of need. The transformation of the meaning of the subpersonality's existence becomes the motivator to achieve the goal while experiencing success as a feeling of fulfillment and deep satisfaction, having enacted one's highest strengths.

The moment when we awaken and participate, exercising a purposeful act of will in the Presence of the Self at once immanent and transcendent, is forever transformational. It is so because from that point the "I", instead of being acted upon, becomes an agent. From being manipulated by subpersonalities it transforms them into useful instruments in the evolutionary process.

This evolution can be considered to be from "ego to eco" in the sense that during the transformational process of the subpersonalities the center around which the revolution takes place changes: from the satisfaction of a need related to the personal dimension of doing, consciousness evolves to the dimension of Being. The need for Self-realization becomes the motivating engine of every goal.

Action will have as its goal the manifestation of Love,

COACHING THE ESSENCE

defined in the *Bhagavad-Gītā*, as Bhakti Yoga, the action par excellence, ecological and sustainable since it is grounded in the Self. In this transformational process at the transpersonal level, the "I" regains access to Will as its ontological faculty, with an evolutionary purpose.

It is by immersing ourselves in ourselves that we can find this timeless dimension, outside of space-time, the dimension of Being, where we find our Ideal Model or Ideal Image, called in Sanskrit *Svarūpa* (the Vedic concept we saw earlier relating to essential form): the personal expansion of the Original Natural Transcendental Identity, the true nature of manifestation.

The Ideal Model is the most authentic and adherent image we can build by choice around our Essence, a representation of the True Nature of Being, with the function of reflecting the Essence, into the personal dimension through the "I". From there we can govern the inner dynamics of superficial, chronically conflicting self-images dominated by basic needs and intense emotions.

Once transformed, a subpersonality becomes a valuable ally, releasing its *Svarūpa*, the transpersonal quality within its core, which can then be used at will by the "I" to act in line with its Essential Purpose and values. Each self-image at this point will be transformed by the light of the Self, providing the unique quality at its core that is essential for creating the larger image that wants to emerge and that calls to us.

The "Call of Self", which we confuse with the incessant buzz of inner voices that distract our attention, needs silence to be received; the incessant surface noise of personality must be quieted to let the background vibration, the note of the transpersonal Self, emerge.

Quieting the changes in the mental field, as suggested millennia ago by Patanjali in the *Yoga Sutras*, is done in Psychosynthesis through the technique of disidentification, as we saw in the previous chapter.

"yogaś cittā vṛtti nirodhaḥ"

- Samādhi Pāda v.2

"Yoga consists of the suspension of modifications in the mental field."

8- Psychosynthesis Concepts and Maps

Silence, the Word of the Self

"Self. The 'Immovable Engine'"

- Roberto Assagioli

The Self will thus emerge through the synthesis of multiplicity, through an Ideal Model, built on the core of many superficial images and more than the sum of its parts: a synthetic and non-static element representing its Origin, within the space of Silence.

The Self always remains the silent motionless Witness of the inner dynamics, while the many self-images as actors play their roles through the "I", creating the reality they want to achieve to satisfy their needs, cast in their abstract future.

Self-awareness is not an unambiguous outcome but the result of constant work on the Self of transformation and empathic love for each subpersonality and its contents. Metaphorically, we want to become "bridges" through which the Self can finally emanate Its energy into the personality, of which the "I" becomes a receptor and transformer, through the essential quality of each part, of each subpersonality, in the synthesis of an Ideal Model created as a bridge for the Self.

In practice, by embodying the Ideal Model at will, we act as if we were already capable of living from the Self, training the manifold personality to gravitate around the "I", living out our humanity as embodied souls, spiritual beings experiencing through manifestation, in the journey of Life whose destination is to arrive at Being Who we already are: Volitional Loving Awareness.

At this point multiplicity in unity will reflect and amplify the Self Image into Oneness in the richness of diversity. Once awakened to its Source, the client can use the higher potentials of the subpersonalities, not consciously accessible previously because of their related dynamics and the unconscious identifications of the "I".

Diving deeper into ourselves we find this timeless dimension, beyond that of space-time, in the full vacuum of the Self's energies mirrored by the Ideal Model, the authentic image instrumental to the Self, the instrument that creates the connection with the soul from which Transpersonal Leadership emanates.

In the process of transforming impermanent self-images, we bring to the surface an even deeper image at the core of the subject. It is by coming out of abstract images that the *Svarūpa*, the most authentic, deepest, and highest intrinsic form emerges, upon which we can build an Ideal Model to manifest the Self.

A subpersonality is an abstraction of the self-image. It exists as a superficial self-image, the one with which the client comes into coaching wanting to achieve a goal, acting as an agent for the deeper Self, but in a distorted way. A subpersonality belongs to the personal dimension of the psyche; it is an idea-force that drives the subject to a purposeful action motivated by a need. This self-image can be considered a clue to a deeper, nuclear image that wants to emerge in all its power: the Self.

Subpersonalities belong to the "Doing" dimension. The Self belongs to the "Being" dimension. The "I" is the middle point where the two dimensions can find a dynamic synthesis when transformed into a useful force for evolutionary purposes. In the crosshairs of our work as PLCs there is the "I", pure awareness and will, without contents but conditioned by contents because of embodiment in a peculiar bio-psychic form and unconsciously identified due to the attraction exerted by the multiplicity.

The "I" is the bridge between two dimensions: the personal realm, represented by subpersonalities/self-images (the "operators"), and the transpersonal realm, represented by the Self (Being). The Ideal Model bridges the gap between these two dimensions. The "mantra" we use in PLC is, "more and more 'I'".

In the coaching process, the client moves forward with the future in mind to achieve a goal by the end of the session. They are, as we all are, unconsciously drawn to a deeper level, toward the broader goal of self-evolution toward the Self, but are also being unconsciously distracted and attracted by needs related to subpersonalities, delaying the realization of Essence. Together with our clients, we cooperate in an inspiring and co-creative way to achieve their imagined future, going even deeper along the path, into the metaspace of the heart to unfold the higher

8- Psychosynthesis Concepts and Maps

potentials already present within them, transforming subpersonalities from obstacles to resources, empowering the "I", in the shared journey of Self-realization.

Moving from the past, into the present, toward the future, we are going further and further into the Egg Diagram, to bring forth the Essence, releasing the highest potentials belonging to the Transpersonal Self Image, bridging the gap between the personal and transcendental dimensions. Along the way, the limiting superficial self-images are transformed and synthesized within an Ideal Model, which becomes the center of external projection and attraction, in the image and likeness of the Self.

"My Lord, You are the One who observes all the goals of the senses. Without Your mercy, there is no possibility of solving the problem of doubt. This material world is like a shadow that resembles You. We consider this material world real because it gives us an idea of Your existence."

— Śrimad-Bhāgavatam, 8,3,14

The Ideal Model is an introspective view. A client always enters coaching from a subpersonality that wants to achieve a goal, thus empowering itself by assuming more power over the "I" and shaping it with a superficial self-image. As we journey together with our clients on the path to achieve their goal brought into the session by a subpersonality, we are aware of this dynamic, so we simultaneously work together with our clients for "more 'I'", toward the emergence of a new self-image more in line with their Essence at the moment.

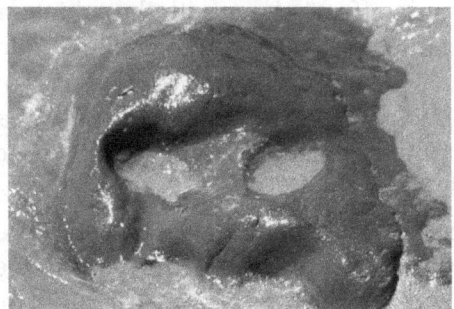

Photo: "Masks", C. Pelizzatt (Rockland, Maine)

COACHING THE ESSENCE

In doing so, a process disempowerment of the superficial self-image occurs in an empathic context, due to the coach's connection with their Self, acting as an "External Center of Synthesis", through which the client can mirror and finally resonate with their Self, while simultaneously resonating with the coach who guides the process, in a safe environment based on mutual trust.

The coach facilitates this positioning or Personal Leadership for the client in a partnership between two Selves at the transpersonal level. This process of empowerment, while sub-agents are disempowered, occurs through the process called IDA: Identification - Disidentification - Self-identification, mentioned earlier. Identify the sub-agent in play, disidentify from it, and identify with it through the "I", empowering the "I" with its nuclear quality.

Transpersonal Leadership or Self-Realization is an ongoing process that emerges from the transformation of self-images bound to the past into new self-images rooted in the here and now, strengthened by the emergence of their fundamental qualities along the journey toward the goal. The Ideal Model for the Self is gradually revealed through the transformation of impermanent self-images, each of them representing an essential clue to completing the whole picture of the Authenticity that wants to emerge.

At this point, the "I" will identify and recognize its True Ontological Nature, from the past to the present, toward the future that demands manifestation in every action. The coaching process becomes a process of Self-Awakening with a powerful outcome as a "side-effect" along with the achievement of the objective brought into session: the emergence of an Ideal Model for the "I". This serves as a conduit for the Self or is available to the "I", around which subpersonalities will orbit, each with their transpersonal potentials, now available to be used at choice for Personal Leadership.

The next step of Transpersonal Leadership sees that the "I" becomes the protagonist of the transformation, the point of synthesis of the bio-psychic subject into the unity of the Self, the motivator of the movement toward the final goal: Love.

Through the use of an image for the Ideal Self which emerges as a synthesis of the essential qualities of the multiplicity, re-alignment with the Source takes place. The "I" finally rests in pure Consciousness, using subpersonalities at will as the best allies in line with its essential values, purpose, and meaning. We position ourselves in pure Self-Consciousness, through an Ideal Model for the Self at the moment, whose bridge is the personal self that has a mission to achieve: ItSelf. The Ideal Model is the Model in "Becoming Our Self".

As suggested by J.Hillman in his "Acorn Theory" or "Theory of the Soul", everyone already has the potential for unique possibilities within themselves. Just as an acorn contains the pattern for becoming an oak tree, a unique and individual soul energy is contained in every human being, manifested throughout his or her life and shown in his or her vocation and life's work when fully realized.

Hillman wrote: *"This intelligence of imagination resides in the heart. The expression 'intelligence of the heart' connotes the act of knowing and loving simultaneously using the imaginative act. (...) The work of the heart is imaginative thinking."*

The Neuroscience of the Psychological Functions

"To become a psychosynthesist requires the attainment of a certain degree of mental polarization. This does not mean developing the mind by repressing or ignoring emotions. Instead, it means cultivating the mind and not just emotions, as well as acquiring a personal center of gravity within a kind of balanced and loving 'reasoning' (in the broadest and deepest sense of the term) rather than uncontrolled emotionality."

- Roberto Assagioli

Several years ago, during one of my studies in Positive Psychology, I performed the "VIA Character Strengths Survey": one

COACHING THE ESSENCE

of my main skills that emerged was "Self Control", the discipline that leads to mastery over one's psychological functions.

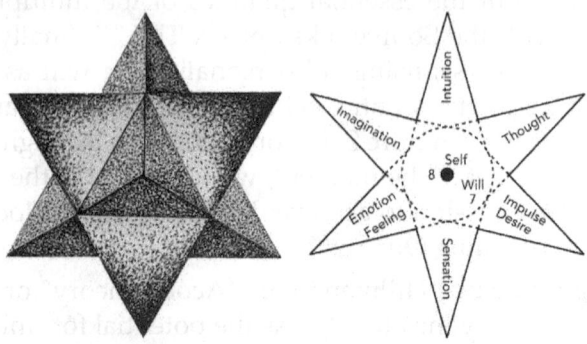

Graphic: Carmen Lenatti, R. Assagioli

I have written three different papers in this area comparing this emerged skill with Psychosynthesis and my more recent study in the application of neuroscience in coaching,:

Neuroscience and Psychological Functions in Coaching

The Neuroscience of Goals: Values & Emotions

Neuroscience and Subpersonality Beliefs in Coaching.

Here I provide a summary of some of the passages in them, about the ability to manage one's psychological functions from a perspective of applied neuroscience in PLC.

Neuroscience and Psychological Functions in Coaching: Facilitating Intuition

This research of mine focuses on a comparative study of the Star Diagram of Psychological Functions, one of the main maps in Psychosynthesis, applied in the context of coaching from the perspective of Neuroscience.

The bio-psycho-spiritual unity that Assagioli introduced almost a century ago in the context of Transpersonal Psychology can be considered an innovation of the current branch of Neuropsychology, the discipline that studies cognitive functions and their correlations with brain structures.

Along with the Egg Diagram Map, the mental field or psychic cell, the other main map in Psychosynthesis is the Star Diagram

8- Psychosynthesis Concepts and Maps

or Star of the Psychological Functions.

A psychological function is a specific psychic activity with the ability to establish a connection between experiential fact and associated brain function in the synthesis of subjective experience. Psychosynthesis defines psychological functions as the tools through which the "I" (the perceiving subject) experiences objective reality and as vehicles for self-expression in the world.

Each psychological function can be placed in its psychic field, and the sum of the fields of psychological functions, except the functions of Will and Intuition, generates the psychic structure shown in the Egg Diagram, according to neuroscientist and psychosynthesist Pier Maria Bonacina.

Neuroscience research provides an additional and valuable perspective on this psychological model regarding how we "function" at the unconscious level and the mechanisms of associated mental models that are activated in the brain during a coaching conversation.

Awareness of the mechanisms through which psychological functions fuel inner dynamics, together with an understanding of neuroplasticity through neuroscience, significantly enhances coaches' abilities to maintain an intuitive presence during the coaching process, accompanying their clients to maintain the same presence as they participate in the process of transforming their psychological content and related mindset.

The ability to train the brain to rewire itself and reconstruct the process of thinking at will can facilitate the emergence of the psychological function Intuition, thanks to the targeted use of the countless instruments that Psychosynthesis provides, particularly the Star Diagram.

The purpose of my comparison is to explore the complex dynamics that occur within the multidimensional realm of the human unconscious mind during the coaching process, among the various psychological functions postulated by Psychosynthesis, from the perspective of brain function.

Coaching has been defined in several ways. The definition provided by the International Coaching Federation that I primarily refer to is: "A Partnership with clients in a creative and challenging process that inspires them to maximize their personal and professional potential."

Coaching essentially provides an intellectual service. Knowing how the mind works during the coaching conversation increases both the coach's and the coachee's ability to manage at will their psychological functions, particularly the emotional field and thinking. This management will enhance the ability to emerge at the end of the session with a clear perspective of strategies to be put into action in an ecological, responsible, and sustainable way, starting from creating an inner ecosystem and tending toward Well-Being, related to Self-Realization.

Since the early 1900s, Psychosynthesis has defined the 4th force of Psychology as Transpersonal Psychology and is one of the forerunners of today's Positive Psychology, outlining its foundations and presenting a rigorous methodology aimed at Self-realization through a dynamic synthesis of multiple dimensions of the human being: physical, emotional and mental, in the unity of the "Self", our deepest source of wisdom and power.

Roberto Assagioli's conception of the human being is an integral and holistic view, incorporating a methodology based on the principle of organizing the personality around a unifying or synthesizing center, the "I", a reflection of the Self into the personality.

The "I" is the experiential subject immersed in the field of consciousness at the center of the unconscious regions of the mental field or psychic cell illustrated by the Egg Diagram, and it is constantly impacted by contents. These contents arrive through psychological functions, instruments available to the "I" to experience and learn from external reality, in a process tending toward evolution, which Assagioli calls "Self-realization".

The "I" is the inner space of pure awareness and will, uncolored by subpersonality or content and therefore potentially capable to observe and manage the incessant unconscious dynamics from a neutral position.

Personal Psychosynthesis, the first and fundamental stage of the process of Self-realization, leads to the ability to harmonize these dynamics through the ontological function "Will", whose

8- Psychosynthesis Concepts and Maps

primary role is to manage and modulate the other psychological functions: Thought, Impulse-Desire, Sensation, Emotion, and Imagination, thereby creating an ideal space for the emergence of the function most closely associated with the Transpersonal: Intuition.

In addition to the more mechanistic functions such as Sensation, Impulse/Desire, and Emotions recognized by the psychology of his time, Assagioli's definition of the Psychological Functions includes Will. The relationship between the "I" and the Will is so intimate that Assagioli considers the experiential discovery of Will as culminating in the realization of "Being Will" or "Self-realization".

This volitional awareness and capacity enables the next step of Transpersonal Psychosynthesis: using the function of Intuition to get in touch with the higher dimension of the psyche, the Superconscious, where the transpersonal qualities of the Self reside. This enables manifestation of meta values through the "I" in an ideal mental model rooted in a personality solidly grounded in the "I", the Leader of one's dynamic and manifold inner system.

Coaching is about change. It is a dynamic process in which the coach flows with the client's subjective experience and mindset consisting of multiple mental models associated with subpersonalities, as taught by Psychosynthesis.

Session after session, the coach collaborates with the client to create and understand the process of unraveling one's mental processes and ways of "functioning", supporting evolutionary transformation and the creation of an ideal mental model as a resource, in the process of achieving the desired outcome in line with the client's core values.

Neuroscience helps us to understand the plasticity of the brain and how it functions, through empirical observations of the activities (electrical and chemical) that occur within it, and how it rewires following the experience of input through the senses or reactivation of memories deposited in cerebral pathways.

Neuroplasticity underlies the changes that occur in the brain as a result of challenges faced throughout life. This process stimulates ways of thinking that create new neural pathways through which thought flows.

The application of neuroscience to coaching offers an additional perspective on conscious and unconscious thought processes, expanding mental models so that we can question how each psychological function can be related to a specific area of the brain and simultaneously also to the entire brain system, in a complex psycho-physical system, underlain by transpersonal life energy.

The dashed outline of the Egg Diagram represents the permeability that allows osmosis between the unconscious and the incessant flows of content generated and filtered by the contact of the psychological functions with objects with which the senses identify. Metaphorically, the Egg Diagram represents the mental container of memories related to experiences stored over time in the various unconscious levels, as potential energies flowing in specific mental pathways.

Once observed, objective reality becomes subjective, filtered by the subject's "functioning" or how the subject's psychological functions store information related to the experience with objective reality, depending on who (what subpersonality) uses it. What remains of the experience is an emotional memory that is stored with other contents with similar emotional valence and associated meaning.

In the Vedas, this mechanism is explained through the theory of "*Samskara*".

The brain always seeks the path of least resistance, and to simplify the process of assigning meaning, it looks forward to associating new content that enters the mental field with similar content that has already been previously stored (thus related to the past). Mental habits are created in this way. Neuroscience does not directly explain our behaviors, but it helps reveal the mechanism by which we construct our subjective world and related mental patterns.

Psychic activity and the nervous system are closely linked through electrochemical processes. The brain receives, processes, shapes, transforms, stores, or deletes information through a

8- Psychosynthesis Concepts and Maps

vast network of nerve circuits, the neural connections.

All information is processed and transmitted using oscillating electrical voltages in the brain generated by rhythmic or repetitive patterns of neural activity, and the frequency of activation of neurons depends on the intensity of the stimulus they receive.

The brain consists of neurons and glial cells. When stimulated by incoming signals, neurons transmit information in the form of electrical impulses at varying wavelengths, conducted forward along filaments in a three-dimensional radial network to the cells where the information is processed. These impulses can be modified or enhanced by the glial cells which themselves act as intermediates or sub-processors within the neural network.

Each ray in the Star Diagram represents the bio-psychic structure of the specific psychological function; each function is interconnected and communicates with the others; in the nucleus is the psychological function of Will. Neural connections enable the exchange of information that stimulates each ray.

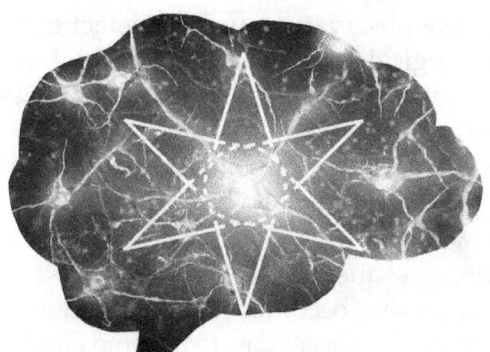

Graphic: Synthesis Coaching Associates

Contemporary research emphasizes brain activity as an integrated system of cellular structures such as receptors and transmitters of data, along with specific functions: an interconnected network of different regions that cooperate and exchange more data and information. Cellular assemblies called "functional systems" cooperate in creating programmed pathways to achieve a specific outcome. Multiple cellular ensembles cooperating and programmed in the processing of one specific set of information can be considered equivalent to a "psychological function".

Neuroplasticity allows the brain to change in response to input and helps create new synapses while the number of neurons remains the same. The enhancement of synapses and creation of neuropathways occurs in proportion to the degree of stimulus repetition: "practice creates habits".

Synaptic neuroplasticity is related to a change in synapses and is about building habits and new skills. Neurons are connected by synapses where chemical and electrical signals are transmitted, and synapses are created by experience.

The process of long-term potentiation described by Hebb's law, "That which activates together repeatedly, strengthens their connection", emphasizes the associated positive and negative outcomes: repetition of limiting habits supported by beliefs engrained in the mind can limit creativity or the creation of new neural pathways, so intuition cannot flow and the individual remains stuck in a mental pattern that loads and unloads data through downloading from the past.

From objective observation, we can detect that the development of psychological functions occurs through repetitive stimuli. In coaching, we stimulate the client's awareness of his or her thought patterns, mental patterns, modes of functioning (use of psychological functions), recurring behaviors, and possibly following new habits, one step at a time, repeatedly.

The brain works systematically however, not all brain processing activity is sequential. Usually, when we learn or form new habits, processing becomes parallel (because it is more automatic and faster). It is necessary to become familiar with a new habit, first by going through knowledge, then associating it with similar memories, predicting probable outcomes, and modifying expectations based on verified information from senses and memories, keeping in mind the outcome to be achieved in the future. Anchoring a new habit occurs through the ability to adapt or recreate connections of the brain: synapses are wired through neuroplasticity, creating familiar neuropathways that can rapidly send messages to related brain regions and the body.

8- Psychosynthesis Concepts and Maps

The brain receives the information and, through its network and nerve processes, modifies, shapes, distorts, or erases it, underscoring the importance of knowing how to most effectively stimulate the client during the coaching process by training awareness of his or her complex mental system.

The cerebral network is constantly active and in Default Mode Network (DMN): two activities that are not mutually exclusive. The DMN is activated when we are not focused on tasks or when we are daydreaming, for example, while the cerebral network remains active. Multiple scientific studies have shown paradoxically that the brain is constantly in high activity even when the subject is not engaged in a focused mental activity, while activity levels actually decrease when the subject is focused on an intentional mental activity.

This mode of high activity of the mental field is similar and related to the mechanism of functioning of a dominant or the most mature subpersonality, as defined in Psychosynthesis. The psychic field (Egg Diagram) remains active, dynamic, and interactive, while a particular habit (subpersonality), the most frequently polled or manifested makes the unconscious subject "work" (use of psychological functions) toward the direction of satisfying the primary need it carries.

Psychosynthesis emphasizes the Will as a central function, without an organ of expression per se but using the entire bio-psychic system to dominate the mind, directing the other psychological functions so that Intuition can emerge.

From the *Bhagavad-Gītā* 2, 67, 68:

"Just as a rushing wind sweeps a boat over the water, so one of the restless senses on which the mind fixes itself can deprive a man of his Intelligence."

"Therefore, O Arjuna with powerful arms, he who turns the senses away from their objects possesses a firm intelligence."

As coaches we work with our clients in a stimulating partnership, facilitating in them a new way of thinking, so that by the end of the session they'll also emerge with a physical change in the brain.

COACHING THE ESSENCE

Once the client is empowered to act on the new awareness, the result is the creation of a new mental habit through synapse strengthening and long-term empowerment. Habits with reiteration structure the neural pathway, discharging chemicals that stimulate the motivational circuits that frame the "highways" in the brain, thanks to neuroplasticity.

We have two main systems of thinking: System 1 (S1) and System 2 (S2).

The first (S1) is unconscious, fast, logical, automatic, and relative to beliefs, influenced by the circumstances of the present moment, without pauses for reflection, mostly related to the limbic system. The second (S2) is conscious, slow, abstract, analytical, and reflective; considers past, present, and future; related mainly to the prefrontal cortex (PFC), where long-term memories are stored.

To synchronize S1 and S2, the use of inhibition is functional. In *The Act of Will* Assagioli describes the volitional project in detail, emphasizing the significance of inhibition and how it facilitates the emergence of Intuition.

Psychosynthesis emphasizes the capacity for choice once the "I" has achieved a state of freedom from unconscious conditioning through the technique of disidentification, which, once the psychic contents have been identified, allows the subject to assume a neutral space from where the contents can be managed at will.

The pre-frontal cortex (PFC) is like the CEO in the brain system, as well as the "I" in the Egg Diagram. The "cold" cognitive function of the PFC is the state of the disidentified "I", defined in Psychosynthesis as pure awareness and will without content, the neutral Observer, with the ability to direct its inner dynamics at will.

In addition to the above relationships, according to Damasio's Somatic Marker hypothesis (see references) the Orbital Frontal Cortex (OFC) plays a central role in decision-making for reverse learning or flexibility during change, engaging the intuitive intelligence of the emotional body system.

8- Psychosynthesis Concepts and Maps

Inhibition: Function of the Will

To plan and set goals in a psychologically sustainable manner the PFC-related skill of inhibition is central. Inhibition is a key ability to protect us from distracting information by suspending habitual thinking or responses during the goal-setting process. The transmission of neurotransmitters with inhibitory function impacts neurons by decreasing the likelihood that the neuron will activate an action potential, thus affecting psychological functions.

The will process of "Inhibition" postulated in Psychosynthesis describes the conscious act of controlling drives associated with the deliberation process, the conscious choice to resolutely restrain an impulse or tendency while deliberating the best next step in the process.

Inhibition involves four stages: recognizing; examining and analyzing; directing or transmuting the emerging impulse; and acting on it at the most appropriate time.

Achieving conscious control through inhibition is the prerequisite for the Deliberation stage in the Will Project, the purpose of which is to lead us to the best possible decision given the various functions involved, through balancing of the psychic contents.

The stage of Deliberation is followed by the stage of Choice and Decision, which involves bringing unconscious motives and factors into the field of consciousness, evaluating them, choosing the best alternative, and letting others go, freeing ourselves from the habit of downloading data from the past.

Often the client presents several goals, and the coach must help him or her in making a clear choice. The unconscious selection process involves an evaluation and deliberation of the various goals, the relative possibility of their achievement, the desirability and consequences of doing so, and any other relevant factors at play that must be kept in mind and explored. The goal presented is closely related to a mental model, a sum of habits, and self-image representations with meaning and associated needs, behaviors, rules, and expectations.

COACHING THE ESSENCE

A dominant mental model or interpreter is related to a dominant subpersonality, the most frequently attended, which adopts any means to achieve its goals. As we have seen this occurs without the subject's awareness and independently or completely against his or her will, as outlined in the Ten Psychological Laws defined by Assagioli in *The Act of Will*, particularly the eighth law:

"*All the various functions, and their many combinations in complexes and sub-personalities, set in motion the realization of their purposes outside our consciousness, and independent of, and even against, our will.*"

The actual application of the Purpose phase, in *The Act of Will*, defines a goal that is determined based on evaluation, which by definition implies a scale of values. The relationships between purpose, evaluation, motivation, and intention are dynamic and reciprocal; motivations and intentions are based on evaluations and are related to our self-image and inner dialogue, as well as to the meaning and values we attach to life, which is fundamentally good and positive.

A purposeful goal generates the intention to achieve it and motivates one to do so. Intention represents a driving force, giving rise to impulses from unconscious dynamics. The function of intention is to use them by obtaining their cooperation in achieving the desired result. Motivation involves the discovery and transformation of any eventual unconscious patterns, distilling their meaning and making them perceptible in the field of consciousness of the "I".

Through awareness we can activate the will to direct our psychological functions, achieving the ability to choose to what extent to give expression and direction to the motive or impulse and access the transpersonal resources of the Self through the primary function of the "I": Intuition.

One of the main functions of the PFC is to calculate and predict the future by making sense of experiences, bringing out memories, changing expectations, detecting patterns, and creating meanings.

Patterns that are familiar to us (habits, beliefs) can hinder

8- Psychosynthesis Concepts and Maps

creativity and access to Intuition as they represent another side of neuroplasticity. Plasticity involves both the potentiation of synapses (LTP, long-term potentiation) and also serves to decrease the strength of the connection between neurons (LTD, long-term depression) for information that is not reinforced and is important because it helps to avoid the state of saturation.

So in describing the role of Inhibition, it is important to clarify that plasticity not only serves to strengthen connections between neurons but can also inhibit them.

The psychological functions are the instruments available to the "I" to experience external reality, constructing meanings associated with memories and also working unconsciously to create mental and behavioral patterns.

When the mind has reached its original nature, under the control of the "I", the transformation of limiting mental patterns takes place and the subject can "function" accordingly with their Self, thanks to neuroplasticity. At that point, freed from unconscious identifications and limiting mindset, the "I" becomes the Observer/Director of its inner dynamics, with the power to choose at will the psychological functions of a particular self-image (subpersonality) necessary to achieve the desired outcome.

A coaching intervention based on Intuition as a state of flow between the heart and brain, through the activation of (S2) related to (S1) at will, by running it through the heart, will expand the awareness of both coach and coachee, using psychological functions effectively and combined with intuitive guidance of the Self, in the transformative journey toward the evolutionary goal.

The application of Neuroscience in coaching the importance of managing psychological functions at will offers an additional perspective on conscious and unconscious thought processes for Self-level Leadership.

Initially, it was assumed that there was a direct correlation between area and function in the brain, but now it is known that each area cooperates and mutually influences the others. This is evidenced, for example, if an area associated with a function is injured and that function is "recovered" by the activation of the other areas that make up for the loss. This is also understood as plasticity.

The hypothesis that each psychological function interacts with others is confirmed by the Ten Laws of Psychodynamics postulated by Assagioli. Each psychological function interacts with the others and simultaneously in the entire psychic system mapped in the Egg Diagram, as well as within the entire brain in a dynamic cluster of chemical-electrical communications.

Can we, therefore, learn to rewire the brain at will to facilitate the emergence of Intuition?

By neuroplastic reshaping of the brain through active management of psychological functions, we can achieve the ability to "function" in resonance with the Self. The primary function of the Will is to manage other psychological functions to bring forth Intuition. By mastering the mental faculties at will, the ability to remain present will emerge as a state of flow from mind to heart and vice versa in an intuitive presence to the Self, in the transformative and transpersonal process of coaching.

Where does your heart lead you?

Reflections on the psychological function of Emotion and its impact on goal setting.

Understanding how we perceive and feel emotions and how to use other psychological functions to manage emotions and facilitate the process of achieving a goal with the best attitude is a key skill in coaching.

Clients invariably enter coaching bringing a goal with an unconscious emotional attachment. They are mostly unaware of the complexity of the thinking, emotions, desires, motivation, feelings, and images involved in the goal-setting process and are also generally completely unaware of which subpersonality is bringing the goal into the session.

Our role as PLCs is to help them become aware of how we function unconsciously and improve their ability to change their mindset by choice (to identify themselves in one subpersonality or another as necessary to reach the desired end), creating new

8- Psychosynthesis Concepts and Maps

habits more in line with their Self.

Neuroscience provides an additional perspective to facilitate the creation of new neural pathways, acquiring a greater ability to manage emotions consciously and at will using the psychological functions related to the subpersonality present in the "I"'s field of consciousness at any given time. Each thought and learning process corresponds to a change in a neural circuit, even at the functional level.

Neuroscience helps us understand that every goal brought into the session has a specific involvement of the brain and the body, with emotion as the main driver. There is a physiological change in clients when they talk about their goals, so being aware of nonverbal communication is a fundamental skill for a coach.

From a neuroscience perspective, values (the value or meaningful system) represent both a goal and the momentum to achieve it, involving a reward circuit in the brain, centered on the nucleus accumbens in the limbic system and related to the emotional system and others in the prefrontal cortex.

Elements of the Mesolimbic Reward System

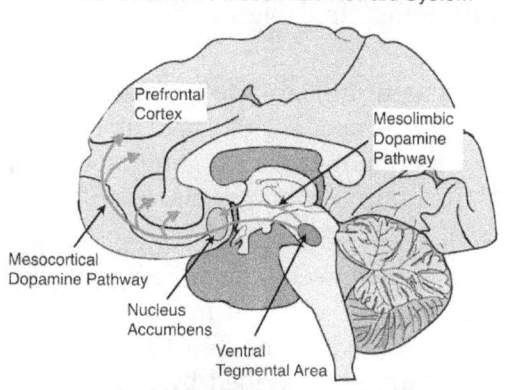

Graphic: Synthesis Coaching Associates

Psychological functions are interconnected and interact with each other. This interaction can be mastered and guided by the "I" as the "Observer and Director" of unconscious dynamics, through the technique of disidentification, learning to respond to events instead of reacting impulsively to them.

COACHING THE ESSENCE

In the field of neuroscience, the physical structure of the brain is considered to function as a system, each part having a specific function in an integrated and interconnected psycho-physical whole: specific functions exist but cannot be separated. The whole is greater than the sum of the parts.

Antonio Damasio, a Portuguese neurologist, neuroscientist, psychologist, and essayist, suggests (1999) that the way an emotion emerges in the brain, and consequently changes in the body occur and are perceived by the subject as a feeling that runs through the sense of self, is a key point to explore from a psychosynthetic perspective.

His research has focused on understanding the neural mechanism from a neuroscientific perspective and the biological impact involving three phenomena: emotion, the feeling of emotion, and knowledge of having a feeling of emotion.

This perspective helps to contextualize the representation of Emotion-Feeling within the same ray in the Star Diagram, as well as how the "I", having achieved emotional detachment and a greater awareness of inner dynamics through disidentification, can manage this psychological function through the purposeful use of Will, in its complete design composed of stages, states, and qualities.

Another key element in Damasio's research, in a parallel to Psychosynthesis, concerns the process that takes place in the brain to form the mental model that generates the image of an object and how the brain formulates a sense of self in the act of knowing.

Imagery is one of the psychological functions defined in the Star Diagram and is a key element in inner dynamics and decision-making, as outlined in the Ten Psychological Laws (or Laws of Psychodynamics) described by Assagioli in *The Act of Will*. One of the very impactful psychosynthetic techniques is the use of guided imagery or visualization.

In a psychosynthetic view, the ability to master the mind emerges when the "I" can disidentify from the various subpersonalities residing in its psychic realm. Disidentification involves maintaining emotional detachment from their demands

8- Psychosynthesis Concepts and Maps

as they seek to satisfy their basic needs, often against the "I"'s purpose, which is always evolutionary. The Laws of Psychodynamics describe cause/effect relationships through which the use of images and sensations affect emotions and feelings and vice versa.

Consciousness is considered the unified mental structure that brings the object together as a neural pattern exhibited in the sensory cortex appropriate for this task, and the self in the act of knowing. Damasio calls this process the "neurobiology of consciousness" and it represents a step forward in understanding the biological mechanisms involved, even if, in his opinion, the intimate problem of the image perceiver remains to be explored.

Psychosynthesis can provide support and a unique perspective in this investigation, through its methodology and maps, within the broad context of Self-Realization: the Egg and Star Diagrams, the Ten Psychological Laws or Laws of Psychodynamics, the innate tendency of the "I" to actualize its transpersonal Source, the Ideal Model, to name a few.

According to Damasio, central consciousness is a simple biological phenomenon that provides a sense of self in the present moment, while extended consciousness provides the broad context of self-identity in a time continuum, from past to future, and is a complex biological phenomenon.

The autobiographical self, a complex sum of the previous two, represents a further distinction, dependent on autobiographical memory, systematized memories of situations that denote the organized recording of major aspects of the organism's biography. The proto-self is the unconscious precursor to the level of self that appears in our mind as a conscious subject participating in the patterns of consciousness.

This process emphasizes the sense of self in the act of knowing and the changes that occur in the organism as a result of contact with an object- a knowing that is continuously created within the brain whether the object is real or imaginary. Consciousness emerges as a feeling once we are in contact with an object, real or as a memory. Damasio asserts that we can say we feel through contact with the object, its experience, and this feeling allows us to say, "I feel through my senses the object itself; the sense of self-knowledge".

Damasio goes on to state that feelings are directed inward and emotions are directed outward, both involving an unconscious biological process; it is through feelings that emotions affect the mind. Separating this process into stages helps make this complicated issue more accessible: an unconscious state of emotion, a state of feeling, and a state of conscious feeling. The feeling can be regarded as the intimate mental experience of an emotion, which in turn is representative of a set of observable responses.

The increasing cycle of emotions perceived through feelings becomes known at the level of the conscious self by specific thoughts and related actions/behaviors. We can learn through conscious thought to partially prevent the external expression of emotion, but we cannot control the automatic change that occurs in the gut.

Damasio's emphasis on viewing emotions and consciousness as a necessity for survival, both rooted in the representation of the body, is reflected in Assagioli's representation of the Star Diagram of Psychological Functions. Damasio's hypothesis known as the "Somatic Marker" suggests that the mechanism of reasoning is no longer influenced, either unconsciously or consciously, by signals from the neural machinery that underlines emotions. He points out that *"We are not emotional thinking machines, but emotional machines that think."*

In less than a fifth of a second following a stimulus, a feeling is generated: the conscious mind recovers soon after with a small delay, and this is reflected externally as the brain circuits controlling the facial muscles create a micro-emotional expression. The result is a manifestation of genuine feeling at the moment, and the brain collects this physiological change as emotional information. The remaining mood that colors the perception of reality is called the refractory period and is a form of emotional priming. Neuroscientific research has shown that moods and emotional priming can influence our decision-making, and this is relevant in the context of coaching.

8- Psychosynthesis Concepts and Maps

By exploring beliefs, values, meaning, and purpose with the client, we help the coachee become more aware of the ramifications involved in choosing from a certain perspective and mindset, in the transition from unconscious to conscious decisions. Neuroscience provides us with the insights to emphasize that values are closely related to emotions, involving us physically by perceiving, through feelings, their importance.

The arrangement of the Star Diagram, particularly the proximity of Sensation to Emotion, suggests that Assagioli had both a scientific and an intuitive understanding of the neurological mechanisms outlined above.

In the brain, the structure most related to self-awareness appears to be the insula, which connects the amygdala, anterior cingulate cortex, and cortical area of the frontal, temporal, and parietal lobes involved in memory and attention. The insula evaluates emotional stimuli, probably by integrating the sensation into a bodily sensation.

Therefore, helping clients to be more holistically self-aware becomes central to their ability to dis-identify from an emotional attachment to an object and maintain an "I"-centered presence. From this center they can decide whether to let the emotion take its course, impacting the entire psyche, or manage it, in the knowledge that they cannot control the initial feeling but can choose how to act based on awareness of their inner dynamics.

Through neuroplasticity and multiple psychosynthetic techniques, we can create an ecological and sustainable inner habit to modulate emotions, allowing our core values to emerge. The benefits of acting on our core values (meta-values) are decidedly and substantially different from acting on the values of others. We can feel this difference and can help clients to be aware of this inner feeling to have more clarity in decision-making.

Emotion represents a key factor in how we make decisions. The brain seeks out memories of experiences with similar emotional content: balancing them against each other tends toward the more positive, as Damasio describes in his theory of the "Somatic Marker". We perceive and feel through the body, providing an emotional summary of the situation in return.

COACHING THE ESSENCE

Comparing emotions and evaluating reward or punishment is a crucial mental process in decision-making.

In 1991, neuro-cardiologist Dr. J. Andrew Armour introduced the term "heart brain", defining that the heart possesses its complex nervous system, has long-term and short-term memory, neural plasticity, the ability to learn, acts like a brain, and functions independently of the brain itself.

A constant interaction of ascending signals sent from the heart to the brain modifies brain activity in the higher cognitive and emotional centers, influencing the process of awareness, feelings, and emotions. The heart is closely connected with the way we think, feel and behave. The heart is also the most powerful generator of electromagnetic energy in the human body, producing a rhythmic electromagnetic field around the body. The heart's electromagnetic field is about 60 times greater in amplitude than that generated by the brain, providing a precise mechanism for the way we feel our emotions and those of others, even before body language.

Through further research in different disciplines at the HeartMath Institute (USA), it was found that the heart sends information to the brain and body through four different pathways: neurological, biophysical, biochemical, and electromagnetic. By consciously suspending the automatic mechanism that occurs in the brain through breathing and focusing the breath in the heart, HeartMath Institute research has shown that the "brain of the heart" is activated, enhancing the intelligence of the heart, and the emergence of "Coherence" in a resonant state.

Researchers at the HeartMath Institute have established the existence of a direct pathway from the heart to the amygdala, where cells at the center of the amygdala itself synchronize with the heartbeat. The heart rhythm pattern in turn provides information to the amygdala helping to determine our emotional state.

Through neuroplasticity we can generate new pathways to the amygdala by replacing old ineffective emotional patterns, strengthening our ability to move from resourceless to resourceful states, and enabling access to our highest potentials through the psychological function of Intuition.

8- Psychosynthesis Concepts and Maps

What are emotions?

According to Damasio, a shared biological core underlies emotions that manifest various characteristics including patterns emerging from a complicated connection of chemical and neural responses- determined biological processes that depend on an innate set of brain structures perfected by evolution. Emotion-producing structures that occupy a fairly narrow range of subcortical regions are part of a set of structures that regulate and represent bodily states that can be activated unconsciously.

He points out that all emotions use the body to represent themselves, affecting the modus operandi of numerous brain circuits, and that the variety of emotional responses profoundly changes both body and brain. The collection of these changes creates the basis for neural patterns, which eventually become feelings of emotions.

Emotions are closely related to reward or punishment mechanisms and have two biological functions: to produce a specific reaction to a situation and to regulate the internal state of the organism, to change the energy balance, and to be ready for an appropriate reaction from a survival point of view. Emotions are perceived in the organism through sensations and have an impact on the mind. The ability to consciously know the experience of having a feeling enhances the impact of emotions internally, permeating thoughts through involvement with the feeling.

Through consciousness we become aware of emotions, increasing the body's ability to respond in the most appropriate way to survive. Damasio continues by stating that when we have an emotional experience neurons located in the hypothalamus, which regulates hormone release in the basal forebrain and brainstem, release neurotransmitters in different regions of the brain, momentarily transforming the way certain neural circuits work.

We can perceive the effects of this process through the sense of the mental process speeding up or slowing down, or the sense of pleasantness or unpleasantness emphasizing the mental experience. Through the psychological function of sensation, we recognize the experience of having a feeling of emotion while the body has energy available to react to the stimulus (whether it is real or as a memory), triggering a chain of internal neural reactions and influencing our mindset.

Certain regions of the brain send commands to other parts of the brain and body through chemical molecules in the bloodstream and electrochemical signals along neural pathways. In return, the body releases chemicals into the bloodstream, changing the state of the body, altering the processing of numerous brain circuits, and thus triggering specific behaviors. Perceiving the consequences of involvement with a feeling forms a resulting collection of neural patterns, which become images that are part of a particular mindset. Therefore, Damasio concludes, consciousness plays a key role in the feeling of emotion.

The mechanisms behind Assagioli's intuitive representation of psychological functions in the Star Diagram now take on further perspective through modern neuroscience.

According to psychologist and neuroscience researcher Dr. Lisa Feldman Barret, the amygdala and other regions of the brain are important but neither necessary nor sufficient for emotions. In her research, she observed that a mental event, such as fear, is created by a combination of different neurons that produce instances of fear.

This process, consisting of a combination of neurons producing the same result, is called degeneration by neuroscience. Since neurons are multipurpose and perform multiple roles, many central brain systems can serve more than one purpose and participate in the creation of a variety of mental states. Overall, research has shown that no single region of the brain contains the fingerprint for every single emotion, and while emotions result from the activation of neurons, no neuron is dedicated exclusively to emotions. Because variation is the norm, Barrett suggests that emotions are best described as emotional categories.

Emotions are mental constructions: a sensory input simulated by the brain generates automatic changes in the organism, changing the feeling. In the process of simulation, the brain uses concepts that are a collection of neural patterns, representing past experiences. The brain combines these patterns in a variety

8- Psychosynthesis Concepts and Maps

of ways to perceive and guide actions at a given time, using concepts that provide meaning simultaneously to internal and external sensations. The brain constructs an instance of meaning from sensations and feelings, creating an emotional concept.

Emotion is thus, according to this perspective, a mental construct associated with bodily sensations related to an event occurring in the real world or the imagination. The brain gives meaning to sensations through massive intrinsic network activity, consisting of collections of neurons that fire together. The result is an example of emotions, often related to interoceptive sensations, the brain's representation of all sensations for the internal organism, including hormones and the immune system.

Barrett calls this explanation the "Theory of Constructed Emotions", emphasizing that we are the architects of our experiences.

The importance of a flexible coaching mindset, the ability to manage emotions, and the client's centered approach, the "Who" of the client among the "What" of the contents, is underscored by recent developments in the world of professional coaching. The International Coaching Federation has substantially revised its Core Competencies, particularly emphasizing the need for a professional coach to be sensitive to identity, experience, environment, values, and the client's beliefs.

Emphasis is further placed on the ability to maintain a flexible, client-centered approach, and this requires the ability to manage and regulate one's emotions during the coaching partnership and in one's personal life.

Conclusion

The ability to transform our thoughts and emotions to facilitate the emergence of Intuition through the intelligence of the heart has a positive impact on our emotional feelings, improving our decision-making ability. By replacing old mental patterns with new and renewable ones, we gain the flexibility we need to challenge emotional beliefs related to resourceless ways of thinking by focusing on awareness of both emotions and feelings we perceive in the body as sensations.

COACHING THE ESSENCE

The realization that we are guided by emotional choices and that these in turn are the result of specific neural and mental processes underscores the importance of self-awareness in achieving the ability to manage one's inner dynamics and the mechanisms that operate at the unconscious level.

It is essential to self-regulate and manage our emotions. Neuroscience has shown that this voluntary regulation results in the creation of new patterns, thanks to the neuroplasticity of the brain, to better manage the impact of the amygdala on the bio-psychic system.

Emotional intelligence emerges from the ability to have many concepts and to know how and when to use them, to find the most appropriate emotional categorization in the service of meaningful and valuable action, to reinforce positive experiences in daily life, and to create new mental pathways thanks to the neuroplasticity of both heart and brain.

Once we reach the state of "Coalescence" explained in Patanjali's *Yoga Sutras* millennia ago, in which mind and heart function in resonance, we are in connection with the Self and can regulate our emotions through the psychological function of Intuition, maintaining a connection with our inner source of wisdom and power that resides, as defined in the Vedas millennia ago, in the metaspace of the heart.

Patanjali's *Yoga Sutras* on "Coalescence":

1.41 *As the pattern of consciousness fades, a transparent way of seeing, called coalescence, saturates the consciousness; as a jewel reflects in the same way whatever is in front of him, be it subject, object, or act of perception.*

1.42 *As long as conceptual or linguistic knowledge pervades this transparency, it is called coalescence with thought.*

1.43 *In the next stage called coalescence beyond thought, objects cease to be colored by memory; now formless, only their essential nature shines forth.*

1.44 *Likewise, the coalescent contemplation of subtle objects is termed reflective or non-reflective.*

8- Psychosynthesis Concepts and Maps

Embracing the evolutionary drive toward Self-realization as a fundamental and inevitable process, Psychosynthesis provides practical tools for using psychological functions at will in emotional management, enabling us to choose consciously our emotional response to the many challenges life presents us.

The ability to discern the client's mental patterns depends on the coach's ability to be aware of his or her dynamics and mechanisms occurring at the unconscious level. Neuroscience provides a necessary background for an even more effective and conscious application of Psychosynthesis methodologies, on ourselves and our clients, in our common journey toward Self-realization.

References

Frawley, D. & Kshirsagar, S. (2016). *The Art of Vedic Counseling*. (pp. 190, 191, 195-196). Lotus Press

Assagioli R. (1973). *The Act of Will* (1st ed. pp. 22,23,46,49,60,62, 65,84,152,153,157,164). David Platt Publishing Company

Assagioli R. (1973). *The Skillful Will: Psychological Laws.* The Act of Will (pp. 49-65). The David Platt Publishing Company

Archivio Assagioli, Florence (n.d.). https://www.archivioassagioli.org

Barrett, L. (2017). *How Emotions are Made: The Secret Life of the Brain.* (p. 51). Houghton Mifflin Harcourt

Bonacina, P.M. (1997). *L'Uomo Stellare* (p. 40,47,48,49,53,54,55). Editor L'Uomo

Damasio, A. (1999). *The Feeling of What Happens: Body and Emotions in the Making of Consciousness.* (p. 41,51) Houghton Mifflin Harcourt

Eagleman, D. (2016), *Incognito, the secret life of the brain,* (pag.4,5,6,7,9,29,33,42,44, 48,49, 50, 56,57,58,64,70,71,72,104,105, 114,116,118,120,124,132,194,240,), ed. The Canons

Frawley, D. & Kshirsagar, S. (2016). *The Art of Vedic Counseling.* (pp. 190, 191, 195-196). Lotus Press

Gazzaniga, M. (2011). *Who's in Charge? Free Will and the Science of the Brain.* (1st ed., p. 43). Ecco

Gazzaniga, Michael S., and Joseph E. LeDoux (2013), *The integrated mind.* Springer Science & Business Media

Goleman, D. (2020). *Rewire the Brain* (p. 10, 29). TH Press

International Coaching Federation. (n.d.). *What is Coaching.*

McCraty, R. et. al. (2016). *Heart Intelligence- Connecting with the Intuitive Guidance of the Heart* (pp. 28-24,29,84,94). Waterfront Press

O'Connor, J. & Lages, A. (2019). *Coaching the Brain- Practical Application of Neuroscience to Coaching* (1st ed., pp. 2,17,18,26,44, 45,71,73,76,87,142,143,144,145,146,147,149). Routledge

O'Connor, J. Coaching the Brain - *Practical Applications of Neuroscience to Coaching. Session Three - The Neuroscience of Creativity*

O'Connor, J. (2018). *Values Lesson 1* (p. 4,12). Neuroscience Coaching Center.

O'Connor, J. (2019). *The Neuroscience of Belief, session 1* (p.2,3,4,5,6,7,8,9,10 4,5,6,7) Neuroscience Coaching Center

https://coachingfederation.org/about

https://www.heartmath.org

CHAPTER 9

THE PSYCHOSYNTHESIS LIFE COACH (PLC)
Guiding the Entelechic Process

"The Lord is located in the universe, in the heart of every being and also within the atom."

- Brahama-Samhita (5.35)

Graphic: Carmen Lenatti (2010)

The Entelechic process starts from the first essential step of Personal Leadership, founded on the unveiling of the Ideal Image composed of the synthesis of every single surface image and the emergence of the Ideal Model for the Self. The next step

COACHING THE ESSENCE

is one in which action is based on one's highest potentialities linked to Essence and brought into manifestation through an Ideal Model for the Self. A process that requires, among others, two major Leadership skills: Love and Will.

The Leader is a Guide who helps a group in the actualization of purposes. The action the leader takes in this direction is called Leadership. Skills or requirements vital in a Leader, competencies of Leadership, are in essence Love and Power. In Psychosynthesis, we refer to Self-conscious Awareness (Love) and Will (Power) as the volitional project in its aspects, stages, and qualities.

By Love I don't mean the romantic disposition, à la Madame Bovary, but the power of Love according to Dante in his Divine Comedy or the Bhakti Yoga in Vedic wisdom. The powerful force moves with motivation and intention, proceeding from the bottom to the top, from the object to the subject, in many different forms. Love is the engine of action, as the driving force that, with masterful design, turns the sun and other stars around a central point.

A process that leads to maintaining a positioning at the center of self in the "I", grounded in the Self, in the flow of the here and now, to govern by choice our inner dynamics through an Ideal Model, composed of the synthesis of multiplicity in a context of dynamic, non-static, ever-evolving and inclusive flow.

So, Leadership is a process that maintains a position both at the center of oneself and simultaneously at the center of one's relational system; an essential step from which knowing how to do finds a foundation in knowing how to be, in line with one's essential values. From this perspective, the Leader possesses the essential ability to know how to bring these values from the transpersonal dimension into concrete action, within one's personal or professional reality, motivating people by example in relating within one's relational system; starting from oneself.

Essentially, "Being a Leader" means positioning oneself as the Observer and Director of one's inner system to balance the two dimensions- subjective and objective- through the Force of Love.

9- The Psychosynthesis Life Coach (PLC)

The Ideal Model of Psychosynthesis that serves as an inspiration in this context puts the person at the center within a "Life-Affirming System" as defined by Mark Horowitz (2014). According to Horowitz these are systems that encourage creativity, reward responsibility, and initiative, and recognize the unique contribution that each person is capable of bringing to the collective.

The person is a resource by the grace of their value as a human being. A prerequisite for this to become manifest is that the system must take into account the human factor, recognizing it as a resource and not devaluing the humanity of participants by turning the subject into an object.

It then becomes a priority for a Leader to recognize the unique contribution that each person can bring to the system in which they are inserted and with which they are interacting. This recognition devolves within a structure that involves the individual at the center, in their "I" (Personal Leadership), and from their center, their Self (Transpersonal Leadership) in a relationship between Selves. The result is a Leadership that flows from the personal to the transpersonal level simultaneously.

A lack of choice is a defining element of a dysfunctional system. This objectifies individuals because it fosters unconscious identification with the system itself. The antidote suggested by the psychosynthetic approach as a primary coaching skill within this context is disidentification, the attainment of psychological distance from the system and gaining the ability to look at the larger picture from another and more elevated perspective: from the Self.

The Leadership process becomes the actualization of the Self where Being a Leader means attaining the awareness that every action chosen potentially brings the Self into action, passing through reconnection with one's purpose, through balancing these two ontological Forces: Love and Power or in Psychosynthesis, Awareness and Will. Over-reliance on both spheres prevents a system from becoming effective. Love balances the limits of Power and Power balances the limits of Love and, if used equally, together can create a powerful reinforcing dynamic to

COACHING THE ESSENCE

produce a high-performing organization, drawing on individuals as human resources because of their core values.

Emotion represents a key factor in how we make decisions. The realization that we are guided by emotional choices, and that these in turn are the result of specific neural and mental processes, underscores the importance of self-awareness, achieving the ability to manage our inner dynamics and the mechanisms operating at the unconscious level that impact the "I", with Love and Power or Awareness and Will.

> *"Love is metaphysical gravity"*
> -R. Buckminster Fuller

Balancing Love and Power requires practice and effective techniques to develop awareness and maintain a certain psychological distance from our systems, creating a neutral space that allows us to identify with the system and observe its dynamics and impact on both ourselves and others, and subsequently to disidentify from it so that we can observe its dynamics from another perspective, as a Self, and finally to identify ourselves by choice with the best attitude at the moment to bring a meaningful and valuable contribution to the system, in a holistic sense. The Leader becomes the source of inspiration for his or her main skill: the Congruence between Being and Doing, becoming a mentor for subjects within his or her organization.

Hence coaching, as a provider of leverage in inspiring the translation of intentions and values into conscious actions from a Psychosynthesis perspective, considers the Leader as a guide in the Process of Entelechy, the full achievement of one's Purpose in line with one's Essence. This means becoming an Authentic Leader from whom emerges a Leadership that brings a transformative impact at the transpersonal level into the system, accompanying people on the journey of Self-realization as they carry out their tasks within it, translating intentions and values into concrete, ecological and sustainable actions.

From the Śrimad-Bhāgavatam, verses 5-6:
"In the state of consciousness and unconsciousness and the intermediate state, he (the perfect person) should seek to understand

9- The Psychosynthesis Life Coach (PLC)

the Self and be completely situated in the Self. In this way, he should realize that the defined conditioned and liberated stages of life are only illusions, devoid of true existence. Through such high understanding, he should see only the Absolute Truth present in everything."

"Since the material body will surely be destroyed and the duration of life is not fixed, neither death nor life can be glorified. Instead, one must observe the eternal time factor in which the living being manifests and disappears."

Reference:

Mark Horowitz (2016),*The Dance of We: The Mindful Use of Love and Power in Human Systems*, Synthesis Center Press

Entering into the Void

A blank canvas

An empty glass

A clean mirror

A pristine trail

From my father, artist and painter, I learned Art expressed through painting.

From the love for my homeland, the Valtellina, I learned the Art of Service, through the profession of Sommelier.

From Authoritative Sources, the Teaching of the Truth to make Love the Art of Living According to One's Purpose.

From the sport of Sleddog Racing, I learned unconditional love and generosity from my four-legged athletes; the union of purpose in pursuit of a common goal, traversing the white snowy expanses of the Great North.

From the desire to share how to make one's life available as an instrument of service in the development of human potential, a book to be written page by page, filling in the blank spaces

COACHING THE ESSENCE

with meaningful and empowering words about how to make coaching an Art of Living.

"Every thought arises in the mind, in its arising aims to pass out of the mind, into the act; just as every plant, germinating, seeks to rise to the light."

-Ralph Waldo Emerson

My father sought quiet, minimalist environments to compose his works. Possibly simple rooms in the old, rural houses of old Sondrio. He filled them with blank canvases of various sizes, canvases begun, others finished, oil paints, pencils, chalks, brushes, magazine clippings, dried flowers, and other objects that might inspire him. In the air the scent of acrylic, tempera, oil, and nitro thinner for cleaning brushes.

Photo: Elio Pelizzatti (1965)

I like to think I grew up among bread and brushes.

Before he began to apply the pencil to the canvas to let what was already precisely outlined in his imagination and emerging

9- The Psychosynthesis Life Coach (PLC)

in stroke after stroke take shape, there was a space of suspended time between him and the canvas, filled with contemplation. I didn't understand then. I was a child and I watched him and in watching him I could feel the fullness of that space between him and the canvas, the intensity of the moment before he entered the canvas and began to create his work.

I'm not even sure today if that work was only his or if he was the artificer of a work that was manifested through his hand.

The blank canvas was in front of my father who contemplated it as if he was asking its permission to be able to "stain" it, taking away that initial whiteness, and entering the space, full of creativity. In the silence, one could feel the energy flowing as a magical connection was created between him and a dimension beyond time, space, and the rational mind where he was about to enter "into the Void Space".

Then it would begin. The hand would take the pencil, the pencil would approach the canvas, and the canvas was ready to receive the stroke that would forever change its pristine whiteness. I still remember those moments as intense, almost sacred moments, dominated by silence, when he would enter the canvas with his hand to bring into manifestation through creativity what in the space had been imagined, shared, outlined, and thanked. Entering the space of the blank canvas was for him the next step in a ritual, if one can call it this way, without which the heart of what was then represented would not be manifested.

I am deeply grateful to my father for initiating and nurturing me with the Love of Art, the Art that accompanied him until his last breath, leaving us the gift of the Beauty of his works, but above all the beauty of his Being an Artist from the Heart.

In this unfinished piece of work of his I've shown on the next page, he was passing on to me the gift of Art, showing me the path of Psychosynthesis, which I did not know then. In the years that followed, I realized that Psychosynthesis waited for me, was pointed out to me on many occasions, and left marks etched in space, in time, and even on a blank canvas, which it is now my task to complete.

COACHING THE ESSENCE

Elio Pelizzatti: "Vaso con Rose", (2006)

In 2006 I graduated as a Professional Sommelier, even though I am not a wine or alcohol drinker. I drink mostly water. In those years I managed an alpine hut on the ski slopes high in the Italian Alps, in the Valmalenco valley on the border with Switzerland, under the shadow of the Bernina Group. Many people would stop between downhill runs and love to taste, in that short time, a good glass of wine accompanied by a typical dish from the Valtellina, the great east-west valley on the northern border of Lombardy, famous for cooking and wine. My passion for learning stimulated me in that context to study the Art of Tasting and Serving. Studying to become a professional Sommelier, I learned that wine is not just a stimulant or a relaxant, or however you want to define it, but is primarily the result of a complex evolutionary process that starts from a seed.

Without the ideal soil, the right context, the necessary

9- The Psychosynthesis Life Coach (PLC)

conditions, and the care of the winemaker's skilled hand, the elixir that finds the customer's receptive palate would not be there. The small seed, struggling to sprout, flower, and manifest the grape cluster, would not and could not be transformed into the final product.

The result of a long process that starts from a seed, the rare seed of Nebbiolo in Valtellina in particular, which, finding the ideal soil, begins to produce deep roots that sink into the rock in search of groundwater, nurturing a plant that can live for many years even with little water and under extreme climatic conditions. With a unique and particular process of cultivation, this seed yields a fruit that, through the skilled care of the winemaker, provides an elixir. A seed that from the very beginning is a living example of "Resilience" as the power of life to manifest itself at any cost, in soil that is poor and arduous to cultivate, finding its way to take root and emerge, manifesting its potential in all its vitality.

To taste a sip of this elixir, which goes through a long process of phases, states, and stages of the fruit, from birth to pouring to the final product, the ideal glass is needed.

Although we seldom bring due attention to it, the glass is essential. The proper glass and the way we hold and manage it enhances the color of the wine, the quality, and the fragrance that will be released thanks to its shape and the particular movements with which it is rotated and held, that essence that the elixir is ready to release if contained in the ideal space. The glass must have a particular shape according to the contents waiting to enter it, and of course it must be empty and pristine.

The void, filled with air that is being moved by the wine entering it, mingling with the contents, allows the release of the previously confused aromas that reveal themselves as they become manifest with clarity to a trained sense of smell. The glass must be crystal-clear, almost as if the empty space of the glass existed only to allow its contents to be fully appreciated in all its potentials, which can now emerge.

The moment the first drop of wine enters the glass is delicate, slow, velvety, artfully handled by the experienced Sommelier

COACHING THE ESSENCE

and first brought to their attentive gaze that begins to read the wine contained in the space, which is now filled with aromas, flavors, color, subsequently beginning to entering into the space of the Void, in a unique experience to be savored with awareness.

Without the ideal glass, empty, crystal clear, and artfully handled, the wine could not be truly appreciated in every step of its long process that brings it to the customer's palate. The Sommelier educates the customer in the Art of Tasting through refined service, facilitating conscious participation in the experience of appreciating each step leading to the result of tasting the elixir, one small sip at a time.

Photo: "Sorsi"

From *The Sutra of Hui Neng-* School of Ch'an Buddhism, known in Japan as "Zen":

"...The fifth Zen patriarch, Hung-Jen, was looking for his successor. He asked his monks to put their reflections into verse. Shen Hsiu, the favorite for succession wrote:

'Our body is the Bodhi tree and our mind is a shining mirror.
We carefully clean them from hour to hour
So as not to let the dust settle there'

9- The Psychosynthesis Life Coach (PLC)

The Patriarch, unimpressed, commented on the submission, saying: 'To attain supreme enlightenment one must succeed in spontaneously knowing one's nature or Essence of Mind, which is neither created nor can be destroyed. From Ksana to Kshana one must always succeed in realizing one's Essence of Mind. Then all things will be free from compulsion. Come back when you have understood.'

An illiterate servant in the temple, Hui-Neng, asked one of his friends to write down these verses and give them to the Master:

'There is no Bodhi tree
Nor support for a polished mirror.
Since everything is empty,
where can the dust settle?'

Hui-Neng became the sixth and last Zen Patriarch."

During my years of competitive practice in the sport of Sled-dog Racing (1988-1994), I won many medals with my team, including a gold medal in 1992 at the World Championships in Austria in Bad Mittendorf in the 4-dog, purebred category. Among the countless skills I learned during those years in my role as "Musher", team building was primary. Communication with my Huskies was empathetic, verbal, and nonverbal, without the use of restraint of any kind, leveraging their innate quality of running and my passion for action in contact with Nature.

In this case, the bloodline of my athletes was Seppala, and to this day, the offspring descended from my team accompany each of our days as companions in life, emanating joy. Yes, they are indeed emitting joy, their joyful attitude is the precious gift they give us daily, asking for very little in return, sometimes a "mere glance".

In their eyes I still see the long runs in the snowy tracks in Europe and North America, the moments of fatigue as well as those of victory, turning every moment of a life lived together into beauty. Every effort led to excellent results, which I always

COACHING THE ESSENCE

aimed for. In the white snowy trails dominated by silence, our hearts beat in unison, and our breath, condensing into a vapor that crystallized on our faces, was the sign that marked the shared performance of the team, which plowed the white trails, leaving the imprint of our passage immediately erased by the passage of other athletes behind us.

Those snowy white trails are in my heart today, moments of a life lived, without which I could not call myself truly congruent in the application of skills and qualities I experienced one by one myself, and only later studied theoretically.

Today I am following the profession that I most love, that essentially represents me, that deeply belongs to me, to which I dedicate my life with passion, diligence, determination, respect, and constancy: helping people through the Art of Coaching.

Through Psychosynthesis, ancient Vedic Wisdom, Ecopsychology, and especially my life experiences, coaching for me is equivalent to being able to act according to my Dharma, manifesting my "Call of Self".

According to the Vedas each living being is born with a unique tendency that must be manifested. Mine is the tendency toward coaching. Whether it was called "Musher", "Sommelier", "Hut manager" or something else, through coaching I can feel an active participation in what I do best, in every activity I focus on. Certainly an exhausting trend, but what could be more satisfying than following one's "Calling", if it is aimed at going beyond one's limiting beliefs and appearances to tap into the vast plane of Being, manifesting it through conscious actions, and helping or training others to do the same?

Like the blank canvas, the empty glass, the clean mirror, the snowy paths I want to be for people who rely on me, so that they can enter the empty space that separates them from their Essence, filling it with their contents and savoring their innate beauty, once contextualized in the ideal container of which I make myself available and an instrument for themselves and for me. In this manner they are able to become what they already are authentically in power, a Self: achieving the desired results and finally reflecting themselves in their Self, through me, realizing their Essence, making their lives the best-equipped gymnasium available to train their qualities and potentials and acquire others, becoming resilient at the transpersonal level.

"Entering into the Void" there is the space of Creativity. In the creative space of the void they can thus write on the content-free and crystal-clear page of their awareness, their new story, the authentic story about themselves that wants to emerge in an unwritten book, thanks to the void which is essentially an space of opportunity.

For essentially, in the Silence, in the traces of life, in the blank pages, in the empty as well as the full, there is only the Self.

The Will to Go Beyond: from Sleddog Racing to Psychosynthesis

Photo: Sleddog Racing, C. Pelizzatti (1993)

"Every Life Converges to Some Center", by Emily Dickinson (1830-1886):

Every life converges to some center
Declared or unspoken.

COACHING THE ESSENCE

There exists in every human heart
A goal
Which it perhaps scarcely dares to acknowledge,
Too beautiful
To risk the audacity
To believe in it.
Cautiously adored as a fragile sky,
To reach it
Would be as desperate an undertaking as
Touching the rainbow's robe.
But safer the more distant for those who persevere:
And how high to the slow patience
Of the saints is the sky!
He may not get the brief trial
Of life, but then
Eternity makes still possible
the ardent momentum.

The dynamics of human thinking are reflected in the reality to which we bring our attention and intention. This statement emerged in me one distant day while walking on the Quai de la Seine in Paris, where for the first time in the 1970s my gaze met the icy sky-blue eyes of a Husky. That meeting of glances generated within a few years a revolution in my life, leading me to the competitive sport of Sleddog Racing, practically unknown in Italy in the 1980s and practiced only by the elite in Europe in the same years.

Born among the mountains of Valtellina, a lifelong fan of mountaineering and skiing, practicing from a young age, I came to sleddog racing through an interesting story that developed moment by moment through the vicissitudes of life and through choices that I followed mostly impulsively.

Meeting the magnetic gaze of that Husky on the Quai de la Seine in Paris was a catalyzing moment as a result of which,

9- The Psychosynthesis Life Coach (PLC)

more or less unconsciously, my path in coaching was profoundly marked, combining a love for Wild Nature and a desire to always achieve the best and go Beyond, motivated by a great passion, with the vague inkling that I was pursuing "a path that had called me".

Sleddog racing allowed me to train qualities that already belonged to me and others that I acquired, which years later I studied through Psychosynthesis and Positive Psychology. These qualities, which I later recognized in the Virtues and Character Strengths (The VIA Classification of Strengths) classifications, were fundamental, especially during the darkest period of my life.

Above all, practicing competitive sport has allowed me to get in deep contact with myself through direct and profound contact with wild nature. Through competitive activity I have been able to harness my anger, transforming the inner conflict into a propellant for my highly competitive spirit poured into the practice of excellence. Through racing I was able to divert the destructive charge of my anger into a creative charge, an attitude that I now practice in coaching and teaching future PLCs.

Catharsis occurs at the transpersonal level, and at that level anger becomes a life force that I bring to the service of my Self, in action emerging from the flow of this energy from mind to heart and vice versa, transformed into positive and creative energy.

Sleddog racing taught me that the transformation of negatively charged energies into positive and productive charge is possible, valuing competitiveness in a joyfully constructive sense, rooted in harmony through conflict, or psychosynthesis.

I also had so much fun in those sporting years and carry with me splendid memories of snowy tracks in European and North American forests, where silence reigned untamed, briefly interrupted by my team's breath and my own, which in the cold turned to steam, clouds of breath appearing and vanishing, a reminder of the impermanence and value of each fleeting moment.

I am truly grateful for all the moments I experienced while practicing sleddog racing, especially for allowing me to be aggressive in my own way, going Beyond my limits to tap into the limitless transpersonal realm.

The first sleddog competition in which I officially participated with my team was in Andermatt, Switzerland, in 1988, in the Swiss championship 4-dog purebred category. This was followed in the following years by numerous national and international championship competitions (in which we were on the podium for the majority of the competitions). I raced during the opening competition of the Olympic Games in Albertville (France in 1992) and finished in fourth place; in the World Championships in Bad Mittendorf in Austria in 1992 in which together with my team we won the gold medal in the 4 dog sprint. This category was restricted to purebreds: the rare bloodline of Seppala Siberian Huskies whose best-known protagonist was Balto, the hero of the 1925 serum run to Nome, Alaska.

The last race I ran in Fairbanks - Alaska, in 1994, in the Limited North American Championship (LNACH) finishing 5th to within a few seconds of first place (I had a rented team and one less dog in the last heat, as I could not participate overseas with my team due to excessive costs). In those years we were on the podium for 95% of the races we participated in, both in Europe and North America.

My mantra was and remains, "in to win, doing my best all the time!"

The "Will to Run"

"The stages of Will are ideal moments."

— Roberto Assagioli

Resilience, perseverance, generosity, beauty, passion, enthusiasm, joy, excitement, determination, strength, curiosity, courage, dedication, respect, unconditional love, grace, harmony, freedom, and empathy, are just some of the qualities embodied by these wonderful "four-legged brothers", my life companions, my teachers. For them, I feel a deep sense of gratitude, since,

9- The Psychosynthesis Life Coach (PLC)

thanks to them, I was able to participate in these qualities by training and strengthening them.

Photo: Sleddog Racing, C. Pelizzatti (1991)

The years of competitive sports we shared were instrumental in the formation of my personality and my evolution as a human being. Without their support and example, because of the devastation I found myself in, fourteen years after leaving competitive sports, I most likely would not be here writing this book.

Huskies run because they were born to do so and they do so with joy. The musher (from the French word "marcher", one who walks with the team) uses their voice exclusively to incite them to keep pace and to issue the various directional commands.

This "Will to Run" is not achieved by trying to force them to run: they run because they were born to do so and because it is a joy for them to be able to do it together. This is an innate aptitude and the musher just connects with this quality and nurtures it, enhances it, and resonates with the team. The musher performs at the level of his or her athletes and the team performs by following the Leadership of the musher connected to the rhythm of the team, to arrive together at the finish line and Beyond.

Between mushers and Huskies, there is a deep respect and

COACHING THE ESSENCE

understanding, a deep empathic relationship, mutual love, passion, and attention to the well-being of each athlete in their specificity and relationship within the system. Team building is one of the fundamental skills to compete in sleddog racing at the highest levels. The Team Leader is the key component and Leadership, while difficult to acquire if not already present in the one who performs it, is an essential prerequisite for both the canine team and the musher.

Being a musher means dedicating one's life to one's team and shared passion, being attentive to the needs, on various levels, of the whole team and of each athlete in particular; diligently studying techniques, theories, and functioning of metabolism to adapt a targeted diet and balancing one's life on various planes to be able to manage energy optimally. This attention is mutual: the musher must be mindful of themselves and know themself more and more deeply, renewing the purpose for all that this sport/lifestyle requires. Motivation is sometimes undermined by too much fatigue on various levels, so keeping alive the question: "why am I doing this?" helps not to lose sight of the course to the finish line, keeping focus, motivation, and concentration on the process, and the final goal. Passion moves one to go beyond fatigue, reaching and exceeding one's limits, together.

The team is selected based on motivation and genealogy, which determines the morphology of the canine athlete. In-depth study of the subject is one of the prerequisites for being successful, and a love of study is one of my characteristics.

> *Every life converges to some center,*
> *Declared or unspoken.*
> *There exists in every human heart*
> *A goal.*

My goal was and remains today to participate by giving my best, to win. Aiming for excellence is my goal, an attitude that has remained unchanged over time. This was the goal of every competition, the motive force behind the hard training in preparation for every competition I entered. Aiming for excellence by performing the best and Beyond is my "mantra". For seven years my life was, so to speak, programmed to win, in a sport

9- The Psychosynthesis Life Coach (PLC)

that I still love deeply and to which I owe so much.

I did not want to win to feel superior to others. Rather, it was my challenge, to always go Beyond, to prove to myself that I could do it, that one can go beyond the limits of one's expectations and beliefs, that one can be faster than one might think, that one can endure exhausting fatigue if one finds that balance between the various physical, mental, and emotional components, an appropriate technique, and above all that understanding with the team that goes beyond what is quantifiable, in a space where immense energies reside waiting to be contacted and brought into action.

The space of the heart.

Love, that to this day connects me to my four-legged brothers and sisters, was the driving force behind the intention to achieve the goal of excellence, rising to the maximum and more.

From heart to heart, communication flows beyond imaginable limits. The heart opens the door beyond the possible we think we can reach, to what is impossible for the rational mind: the field of infinite potential possibilities.

What I am writing here speaks of my lived, experiences, witnessing them with sincerity and non-attachment. The results my team and I have achieved over the years of international competitions have gone beyond expectations, medals, and the stopwatch. They are experiences of the power of Unconditional Love, the transpersonal Love that is not quantifiable, but real and tangible. Even my extreme labors are facets of Love experienced and lived. If what I have done, what I am doing, and what I intend to do has Love as its beginning, middle, and end, then every action in its way is a manifestation of the Power of Love.

I experienced moments of extreme fatigue, where I thought that my strength had run out. Drained by intense fatigue, I had no voice left to cheer the dogs on or breathe in the frigid air, continuing to run for mile after mile at the same speed as the team (30-35 km/h), as the musher does not stand on the sled passively but runs alongside it or pedals to lighten the weight the dogs have to pull, keeping the pace steady throughout the course.

I arrived at the finish line more than once covered in blood from the nasal hemorrhaging which was my body's response for giving more than it could offer at that moment. Today I carry the memories of such labors in my body, which also appear as scars, pains, and activities that I can no longer do for various reasons, as the price of success sometimes requires a counterpart of giving up, recapitulating and closing down, and then opening up other avenues.

I always gave my best, trying to go beyond this "maximum" of mine every time, in a space that I did not know theoretically at the time, but that I lived and experienced as existing in its power. My passion was the only driver at times when doubt and fatigue seemed unbearable. Today I know that this space is called "Transpersonal" and that one can experience this dimension as one crosses the threshold of one's physical, emotional, and mental limits, and the limits of one's beliefs.

When I found myself at the limit of my energies, recalling the motivation for why I was doing what I was experiencing, focusing on what I wanted to achieve, and simultaneously entering a space Beyond personal space, connecting to my team simultaneously to share a force needed to continue in the intent, I became able to go beyond being exhausted. I was able to tap into forces that were not otherwise available because I could not usually access them due to my mental limitations. These would say, in an inner little voice. ... "I can't take it anymore, I give up, enough is enough, I've reached my limit, give up Cristina", as my physique was burning from intense fatigue.

Observing myself from a perspective beyond fatigue as I was going through these experiences, I participated in the power of directing my will by choice just when I thought I no longer had any choice except to slump down exhausted. This shift in awareness, that was then unknowingly already present, allowed me and my team to arrive victorious at the finish line for many years.

Winning did not mean for me then (nor does it mean today) to show others that I am better, but to show myself that I can always improve, and this involves sacrifice...sometimes to extreme levels.

9- The Psychosynthesis Life Coach (PLC)

Life has taken me on many paths after this "life juncture" of mine, but my attitude has remained solid on the principles I learned in my years of competitive sports, in intimate contact with Nature.

To always give my all and go one step Beyond what I know is possible, to do everything in my power when I devote myself to the achievement of a goal is a duty for me, aware that there is a limit beyond which I have no power but surrender to what belongs to the Beyond, where potentials are immeasurable.

To go Beyond, the presence of a Master Guide is indispensable.

The teaching of those years solidified the foundation of my personality and showed me the way, what I now know as the process of: "Individualization" (Carl Jung), "Actualization" (Abraham Maslow), "Realization" (Roberto Assagioli) that is achieved by knowing, training and practicing the intrinsic qualities that we have always carried.

> *"1. Self-realisation*
> *2. Self-identification*
> *3. Self-actualisation*
> *Stage"*
>
> -Roberto Assagioli

The action that brings into manifestation the best of ourselves moment by moment, with dedication and passion, grounded in Love is defined in the *Bhagavad-Gītā* as *Bhakti Yoga*.

The chemistry with my athletes was incredible. Without having studied back in the day what empathy meant, I learned it by running mile after mile of snowy trails. I communicated perfectly (and still do today) with my Huskies, we understood each other through and beyond verbal communication, on a level that I know today to be the transpersonal level, synchronized with shared passion, tuned to the Power of Love. Combining Love and passion is the ideal formula for going beyond one's limits: in my years of competitive sleddog sports, I was able to experience this winning formula. Today it is a fundamental prerequisite in my Being Coach.

The dedication with which my four-legged siblings accompanied me from those years, always giving their all, remains a gift that life has allowed me to experience and for this, I feel deep gratitude. My role even then was to be a Leader for my team and to be a Leader for myself, simultaneously programmed to win, through the Power of Love.

Today I carry out and teach the practice of the same profession, although on another path: that of Psychosynthesis Life Coaching. To be a coach in synthesis means to be a Leader, starting with oneself. By this, I am not saying that the coach directs the coachee during the session, but I am emphasizing that to be effective with our clients we must be able to manage our inner dynamics so that there is no interference as we journey together toward their goal. By training our aptitude for Leadership we can truly set ourselves up to serve our clients as an Ideal Model so that they can learn to become their own Leader.

Everything is correlated.

Competition has been running through my veins since I was young and I do not feel it as a negative point or something colored with boastful pride. The winning attitude that I carry within me has helped me reach the podium for most competitions since I have experienced it, practiced it, and conquered it with much effort and passionate love. A mindset that was solidified during those years and helps me today in my work and life.

Competitiveness first and foremost is for me an inner attitude, a motivator to achieve the chosen goal/objective by giving my best at every moment. Constant sacrifice in favor of achieving a more coveted goal was the routine that I have now transformed into awareness, thanks to the studies I undertook in the years following my time in competitive sports.

Purpose, intention, motivation, choice, deliberation, planning, determination, and execution of action were the daily map in those years, all embedded in Nature, in contact with beautiful beings and meeting people united by the same purpose.

Later I discovered Assagioli's Will Project, which describes

9- The Psychosynthesis Life Coach (PLC)

in masterful detail what I experienced in my younger years through the practice of sleddog racing.

To strengthen myself, to compete, to breed the best specimens for performance at the highest level, to compare myself on shared goals, to educate myself to respect the environment and creatures, to co-participate, to experiment to always go Beyond, to study, to overcome my limits which, as I have long experienced on my own skin, are always limits related to beliefs related to one's self-images, are attitudes that today have become deeply rooted in my personality.

The beauty of the competitive sport of sleddog racing has enabled me to develop my highest human potentials and in the later stages of my life, these qualities have served as a foundation during the vicissitudes that awaited me, including the encounter that occurred "causally" on a train fourteen years later between the Vedas, Psychosynthesis, and Ecopsychology.

COACHING THE ESSENCE

CHAPTER 10

BEING PLC
The Self, Leader of the Process

Encountering Psychosynthesis, fourteen years after my last competition, showed me the way that I "ran together with my team" back in the day, which allowed me to have many incredible experiences and to be able to testify with certainty that the transpersonal dimension exists, that it is not "out there" but is always present, inside and outside of us at every moment, if we are aware of it and willing to go beyond our limiting beliefs and self-images.

Training awareness and activating the will according to the blueprint that Psychosynthesis teaches, in line with Vedic Wisdom, is my main passion and purpose today.

Replying to My "Call of Self"

Activating self-awareness to bring it out in a prepared personality is the main goal of my way of living and my work. Helping people get in touch with their inner Source of wisdom and power in any area of life, personal or professional is a source of joy and deep gratitude for me. To be able to be a participant in this intimate journey of unveiling the authentic image veiled among the many self-images is an honor.

Approaching such intrinsic beauty occurs with an attitude of

COACHING THE ESSENCE

respect and devotion, for at that level we are truly and essentially One, interconnected, interdependent, different yet similar, in the paradox we intend to explore with our clients.

In my role as PLC, I bring emphasis to the importance of being able to develop and maintain the attitude of the Observer-Director. This positioning of myself, in myself, in the field of consciousness of the I-Self, the Silent Witness, allows me to observe the various parts at play in my personality (my content) while simultaneously being present in my client's coaching process.

In this state of Presence in the flow of becoming, I can truly observe from another higher perspective how these contents impact by facilitating or interfering with the mental, emotional and physical field of my client and my own simultaneously, so that I can momentarily distance myself from them (disidentify) and identify more and more with the "something else" that is behind all these planes of Being, the "True Essential Nature" that underlies everything.

"The Self is one; it manifests itself in different degrees of awareness and Self-realization."
- Roberto Assagioli

I can perceive Unity in multiplicity, an inconceivable concept for the rational mind working only with the psychological function of Thought, as a condensed feeling of thought, emotion, sensation, imagination, and desire to know more, that is, to participate in the flow of Being myself, moment by moment, and simultaneously being present to the experience of my client, through a transpersonal field of infinite possibilities.

At this point, my Presence goes Beyond Me. I move into the field of transpersonal energies, the Superconscious, where the energies of the Self emanate most distinctly and I place myself at the service of my client as an "External Center of Synthesis", in a game of refractions, if one can call it that, to facilitate the client's access to this dimension within themself. Through me the client finds more and more of themself, their authenticity, which now

10- Being PLC

emerges through partnership at the transpersonal level, guided by the Self.

The attitude of the Observer-Director is not only a self-analysis but a way of looking at oneself from another and higher (transpersonal) perspective, from the Witness Self, an inner positioning that allows awareness to unfold, rather than reaching it through speculative analysis. When one can position oneself and maintain the positioning as an Observer-Director in touch with the highest state of consciousness, one can act from the Self, the Silent Witness, rather than from the personal self, which is always influenced and agitated by thoughts and emotions of one subpersonality or another, keeping the individual in a disempowering state of confusion.

Positioning and establishing oneself in the attitude of Observer-Director in touch with one's Transpersonal Self, reaching a higher state of consciousness, opens the way to true freedom: the freedom of being able to choose which attitude to use, which part of us to identify with, and which qualities to use as we move forward on the path to achieving a desired goal.

From this positioning, or Presence, as we mean it in Psychosynthesis, one can experience a state of Being free from all mental, emotional, and physical movements, a presence that always remains unchanged, a presence that connects us with a sense of a-temporality and universality at the same time, in a perfume of Peace.

The process of achieving and maintaining this state of Presence, or Flow of Being, is known in Psychosynthesis through the IDA Stages: "Identification-Disidentification-Self-identification", which we've seen earlier.

As a PLC, I work, focusing on personal-level development and transpersonal-level evolution of awareness, toward a consciousness of one's subjective reality, through the techniques and educational approach of the Vedic Wisdom Tradition, Psychosynthesis and Ecopsychology.

Psychosynthesis is, so to speak, "simply" a name for the process of personal growth, the natural tendency in each of us to harmonize and synthesize the various dynamic aspects at increasingly inclusive and elevated levels of organization. It is the conscious attempt to cooperate with the natural process of actualization and personal development toward transpersonal development. As Assagioli underlines and we see in all the great Wisdom traditions, Simplicity is the result of a long journey.

All living beings contain within them a drive to evolve, to become the full realization of themselves. Psychosynthesis consciously supports this evolutionary process. Through theories and direct experience, it provides a well-defined structure designed and tested to support the individual, groups, and the entire planet in the evolutionary process. We help accelerate the process of inner perspective change to catalyze change in the outer world, starting from one's inner realm, everything being interconnected and interdependent.

Psychosynthesis integrates through synthesis many millennia-old wisdom traditions of various origins and provenance. It is a science of the spirit, a holistic, comprehensive, inclusive, non-dual praxis that insists on the need to find purpose, meaning, and elevated values in every goal, starting with knowing, mastering, and transforming ourselves.

An inclusive approach to human growth, as we've seen earlier Psychosynthesis dates back to around 1911, founded by Roberto Assagioli. Psychosynthesis is a process, a task that is considered by its founder open-ended and never completed, inviting each of us to participate in the development of Psychosynthesis according to time, place and circumstances, staying strictly within its fundamental parameters or Experiential Facts.

Psychosynthesis recognizes the presence in each living being of a transpersonal essence: the Self, while maintaining that the primary purpose of life is to manifest this Essence in conscious actions congruent with It. The focus of the pragmatic psychosynthesis approach revolves around the realization and experience of already being the Self, whose counterpart, the "I", is immersed in a bio-psychic field, in a particular and not always stable personality. By definition, the "I" is that much of awareness available at any given moment from one's Original Source, the contentless center of awareness and will, represented by the point at the center of the field of consciousness shown in the middle unconscious of the Egg Diagram, the "psychic cell".

The "I", a reflection of the Self in the personality, has the same ontological qualities, but different available quantities of the same which can be used once contacted and purified by contact with the personality. The "I" experiences itself as the Observer and Director of manifest and tangible reality, through identification with subpersonalities, its sub-agents, and subsequent dis-identification from them.

The Self never becomes identified with content since it does not belong to the objective material dimension; paradoxically it participates in experience through the "I", always remaining in the position of Silent Witness.

When the I-Self connection is reestablished, the "I" acquires the ability to choose how to act ecologically through the multiple identifications, observing their dynamics and directing them at will, remaining in line with Dharma, the Ethical Cosmic Order or Universal Self.

The ability acquired by the "I" to act by manifesting transpersonal values in the personal dimension, using the various subpersonalities as allies in the service of the Director "I", always supervised by the Self, is the essence of Self-Leadership.

When the "I" is acted upon by subpersonalities it becomes their servant, deviates from Dharma and generates karma, binding itself to suffering which is essentially rooted in Ignorance of one's True Nature.

"Let us try to fully understand the full significance and immense value of the discovery of the will. However it happens, whether spontaneously or through conscious actions, in a crisis or the stillness of inner recollection, it constitutes a most important and decisive event in our lives."

- Roberto Assagioli

COACHING THE ESSENCE

The Will to Want What I Want

"Daily life is a constant testing and training"
- Roberto Assagioli

"In Truth, it is also said that man is made of desire: but what is desire, such as well, such as well, such as action, such is the result it achieves."
- Bṛhadāraṇyaka Upaniṣad IV.4.5

The recurring phrase I heard as a child when I wanted something was, "the weed 'I want' doesn't grow even in the garden of the King!". Then, since I was already determined and resolute, I would somehow get what I wanted, obviously with the compensation of a good punishment.

So I learned to restrain my will in a way divergent from my natural aptitude and, to get what I wanted, I learned not to want. The sense of not deserving what I wanted grew more and more and if I got it one way or another the sense of not being deserving and thus the need to hide went hand in hand and fed on each other. A strong sense of anger toward myself grew inside me, which I contained with a will directed to the repression of my desire of the moment. However, inevitably this emerged with cutting, direct remarks or with impulsive actions which were not exactly ecological, so to speak.

Having since childhood grown up between two worlds, rural Valtellina and France, I have been able to shape this strong-willed attitude of mine creatively over the years, and certainly the practice of competitive sports and the conquest of the mountains ringing the Valtellina has allowed me to use my propellant energy, directing it toward ambitious goals in which excellence was, and remains, the minimum level of performance accepted.

In France, I learned early to walk across the vast expanses of the Normandy beaches where I spent summers with my grandmother, who had a residence near Deauville. Contemplating the powerful tides of the cold northern English

Channel, I participated in the magic of the appearance and disappearance of the event horizon. Then, walking together along the winding streets of the Paris that used to be, she took me on a discovery of museums, of tastes and scents that even as I write I remember, a multiplicity of ethnicities that did not exist in those days in Valtellina and that nurtured in me a deep sense of unity in diversity and of belonging, despite the differences in origin, gender, and culture.

I learned to appreciate the smallest details of a diverse multi-ethnic representation, in a context that had something magical for me. The Paris I carry in my heart is "La Ville Lumière" of the bright moments of my youth, which accompanied me for many successive years growing up between two worlds that had nothing to do with each other: my mountains, "La Ville Lumière"- and me in between.

From the closed perspective of the Valtellina in which I was born, a splendid valley running east-west and positioned between the Rhaetian Alps and the Pre-Orobian Alps, I learned that to see Beyond, I had to painstakingly climb the lofty peaks, and from that perspective, the emerging awareness was the "redimensioning" of me.

Later I learned that in Psychosynthesis this is called "Disidentification". Achieving this inner positioning and maintaining it requires constant practice, and is neither a walk in the park nor a goal to be achieved. It is not even a permanent goal once learned or studied by heart at best! It is the inner attitude or positioning in oneself, in one's observing center, that is necessary to achieve self-mastery at any given moment so that one can practice excellence in achieving any desired goal.

It is a competency that must be trained constantly and rigorously for it to become effective and efficient.

From practicing the competitive sport of sleddog racing I have learned to participate in team activities as a Leader, to love unconditionally, to compete at the highest level, to put myself out there by giving my best, by going beyond my limiting beliefs, to become aware that there is an intimate feeling of connection with naturalness in me and that I truly and essentially need to be in direct contact with Nature, to which I belong.

COACHING THE ESSENCE

I Am Nature, Nature Is Me.

Photo: Cris and Seppala Siberian "Pirat" (2018)

My Being Coach today carries with it all the seeds of these junctures of my life. I have lived fully, true to my way of being myself fully and authentically, following my essential Nature, and bringing my uniqueness to the service of those who feel the time has come to move beyond their masks and limiting beliefs.

If I want to be myself truly, I have to be myself Naturally.

Encountering Psychosynthesis, Indovedic Psychology, and Ecopsychology allowed me to take the next step and contextualize my attitude of willingness in a personal way, thanks to the realization that willingness is a right and a duty to be manifested responsibly and through an ideal project. First, I learned along the way that there is no separation between the objective world and me unless I cause this separation by feeling separate myself.

I am a participant subject to the objective reality which, paradoxically, exists between me and my experiences while

10- Being PLC

simultaneously there is no separation in the process of participation. I remain myself, and in the grace of presence at my center, I can truly be a participant in objective reality, learning its evolutionary lesson through the opportunity it affords me to train my skills and possibly acquire others.

At this point, it is my responsibility to anchor them in my awareness, through a precise, ecological and sustainable inner project.

As with any project, there is a phase of exploring ideas about a goal that initially belongs to the world of ideas or is idealized, with a motivating or desired purpose and meaning that must then be manifested through an Ideal Model.

A goal is an Ideal Model.

The next step is the evaluation or exploration of the intrinsic and extrinsic value of the desired goal to check in detail the motivation for action, which at this stage is still the inner action or interaction of parts in play, each with its specific task and way of functioning (use of the psychological functions). In other words, this is the stage when subpersonalities and related dynamics which can undermine the volitional act by diverting the subject's intrinsic motivation toward the fulfillment of their needs come into play.

At this point, the person is ready to deliberate the strategy to undertake toward the desired goal and resolutely must make the choice to let go of what has not been selected. This is not an easy time as the attractive and viscous grip of subpersonalities, which are deeply ingrained modes of thought with which one associates self-images within an insulated system, hinder creative thinking, binding the subject to known modes emerging from the past.

As today's neuroscience confirms, cerebral activity prefers downloading from the past, creating patterns that keep the system in which the brain is embedded functional by associating the unfamiliar with the known. To enter the unknown, once again positioning oneself as an Observer allows the subject to pause the mental system and from that disidentified perspective to be able to redimension and metaphorically put the parts

COACHING THE ESSENCE

in play at the moment on the scales with their relative ways of functioning. This enables an objective and resolute choice, selecting the most functional and suitable for empowering the "I" in achieving the desired goal, while inhibiting the others.

The deliberation phase necessitates choice, which without positioning in one's command center, the Observer and Director, cannot take place. For the process toward the desired outcome to truly be achieved ecologically and sustainably, disidentification from one's inner ecosystem shown in the Egg Diagram is a fundamental prerequisite.

Having made the choice, and having let go what has not been chosen with unconditional acceptance of the choice, activating the fire of Will takes a synthetic and symbolic affirmation. This catalyzes all the energy needed to set in motion the direction of the next action that from inner now becomes outer, through the manifestation and execution of a planned and scheduled project consisting of specific, measurable, actionable, realistic, and time-based actions (the "SMART" model).

Assagioli emphasizes in his writings that the concept of Will is difficult to describe, it cannot be fully expressed in words but there is evidence to be gathered that leads to it, as well as the conditions that foster its direct experience and the impact on ourselves and in the context in which we operate.

Self-awareness or the awareness of Self occurring in the personal self or "I" appears as being a willing or volitional "I" with two closely related characteristics:

1- The presence of an introspective factor, or inner action of pure Awareness;
2- The presence of a dynamic element or outward action: the Will as a dynamic force that emerges from within and later manifests outwardly in actions and behavior.

Will is, so to speak, the muscle of consciousness and must be discovered, activated, trained, and practiced. Being an act that moves from within ourselves outward, it requires the presence of a coordinating agent who is aware of what then takes place in dynamic mode: the "I", the non-dual reality with the Self, its Source.

10- Being PLC

Assagioli writes in *The Act of Will*:

"At any given moment, perhaps during a crisis, one has a vivid and unmistakable internal experience of its reality and nature. When danger threatens to paralyze us, suddenly, from the mysterious depths of our being, there springs forth an unexpected force that enables us to put a firm foot on the edge of the precipice or calmly and resolutely face an aggressor."

Emphasizing congruence in his work and life as Being in the flow of becoming, Assagioli models the experiential fact that the discovery of the will within oneself and the intimate interconnection between Self and Will, can effectively and radically change our self-awareness or awareness of our essential Real Nature. Thus our attitude toward ourselves, others and the context in which we are interacting also changes. This brings the "I" to gravitate to its essential core, changing the paradigm of revolution, in which it would otherwise revolve around one subpersonality or another, like a feather carried by the wind, at the mercy of the direction in which the wind carries it.

"Will is a specific power that rises within us, and this inner energy gives us the experience of 'willing'."
- R. Assagioli

The awareness of the reality of "Being a volitional living subject" endowed with the inner power to direct and choose one's direction, thus bringing about changes from the inside out, is deeply transformational and roots the transpersonal dimension in the personality. In other words, when the subject stands in the I, pure awareness and will without content, it has the power to direct by choice the content that is most appropriate for the desired end and evolve.

There are three main steps or stages associated with the experience of Will:

The first is to recognize that the Will exists as a psychological function and as a capacity to act in response to an external event.

COACHING THE ESSENCE

This step is, in my understanding and experience, the pre-personal level or stage of Will.

The second is the experience of having the Will as propulsive energy, an inner force bubbling up from within, and we can feel the intensity of this powerful inner energy pushing to emerge externally with an impulse. I think of this passage as the personal level or stage of Will.

The third step is the realization of being a Willing "I" or Being Will. I consider this step to be the transpersonal level or stage of will.

Will emerges through awareness, toward action that is in line with Dharma, the evolution of consciousness brought into service for the evolutionary purpose of the system in which the subject is embedded and interacts.

The training of this fundamental experience of Being can likewise be divided into three moments or stages:

The first consists of recognizing the central position of Will in one's personality, thus of the Observing "I" and Director of one's inner system, due to the intimate interconnection with its core, the Self.

This stage depends on the level of disidentification that the subject can maintain, simultaneously remaining present to the Self and in a space where, by observing their inner dynamics, they exercise decision-making power over them and using them for the purpose of evolution rather than forcing them to remain unused.

The second step is to delve into the real function of Will as the driver of decision-making and choice in directing other psychological functions for the desired end, using one's abilities and resources to overcome obstacles present in the process toward the goal, consequently training resilience.

The third step is the direct discovery through experience of the existential reality of Being Will, or having the power to consciously act for the common well-Being and development in consciousness. In other words, acting according to one's "Call of Self" is in line with Dharma, and therefore not generating karma.

10- Being PLC

In summary, awareness and will are considered a flow of Presence or "Flow of Being".

Presence: "Being Flow"

Photo: Cris and Carpathian Wolf "MyDream" (2015)

Awareness is a flowing process that allows us, moment by moment, to become the Observer of any content that enters the field of consciousness of the "I", through the key psychosynthesis technique of disidentification. This is the creation of a neutral and safe psychological space that allows us to achieve the optimal psychological distance from the contents with which the "I" relentlessly and unconsciously identifies, restoring freedom from unconscious influences due to interaction with the subpersonality that acts on the "I" at any given moment.

As an impartial Observer, we can become a Director who can use the Will to choose the most effective subpersonality for the desired goal and act in line with the "Call of Self" the True Source of empowerment and wisdom, acting ecologically and sustainably in line with the Ethical Cosmic Order.

It is essential to realize that one has always and forever been self-immersed in the bio-psychic field through its reflection and that the "I", having the dual power of neutrality and will, is a pivotal aspect in Psychosynthesis. This provides a revolutionary educational model that considers every event and content an opportunity for evolutionary learning and resilience training, as Assagioli points out when describing the volitional act as the ability to perceive oneself as a "living subject endowed with the power of choice."

The will, therefore, is an ontological energy force of the Self, which is reflected in the personality through the "I" who uses a certain portion of this force, depending on the subpersonality with which it is identified at any given time.

If a client can create a certain psychological distance from a psychological content and then draw on a sufficient capacity to choose to direct that content, transforming it from a limiting belief to an enhancer and going beyond the obstacle presented in the session, then our work as a PLC can be undertaken effectively.

In other words, the power to disidentify from the dynamics related to a subpersonality that hinders progress toward the goal is a key factor to consider in the coaching contract phase and goal-setting.

In the assessment phase of coaching we want to clarify the direction the client wants to go, getting help by connecting with the heart, in the metaspace within which the Self resides. We create a space free from ambiguous content to the point of emergence of what is truly meaningful to the client, having value with a clear, essential purpose.

At that point together we connect to what emerges from the heart, and then bring back into the heart what is encountered along the way, for the heart to take care of, a caring which in synthesis comes from the Self. The transformation of obstacles into evolutionary opportunities from this perspective is no longer tied to the dimension of doing (personality). One must trust (rely on) and let this "alchemical process" happen from the superconscious, staying in the flow with mind and heart connected in one's center of synthesis, the "I", supervised by the Self.

Assagioli emphasizes that we are guided by whatever content we are unconsciously identified with, and we can gain mastery/leadership of our inner world once we become aware of the dynamics related to these contents and their subtle power

10- Being PLC

over the "I". Once we become aware that we have the power of choice, we gain inner freedom and can manage and regulate our emotions as well. Otherwise, we are unconsciously guided, pushed, or pulled by the goals of subpersonalities, each with a specific emotional and mental apparatus, needs, and desires that demand satisfaction, impacting the process of achieving the desired goals and awareness of our True Nature.

Once we gain the ability to become the Observer, we awaken to the realization that we have the power of choice, and desire, the driving element of the entire volitional process emerges. As was written millennia ago in the Vedic Wisdom tradition, we are made of desire.

Every goal brought into coaching is intrinsically related to the desire for the actualization of the Self.

One of the fundamental purposes of psychosynthesis is to fulfill our need to discover the deeper desire related to the project of the Self, the one that allows us to manifest our uniqueness. On the other hand, when we achieve any desire related to a subpersonality, there is always an aspect that seems incomplete, that something more important is missing. We thus wonder why after so much effort, sacrifice and energy we still do not feel completely satisfied.

The "Call of Self" as defined in Psychosynthesis is the inner voice that, although it whispers, exerts a powerful attraction, is always present among the incessant clamoring of subpersonalities and seeks to emerge and manifest itself through the "I". In Psychosynthesis Coaching, we work together with the coachee to reach this deep "seed" of our being that asks to manifest itself, as defined by American psychologist James Hillman in his Acorn Theory.

Will is the driving force that enables us to achieve the larger goal in life: the emergence of the seed of authenticity that in its process of Self-realization trains resilience, consolidating the I-Self realignment. Without this alignment, the will can readily dissolve into the meanderings of the multiplicity, leaving us unsatisfied and constantly wondering what the meaning of life is in the end.

COACHING THE ESSENCE

Through the process of synthesis of the subpersonalities in the "I", we achieve a broadening of our awareness and the ability to clearly say to our subpersonalities, "I will not give you what you want but I will give you what you need"- in other words, facilitating their evolution.

Assagioli remains of the pragmatic view that the description of the discovery of being a Willer cannot be adequately represented by intellectual speculations or words. However, the process leading to this existential experience can be formulated and expressed in detail.

The sequence is characterized by the unfolding of the Awareness of being an "I" with the power of will or Being Will, through the steps of Identification/Disidentification/Self-identification or IDA process. When we realize that most of the time, as Assagioli said, we use the name of "I" in vain, that is, we may think of ourselves as "I" even though we're passing through identification with many subpersonalities, at that point we gain a greater awareness of the inner multiplicity, of the dynamics to which we are unconsciously subjected. We become aware of those who use the will to satisfy their own needs by achieving evanescent goals from an evolutionary point of view, wasting precious resources and time that can instead be better used for evolutionary purposes.

The ability to use such resources to satisfy the desire related to the essential need related to the "Call of Self", that is, to become a Self in expression through the "I", identified with a peculiar personality to be placed under Its direction, defines, according to my perspective, Self-Leadership or Transpersonal Leadership.

For this reason, we carefully explore the meaning, values, and purpose of the goal brought into the session by the client, listening to the energy of the field in which the words are expressed. The word has power and the energy with which it is expressed defines its power as a psychic object. Once expressed it has in itself in power, a specific direction motivated by the intention from which it emerges.

This intention impresses the field of the coaching relationship

10- Being PLC

with a specific energy. The attentiveness with which we actively listen to the energy of verbal and nonverbal communication helps greatly to listen to the energy of the field in which the coaching relationship takes place. We stay in touch with what, although it has not yet emerged, is more evident than what is being injected into the conversation by the coachee.

In practice, an experienced PLC, simultaneously present from their Self to the client's Self, listens to the Call that is asking to emerge and wants to be actively manifested in the process of realizing one's essential authenticity, in a dynamic process of flow between historical personality and ontological identity.

We can recognize the client's degree of alignment with their will as the Volitional "I" through phrases such as "I would", "I should", "I must", "I could", "yes but maybe", "maybe", "it would be nice, but", and so on, which indicate the presence of a subpersonality, thus of a non-I-Self alignment but an I-subpersonality alignment.

The alignment of the I-Self will occur through a process of recognition in an empathic, nonjudgmental environment of listening to the positive intention of the surface self-image present at the moment in the "I" field of consciousness and subsequent acceptance.

Through a five-step process (Recognize-Name-Accept-Coordinate-Transform) we arrive first at Synthesis, then at the change of the energy level of the field in which the coaching relationship takes place. At this point, the partnership between coach and coachee is illuminated by transpersonal energies, and higher potentials finally emerge to be used consciously and responsibly by the client to arrive at the goal he or she truly desires to achieve, as "I, Volitional Being".

The loving, caring acceptance and understanding on the part of both coach and coachee of the critical transformational process in which the expansion of content and context perspective in the transpersonal coaching process takes place is a fundamental attitude.

Placing oneself under the guidance of the Self as Leader of the process will enable Its reflected image, the "I", to gather information about the energetic qualities of the underlying reality that forms the manifold appearance of manifest substance.

In synthesis, the coach in their role as the External Center of Synthesis facilitates the client in becoming more authentically themselves and tapping into their Internal Center of Synthesis as the Leader of their own complex psychic system.

The form that takes the likeness of that which underlies it, which informs and gives form to the substance, is the Ideal Model for the Self. It is an ideal self-image that, once created and identified with at will by the "I", then must be acted upon immediately as if the subject already functions from it (already has mastery over psychological functions through the purposeful use of the will in line with the essential purpose). Repetition is the basis for the solidification of mental patterns, as confirmed today by neuroscience.

Becoming what we choose to identify with in order to manifest the best version of ourselves is possible if we train with determination, perseverance, and passion. Acting as if we are authentically ourselves, perfectly imperfect on the path to perfection, aiming for the excellence of which we are essentially composed is, ultimately, the only way forward. Knowing how to walk this path makes all the difference, aiming for the management of one's inner resources in an ecological and sustainable mode. This attitude will also have a positive, meaningful, and valuable impact on the system in which we are embedded and interact.

This is the wonderful promise of what we can become: essentially and authentically ourselves, as Assagioli points out in his Psychosynthesis- the psychosynthesis that each of us as professionals and especially as human beings must experience in depth through constant practice to be up to the task of helping others realize their original uniqueness. For each one is unique, unrepeatable, and valuable with a purpose to fulfill.

By following the seven key concepts that define this "Way to Self-Actualization" Self-Leadership becomes realistic, achievable, and sustainable when ideally trained. Already from the concept of "training" we can see the attitude of the coach as the

10- Being PLC

ideal partner for learning to practice Psychosynthesis in Self Actualization, starting from the very foundation: the synthesis of multiplicity in the bio-psychic unity that takes place in the "I" supervised by the Self, the Leader who asks for manifestation in evolutionary actions.

Fantasy or Reality?

The American existentialist psychologist, Rollo May, in his text *Love and Will* writes: "*Fantasy, one of the expressions of imagination, is the capacity through which we give particular meaning to something elusive; its etymological origin 'phantasm' means 'capacity to represent,' 'to make visible'.*"

Imagination and images are the language of the Self which communicate to us, through various forms, the expression of desire as the motor of volitional actions through projection in any given situation, as confirmed by the *Bṛhadāraṇyaka Upaniṣad* millennia ago. Repeating a quote we've seen previously:

"In Truth, it is also said that man is made of desire: and as is his desire, so is his will; and as is his will, so is his action; and as is his action, so is the result that is obtained."

- Bṛhadāraṇyaka Upaniṣad IV.4.5

Symbols speak to us through images and are energetic catalysts. The unconscious speaks through symbolic images. The use and management of symbolic, metaphorical images are essential in coaching.

COACHING THE ESSENCE

Graphic: Carmen Lenatti (2011)

It is desire that moves the will, putting the mental-emotional apparatus into action as indicated by the Ten Laws of Psychodynamics.

Rollo May also defines desire as an element of meaning and purpose. Indeed, it is the particular confluence of forces and meanings that constitute human desire.

Desire is the beginning of an orientation toward the future, acceptance through an affirmation that we want to direct ourselves toward the future, to be as we wish to become, giving us the ability to reach the profound depths within us and to arrive, through engagement with experiences, through understanding their underlying meaning and value. We are co-participants in creating the future that calls to be manifested, through us.

As we saw in the quote from the *Upaniṣads*, there is no will without first a desire. Desire is a progressive and propulsive element that comes from within; desire carries meaning and all its power. The potent engine that resides in the synthesis of these

10- Being PLC

components: meaning, purpose, and will, is ontological desire.

Coaching is a dynamic process. Session after session, we coach the client to create and understand the process of unveiling the Self, trust the process, and support him or her along the path to achieving the desired goal brought into the session.

The small steps taken toward the goal increase the client's self-esteem and confidence to put their potential, qualities, and abilities into play. For this reason, it is essential that there is more than just an objective for its own sake or a process of problem-solving; each session needs to have a meaningful goal that we help contextualize along the trail of the client's manifestation of Self from the past, into the present, into the future.

Each goal achieved in the sessions represents a step toward achieving the larger ultimate goal, which we know is directed broadly toward the client's Self-realization, or in other words the goal of becoming fully and authentically themself.

We work to achieve "more 'I'", an expansion of the space of consciousness of the personal self, transforming limiting beliefs, increasing awareness and power of choice. More "I" equals more will, a wider range of choice, more inner freedom, and consequently more personal power.

The "I" is the starting and ending point of our work in PLC.

Assagioli noted, *"Execution-The task of the Will is the use of attention; at the center of the field of consciousness, the ideas, the images concerning the actions to be performed, the program to be executed."*

As PLC, we assume that the coachee arrives in coaching through an act of will related to the desire of a subpersonality of which he or she is often unaware: a desire to change, to achieve a goal, to improve one's life in some area, a desire for something that he or she cannot yet clearly define but feels to be present as an engine toward change; a desire that is often mixed with a need. Therefore, it is important to get to the underlying need and be able to process it through an ideal partnership.

Using the Egg Diagram, we travel together with the client, bringing awareness to light in the field of consciousness of the "I", potentially present as the motive engine to action.

COACHING THE ESSENCE

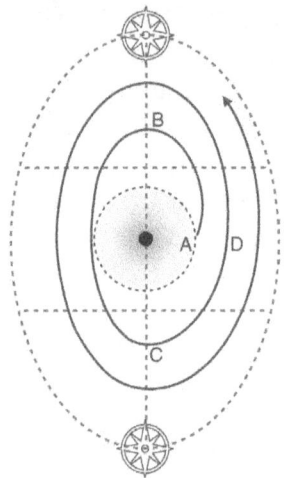

Graphic: Synthesis Coaching Associates

Always starting from the center, the middle unconscious, point A in the diagram, the present, we ask the client, "Where are you now?" Then, we continue with the question "Where do you wish to be at the end of the session?" This moves us into the higher unconscious, the realm of higher aspirations and potentials, the future- point B.

The next question takes us to the lower unconscious, C, the past, where less recent memories are hidden, memories related to important emotional experiences, traumatic, unmet needs, unrealized desires, drives related to basic needs, outdated self-images that the subject continues to wear unconsciously and which are often the source of blocks. We ask:

"What energy, dynamic, or force within you can interfere with the realization of your vision/goal?"

Subsequent questions are intended to take the coaching process forward to the goal, point D, actualizing the emerging awareness to the context of manifestation, with the question:

"What concrete action can you take as of now to move from the present to the realization of your goal?"

This process continues in a spiral movement, expanding the field of consciousness of the "I" ideally throughout the Egg Diagram. At the end of the session, the client will not only have successfully achieved their goal but will have learned more about themself through a transpersonal-level partnership focused on designing and implementing specific meaning along the changes encountered in their life's journey.

Through a partnership rooted in the Self as a transpersonal flow state, we help clients accurately formulate their goals, resources, and obstacles and express the mind's incessant hyperactivity through expanded awareness.

We work as allies in a co-creative way, accompanying clients toward an increasingly positive and proactive attitude, looking at the future outcome with an attitude of mind and heart in connection, openness to change as an opportunity for evolutionary growth, designing what will be the new future that calls for manifestation and how the client intends to present themself in that ideal future.

The most effective tool in this process is the Ideal Model, the creation of a subpersonality to be adopted as one chooses by acting as if one were already that model with all its qualities and abilities to use the psychological functions purposefully in successful achievement of the desired goal in a context of growing awareness.

"Imagination is more important than knowledge. Knowledge is limited. Imagination surrounds the world."

-Albert Einstein

We are Universes on a Journey, Toward the One

In the journey we take with our coaching clients, we follow them in a segment of space-time in becoming themselves as they achieve the goal brought into the session. In this space-time segment, they have the opportunity to expand the awareness of their finiteness and at the same time non-finiteness, a paradox that in the Vedas is defined in the *Achintya-Bheda-Abheda Tattva* theory of Sri Chaitanya Mahaprabhu: the inconceivable simultaneous equality and non-equality between the Creator, Creation and the creatures.

COACHING THE ESSENCE

This is a paradox of which conscious understanding can hardly be sustained on one's own, as it has the power to unhinge old beliefs, mental habits, and self-images to which we are attached, adherent, and accustomed, which still give us a certain sense of identity, which we certainly need, up to a certain limit. Beyond that, they become an obstacle that is practically insurmountable without the support of an ideal guide.

In the role of External Center of Synthesis, the PLC is prepared and qualified to support the coachee in this process. The trained PLC is positioned in their center, maintaining a presence to their Source, their Self, and simultaneously to the client's Self as the moment-to-moment Guide, paradoxically identified in the client's unconscious experience and at the same time disidentified from their psychic contents, thanks to the process of disidentification.

The PLC serves in this context as a guide in their role of External Center of Synthesis for the client's Self, the true Leader of the metaphorical climb to the profound peaks of the psyche, in a clear move into the future.

The PLC thus stands at the service of the client so that the client learns to trust the field of infinite possibilities more and more while becoming the Leader of themselves, the guide of their own inner realm, thanks to the transpersonal partnership with the coach.

The Ideal Model, whose congruence the coach exemplifies, allows the coachee to bring into action the qualities present in their multitude and truly available, once placed at the service of the "I". These qualities will go on to empower the client in their process of Personal Leadership and the creation of their Ideal Model that catalyzes qualitative energies to achieve ecological and sustainable results from their inner universe. At this point, they will be ready for the next step of Self-Leadership-Transpersonal Leadership, which corresponds to the level of Transpersonal Psychosynthesis.

The Stages of the Act of Will outline the process of moving from defining purpose to manifesting action through execution. These phases are concatenated like links in a chain, and like a chain, the act of will is only as strong as the weakest link. Thus an act of will is successful and effective relative to the extent that each of the steps is executed with determination and clarity to successfully achieve the initially agreed-upon result.

When I raced with sled dogs the same dynamic happened: the team was winning to the extent that the performance among the components was balanced, as the top speed was determined by the slowest athlete, including the musher!

The goal to be performed provides a clear vision of the result to be achieved and sets the direction of the action to be performed, which in turn is related to the management of willpower in all its aspects, stages, and qualities. The choice of the goal is based on the assessment of values for the subject, inherent in the goal or evaluation. This gives rise to the intention to achieve it and provides the motives to start setting the volitional act in motion.

The first phase involves defining the purpose or goal based on evaluation, intention, and motivation.

The second phase involves deliberation, choice, and affirmation.

The third phase is inherent in planning and scheduling the steps necessary to manifest and execute the action toward the goal.

How Do We Work with the Will in Psychosynthesis Coaching?

"Capacity to direct energy (through understanding and intent) toward a recognized and desired end, overcoming all obstacles and destroying all that stands in the way."

- Roberto Assagioli

We always work for "more I" through a broadening of the space of consciousness, awareness, and will, free of limiting content. "More I" means more will through greater awareness of multiple unconscious dynamics, a wider range of choices, more

COACHING THE ESSENCE

freedom to manage inner resources, and consequently, more personal power.

The statement, "I am a center of pure awareness and will", generally used in the disidentification exercise, is fundamental in our transformational process of unconscious content. I am both the starting point and the ending point of the psychosynthesis coaching process.

In Psychosynthesis, Presence is considered a flow state of being or self-awareness. In this "Flow State", the "I" merges with the content through a voluntary process, fully experiencing the content while remaining in the neutral space of pure awareness and will, the Observer of psychic contents, from which it derives the ability to direct them as it chooses in the role of Director.

Disidentification from unconscious content is essential to achieve and maintain a state of flow of Being at the transpersonal level.

We help the coachee build a "context" consisting of a strong sense of ideal identity that exists in power at the transpersonal level. By exploring, expanding, and empowering the client's "I" as the center to anchor to, through the process of identification, disidentification, and self-identification, we generate and solidly define the creation of an inner space of neutrality on which to position ourself and which we can return to should the need arise.

From this space it is possible to observe, contain and transform any emerging content into an evolutionary opportunity through reconnection with one's inner source of wisdom and power, the Self, a positioning that activates the power of choice on how to move from a limiting belief to the desired state, through a renewed mindset involving the wisdom of the heart.

All this in a coaching process that, as you see in this image, proceeds along the steps of creating and understanding the process, trusting the process, and supporting the process of the emerging Self.

10- Being PLC

                                        Support the Process
                                      Planning and Scheduling
                               Project Management/Execution

                    Trust the Process

       Create and Understand   Affirmation
              the Process

Purpose, Evaluation, Motivation
         Deliberation
      Choice and Decision

                        Graphic: Synthesis Coaching Associates

The force of inner dynamics is powerfully solidified and inscribed "in cerebral highways" because of repetitions, which are constantly being retraced, reinforcing themselves, as indicated by the Ten Laws of Psychodynamics and today's neuroscience. The person becomes that way of thinking of themselves, perceiving themselves, and limiting themselves to the relative self-image which, as I have repeatedly pointed out, binds the subject to its own needs and way of using the psychological functions.

Correlated with the need to make a significant change in one's life, the subject realizes the need for support from expert guidance, to be able to journey safely in one's inner territory, to discover one's potential treasures that lie dormant, in the profound reaches of the psyche.

When the time comes, awakening to one's inner power is the necessary and fundamental prerequisite for reaching the coveted summit, the larger goal: Being the Leader of oneself, from one's Self.

Coach and coachee united in the same metaphorical lifeline, in thought-provoking partnership between two human beings traveling together toward a common goal, their evolution.

We have significant examples in this regard in learned literature- Dante in the Divine Comedy and Arjuna in the *Bhagavad-Gītā*, to name a just a couple.

The PLC plays the role of a guide in that we set ourselves up in our Self to Be an External Center of Synthesis for the client. From our center to the client's center, with the client at the center

COACHING THE ESSENCE

of the coaching relationship, which takes place at the transpersonal level, between two Selves.

This role is hard-won, a difficult and wonderful journey that first the coach must make within themself, leading into the depths of their psyche to the lofty heights of the personality, and then back to the center, the "I", becoming instrumental to the Self and at that point being able to serve their client. Two fully human beings are on the way to the desired goal, while at the same time traveling to both essential centers.

When I was young, I read this inscription, engraved in a stone on the 3,851m (12,634′) summit of the beautiful mountain, Gran Zebrù in the Ortles-Cevedale group that I climbed twice in those years, and it has remained forever etched in my mind. Today I use it a lot as a metaphor for the inner journey with my clients and students:

"The strenuous conquest of lofty peaks invigorates the body, mind, and heart and brings us closer than anything earthly to the Divine Creator."

Elio Pelizzatti: "Badile" (Bernina Group, 2002)

10- Being PLC

A PLC is a guide who is guided by themself, the True Guide. As the expert, they accompany the client on the path to their summit, their goal, revealing step by step the presence of their essential center, their Self, from which they learn to finally be guided. The metaphor of Psychological Mountaineering that Assagioli tells us about in his writings, sees the coach as a guide - a mountaineer of the spirit, expert in traversing the inaccessible inner territories while simultaneously securing themself and their client, as together they prepare to make the ascent to the summit of their essential Authenticity.

We can think of Psychosynthesis as an educational process of discovering one's Essence, which passes through understanding the true nature of psychic phenomena, their origin and positive intention, and limits and possibilities of interaction with other contents, all related to the life force underlying them.

Only such understanding can show us the correct attitude to take at will toward the multiplicity of which we are composed at the psychological level. Understanding means being able to transform, as Assagioli points out in his Psychosynthesis.

Thanks to the resonance between the two Selves, a co-creative and pro-active partnership is created during the coaching process, in a field where the energies of the superconscious can be contacted and flow unhindered. This process takes place at the transpersonal level, guided by the Self, the True Leader who has the power and intention to transform any hindering content into its true positive intention, for the evolution of the subject.

The multiple facets of self-images, seen by the Self, observing them from another and elevated perspective, through the disidentified "I", find synthesis in the Ideal Model as the bridge that unites the two dimensions of Being and Doing. Immanence and transcendence find resolution in the field of consciousness of the "I" that has realized its own True Nuclear Nature and manifests itself with an authentic image of its own ontological Identity.

We share a mutual need with our self-images. Masks give us from time to time a sense of identity and belonging, allowing us to be in the world and become functional persons embedded in a certain historical context. Essentially they are instrumental to the potential that calls us, to which we tend, that is actualized along the way, leading us to the larger goal in life: become who we already essentially are, ourselves.

The problem is that, through wearing them, we become the masks themselves that overlay our ontological authentic identity.

Elio Pelizzatti: "Maschere" (2000)

These instrumental, transient, and objectified self-images possess a strong attraction, they are idea-forces, strengths, as Assagioli also defines them. They serve us, but forgetful of our true spiritual identity we place ourselves in their service, objectifying our subjectivity, hooking ourselves into them until we trap our essential identity that keeps asking for manifestation.

We are still us but trapped in ourselves, in the superficial self-images that allow us to function optimally in certain aspects of life, while, if not consciously managed, simultaneously dysfunctionally in other areas.

We are in the domain of their chronic conflicting dynamics. We spend so much time and effort to conform to them, to that model that tends to perfection but because of unconscious identification with multiplicity is diverted into idealized models related to dynamics aimed at the satisfaction of basic needs, hindering the emergence of the intrinsic work that asks to manifest itself: the Ideal Model for the Self.

The process of Transpersonal Leadership or Self-realization finds in the Ideal Model a phenomenal instrument (related to the phenomenal world), that potentially can connect the subject with the transpersonal dimension, transforming past-bound self-images into new ones, rooted in the here and now and tending toward the future. In this process, they are renewed and re-contextualized by the emergence along the journey toward the goal, of their fundamental positive qualities.

A process of Self-Leadership that takes place around the unveiling of the Essential Image composed of the qualitative energy of each surface image and the consciously chosen action based on one's highest potential, related to Essence.

We are born with a unique and unrepeatable blueprint, a seed that lies dormant in the depths of our psyche, and the journey of life seen from this perspective represents a wonderful opportunity to germinate this seed, experimenting step by step with our potential, training skills, acquiring new competencies and finally, with love and gratitude, nurturing that little sprout day by day with joy, so that it can emerge into the light in the grace of its resilience, having transformed its weakness into a propelling life force.

Our Source whispers to us among the myriad inner voices, motivates us to grow and evolve, becoming adept at handling the dynamics related to psychic contents, urges us to go beyond the primary needs belonging to transient self-images, once these are sufficiently satisfied, drawing us to the Self with a "Natural Tension" that follows the Order of Things, the Dharma.

The philosopher, architect, poet, engineer, scientist, and futurist Richard Buckminster Fuller, our family's great-uncle, called this natural tension to dynamic equilibrium *"Tensegrity"*.

"The word tensegrity is an invention: it is a contraction of tensional integrity."

- R. Buckminster Fuller

COACHING THE ESSENCE

CHAPTER 11

FROM DOING TO BEING
Embodying Awareness

Graphic: Carmen Lenatti (2011)

The Self seeks its expression through its counterpart immersed in the personality, the "I" or personal self, described by Psychosynthesis as equal to and simultaneously different from its Source, but encapsulated in the psyche and ceaselessly subjected to the attraction of psychic contents. Being ignorant of its True Nature and identified from time to time with different transitory contents and self-images, the awareness of its True Reality is veiled to the point of forgetting its origin. This forgetfulness chains one to the dimension of doing, feeding one's karma, inevitably tying oneself to suffering.

The Self is the transpersonal reality, at once transcendent and immanent through the "I" that is chronically at the mercy of the inner dynamics caused by the Ignorance (*Avidyā*) of one's ontological Identity. The "I" from time to time takes on the connotation of the various parties involved who have purposes aimed at satisfying their primary egoic needs, living life exclusively from an objective perspective.

The "I", unconsciously identified with psychic contents, is diverted from the realization of its True Nature. Ensnared by the egocentric dynamics of subpersonalities, it remains ignorant of its rights, which correspond to the rights of the Self postulated by psychosynthesist M. Rosselli to act out its Purpose as a motionless agent through its manifestation in the personality.

The Ideal Model for the Self is the instrument that the "I" creatively can project at will, to be able to convey the highest potentials, the meta values, orienting itself toward the universal transpersonal element, which, being transcendent, needs to become rooted in immanence before it can emerge in its fullness.

The Self calls, pushing to emerge in the desire to manifest itself, and has the right to do so. Its actualizing tendency through the "I" is the same evolutionary drive that belongs to life itself. The direction is not always clear but is always present as an impulse that manifests itself through the goals that our self-images, in their dynamic existence, want to achieve.

Let us explore the dimension of "Being" through the dimension of "Doing" in the context of Psychosynthesis Coaching, the common thread of this book, which I define as my Ideal Model. This is the self-image that allows me to manifest the energies of my Self through a role that I feel is of great value since it fosters the expression of my authenticity. Being and Doing find synthesis in feeling my authenticity through that image which in an ideal way allows my Self to become manifest.

11- From Doing to Being

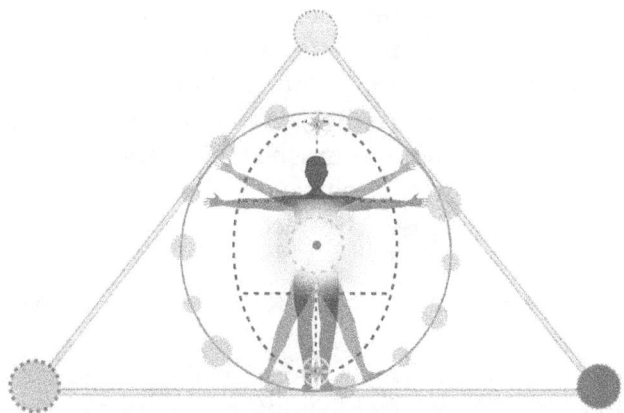

Graphic: Synthesis Coaching Associates

In the imaginary journey that I take with my clients during the coaching process I immerse myself in their inner universe and illuminate myself with their beauty. I place myself as a point of light external from my Self, so that they can bring to light their Essence, having learned to see it reverberating through the multiplicity of which they are bearers.

A game of empathic mirroring that has Love as its foundation: the attitude of mind connected to heart, to be able to welcome without judgment the emerging contents in the coaching conversation, indicators of the presence of a "Greater Force".

The transpersonal dimension is the invisible substrate within which the process moves toward the achievement of the established goal. It tends toward the manifestation of subjective spiritual energy that has a different vibratory frequency from that on which the objective dimension flows and finds synthesis through the actualization of its reflection immersed in the bio-psychic field, the "I", which is identified at will with an Ideal Model to manifest the Self.

When the "I" is ready to receive the energies of the Self directly, each self-image begins to show itself in its authentic positive intention, releasing the essential quality that can thus flow into the psychic field as elevated potential, finally available to the client's "I". This can now freely choose how to act, being aligned with its Purpose, Meaning and transpersonal nuclear Values.

COACHING THE ESSENCE

Each subpersonality corresponds to a mental model and represents a deep belief that needs to be contextualized through renewed awareness. At that point, working with the symbol or image that emerges with either a name or a form, requires the coach's ability to be able to grasp the metaphor and help the coachee unveil its intrinsic message, which is always useful for the evolutionary purpose when accepted for its positive intention.

From *Transpersonal Inspiration*, Roberto Assagioli, M.D:

> "That imagination has a close relation to intuition is demonstrated by the fact that intuitions often do not present themselves to consciousness in an abstract, simple, and 'pure' way, but rather in the form of images. This entails a primary task of distinguishing the content, the essence, and the idea inherent in an intuition, from the form, the vestments, so to speak, it takes. The character of the form is symbolic; the complex and important question of symbolism arises. Since I have dealt with this elsewhere, I will limit myself here to emphasizing the dual and, in a sense, contrasting nature and function of the symbol. It can both veil and reveal. When mistaken for the reality it expresses, it veils it and is thus a source of illusion. When recognized for what it is, a means of expression, it constitutes a useful and sometimes indispensable aid in 'capturing' and thus illuminating a transcendental reality... The capacity to store and recall images is immense, one might say virtually unlimited."

To participate empathically in their symbolic experience as guides, we must also follow the images brought by the client and willingly position ourselves in the same imaginative space:

"The unconscious speaks to us through images, symbols, dreams, fantasies: we can address this hidden part of our mind in its forgotten language, which is its mother tongue."

— Martha Crampton

11- From Doing to Being

What, then, is the PLC's Role?

During the sessions, side by side with the client, we walk together as expert guides in the use of the tools and maps, so that the coachee in the role of the traveler of their own inner realm can achieve the chosen goal, exploring along the way their values, meaning, and purpose, participating in the emergence of a new and deeper meaning in the process of changing their life.

Our role is to facilitate this process. We are trusting that the client is already in possession of all the inner potentials needed to achieve their goals once they are aware that they have these potentials and know how to tap into them as they create and manifest the "New Future" that is asking to emerge.

We help the client build a new "context" of their sense of self, the inner center of synthesis, from which to generate the flow of Presence of the Witnessing Self.

By exploring, expanding, and empowering the "I" through the process of Knowing-Possessing-Transforming, any content that emerges during the sessions that initially presents itself as an obstacle to achieving the chosen goal, may be transformed into an opportunity to train one's skills, acquire others, and acquire a degree of discrimination regarding which to use and which not.

The guide-coach supports the traveler-client in creating a specific meaning and inspired actionable step leading in a specific timeframe to effect change in a specific area, actualizing the new awareness, thus the realization of one's desires and the achievement of full potential, to be acted upon responsibly.

In this transformational process at the transpersonal level, obstacles are transformed in light of the awareness of the "I", devoid of content, into an opportunity to learn to train one's resilience.

As PLCs, we hold the space of Presence, being attuned to the "I", the space of pure awareness, will, and no content. In the role of Observer and Director, we form an External Center of Synthesis through which we accompany our clients as they progress

COACHING THE ESSENCE

toward their own Internal Center of Synthesis, in the process becoming more and more the Leader of their own personality.

We can do this as professionals in that we have been there and traveled that path ourselves. We've gone before, we've done that work, and opened ourselves to a continuous progression toward our own authenticity. We have learned to recognize and accept, discovering the hidden meaning, value, and purpose in every change in our lives.

We represent an external resource for the client, from which we maintain the state of Presence, or Flow State of Being, through a volitional act, an Act of Will, with trust in the process we are going to build together with the client.

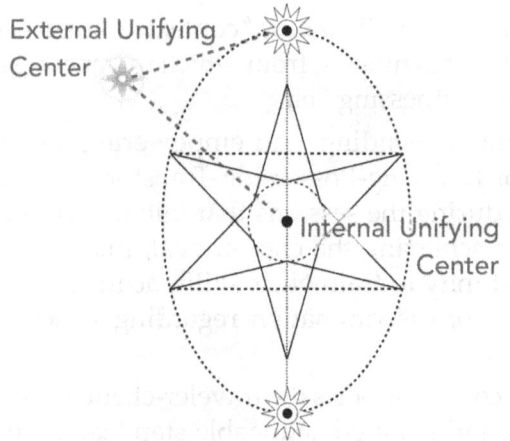

Graphic: Synthesis Coaching Associates

Our role is to facilitate and support the same process in the client, who in the process connects with his or her own higher inner resources, training the ability to create his or her own "New Future" in line with his or her Life Purpose. By learning to bring its meta-values into play, the client trains ontological resilience, that is, the ability to let emerge that potential seed I mentioned earlier, which wants to manifest itself. This is the Self that asks to emerge through the "I", more and more in line with one's essential image or Ideal Model.

11- From Doing to Being

We support the client's inner process by showing congruence with the "Call of Self "as a way of living from the soul, in the here and now.

Assagioli teaches that to formulate the goal clearly and concisely, there must be an active willingness in us to prepare the soil, sow it and fertilize it before we can reap the benefits.

Most people do not have a clear program toward a specific goal. There are several reasons for this, including fear related to a poor self-image, and our self-image is a decisive factor in everything we do.

Without concentration and discipline, we cannot achieve any goal that we have never clearly set for ourselves, because we have not even managed to set it as an ideal. People often fail to achieve their goals not because they lack the necessary skills and competencies, but because they do not recognize the inherent abilities they possess, due to low self-esteem and lack of a self-image that serves as an Ideal Model to actualize their authenticity.

The key point in a psychosynthesis coaching context, as demonstrated by the cause/effect relationships postulated in the Ten Laws of Psychodynamics, is that it is impossible to act incongruently with one's self-image. By changing the self-image, we can change the mode to which performance is hooked.

American motivational speaker Zig Ziglar suggests:

"We must be before we can do and we must do before we can Realize."

Often those with low self-esteem choose to serve others because of this diminished sense of self-value: their service helps them maintain a certain joy in life. In themselves, their self-image ends up defining the capabilities of what they can become and what they can do.

So, it is our job to ask ourselves and guide our clients to ask themselves:

"What is the Ideal Image for my Self that asks to manifest itself through my "I" at this moment?"

COACHING THE ESSENCE

Here we fully enter the realm of the Ideal Model, which needs a neutral space among other self-images to emerge.

Disidentification is a key element in the flow state of Being. Achieving this flow state requires the use of the qualities present in the Aspects of Will.

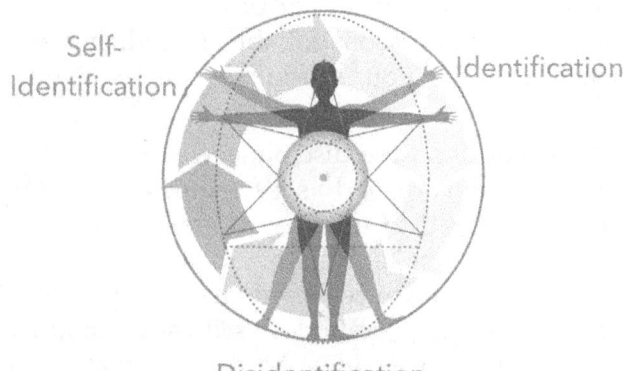

Graphic: Synthesis Coaching Associates

This flow can also be described as the continuous process from Self-Identification, to Self-Realization, to Self-Actualization and Its manifestation through the "I" in a well-integrated personality, gravitating around a point of synthesis defined by an authentic Ideal Model.

Psychosynthesis offers a realistic model that is not only valid in the here and now but is constantly evolving, in tune with the constant motion and change throughout our lives.

Assagioli suggests a positive approach that is identified with the development of self-awareness as a motivational tendency. He says that, to experience the will, *"We must have a positive sense of life"*.

Furthermore: *"Volitional action presupposes that life has a positive aspect and meaning, and not only individual lives, but all of life. For man is not isolated, but intertwined, not only in life inter-individual and social but in the entire flow of the becoming of universal life."*

These are also the foundations of Positive Psychology, of

11- From Doing to Being

which Psychosynthesis has been a precursor for nearly a century.

Maintaining Presence is a constant act of will aimed at renewing awareness of our Essence, of the intimate relationship between the Self at the transpersonal level and the "I" at the personal level or "continuous reconnection" to the Center, since the Self is always Present throughout all changes and constantly calling the "I" to manifest its Purpose.

The "I" is the instrument of the Self at the level of personality and as such its purpose is to serve the Self through volitional action, by governing the functioning of its sub-agents, the sub-personalities, successfully achieving sustainable goals while at the same time evolving.

Will is thus fundamental to maintaining Presence in the coaching conversation, highlighted by the ICF as their Core Competency No. 5. Being present means using every means to be masters and directors of our inner realm, recognizing that there is always the possibility of choosing our inner attitude.

The choice to be present is not always easy. It is the choice to be aware of ourselves, distancing ourselves from conscious and unconscious mental contents and related dynamics, to be able to be the most of what we can be to act in the moment. Reconnecting with the will as the ontological faculty whose primary role at the personal level is the management of psychological functions facilitates the experience of being more and more authentic, beyond the contents present in our lives.

The awareness of being a volitional self that experiences contents in the process of evolving toward our Essence, the Self, represents the concept of Personal Power postulated by American psychologist Carl R. Rogers, the Leadership that we aim for, the will to choose that comes from the state of Flow of Being.

"In every organism, including man, there is a constant flow tending toward the constructive realization of its inherent possibilities, a natural tendency toward growth. This tendency can be deformed, but not destroyed without destroying the whole organism."
- Carl R. Rogers

COACHING THE ESSENCE

Clients enter coaching in response to their "Call of Self", feeling the need to grow, refocus, expand or even reinvent their lives. Whether they are aware of it or not, the Self is always calling! Since it requires clients to be true to themselves, the "Call of Self" is the Inner Wisdom Guide we go to evoke. We learn to listen to it ourselves and guide them to do the same, engaging in each client's deep connection to that Calling through the various inner voices and tapping into the potentials needed for their manifestation.

The "Will to Change" is the power of the Self to call the "I" to reorient itself from egoic or egocentric awareness related to the needs of subpersonalities to Self-centered awareness, moving the "I" toward the Self, like a pendulum.

Moving through the various regions of the mental field shown in the Egg Diagram, the subject comes into contact with various psychic contents, remaining fixed in its Center of Synthesis, the "I" aligned with the Self to which it is anchored at the apex of the Egg Diagram, continuously moving among the contents in a state of flux.

The process of actualization toward "more and more I-Self" is like a constant inner movement or flow that we learn to maintain, remaining anchored in the Higher Unconscious with a volitional act renewed moment by moment. The Self is always there, during all changes, it is available in all circumstances. It exists in the dark night of the soul, when the personality seems to be shattered, when darkness surrounds us, as well as in the bright summit experiences.

The "Call of Self" is the Reality of the eternal Presence in us of the Source deeply rooted in the higher regions of the psyche, the Superconscious, calling the "I" throughout the Egg Diagram.

The Self is always calling us to manifest our Unique Purpose. Sometimes it is clear. Sometimes it is hard to hear it. Sometimes we hear it and ignore it. It is our choice to follow this Call through the changes and incessant voices or to deny it. Through the state of Presence we learn to remain stable in "Who" does not change all the time and during the constant changes: we remain genuinely ourselves.

11- From Doing to Being

We learn to recognize the Presence in us of the unchanging Reality of the Self, through disidentification from the contents present in the field of consciousness, choosing to apply the meaning, value, and purpose of any changes with a positive attitude, mindful of the underlying evolutionary lesson.

Embodying Awareness of "Being a Self"

Cris: Cabo Verde (2004)

The "Call of Self" is the focus of our work and embodies the assumption that everyone has within them the capacity to empathize, deeply, with a higher sense of Purpose in life. It is the "Thread of Ariadne" that we can choose to follow, enabling us to reconnect to our highest and deepest Nature, manifesting it through action in line with Dharma, action based on mindfulness and the will for meaning.

Assagioli referred to this process as "Becoming a Self in expression through the personality" in an ongoing creative and dynamic search for harmony through conflict. Changes, in short, are the opportunities we can choose to seize in difficult moments to set our personal abilities and potentials in motion and tap into transpersonal ones, making ourselves protagonists of the evolutionary purpose which is going to happen anyway whether we like it or not.

COACHING THE ESSENCE

If instead we actively participate in it by knowing how to make opportune choices, we move toward an ever-increasing synthesis in the service of Self Purpose, which is ultimately our Life's Purpose.

From a transpersonal perspective therefore we can consider changes as "basic needs" of the Self calling the "I" to transform and actualize itself along the evolutionary pathway, thanks to the synthesis of the multiplicity of which it becomes Leader.

The Director (the "I", as Leader of the multiplicity which makes up the personality) follows the directives of the Self, the Leader of the whole bio-psychic system through the flow of Presence from the Essence.

It all takes place through the instrument of the Ideal Model, as a way of acting as if one were already that model, designed to embody the awareness of "Being a Self" in action.

From the transpersonal perspective, the objective manifestation of the spiritual Being (the Subject) that, for evolutionary purposes is embodied in a specific form in a specific time and context involving many stages, phases, and states of consciousness, has as its larger goal to evolve and reconnect to the Ultimate Source, the Universal Self, the One.

By cooperating with change in a meaningful way, through the state of Presence, we achieve more and more awareness of the "need for change and growth" as a calling of the Self to Its Actualization.

As Maslow suggested, *"What a man can be, he must be. We call this need 'Actualization of the Self'."*

By helping clients expand their identifications, exploring their limiting beliefs, and stepping out of the comfort zone of a particular subpersonality (usually the most mature or dominant one), we participate in the client's process of empowerment as they gain awareness of being more than a particular identification.

The will is the ontological energy of the "I" that, passing through conflict, once realized and aimed at evolutionary growth, facilitates the process toward Self-realization: a process

11- From Doing to Being

of transforming the perception of separation and conflict associated with change, through acceptance to integration and synthesis, empowering the "I" to manifest the Self in daily life.

Maintaining the state of "I" Presence makes it possible to use psychological functions to manifest the Essential Purpose, taking into account that Intuition is not a psychological function under the control of the will. Intuition emerges once the other psychological functions have been voluntarily placed under the domain of the "I", free from the attraction and dominance of subpersonalities.

Intuition is the only psychological function that can directly receive the higher qualitative energies emanating from the Self. Subpersonalities block access to Intuition, which is diverted for the fulfillment of their own egoic purposes.

We help clients reconnect to their Source by asking powerful questions to change perspective, specifically to embody the higher vision after exploring the limits present in the personality, then anchor the new awareness and choose to act in line with the emerging transpersonal vision.

The process of Self-realization is ultimately a path to the awakening of the highest point of motivation or Purpose of the Self, leading to the ability to choose to act responsibly on this renewed awareness.

The mental field shown in the Egg Diagram can function as a connector between psychological functions at the subtle level and also as a connector of the sensory organs but can also function without them. As indicated millennia ago by the Vedic texts, particularly in *Ayurveda*, the mind resides not in the brain but in the heart, where the Self also resides. Rooted in the heart, the mind expands its activity through the brain, combining the influences of both.

Through decades of research by the HeartMath Institute, this wisdom is grounded in scientific evidence: once activated the intelligence of the heart determines the state of Presence, moving from a state of incoherence to the state of "Coherence". This state is referred to by Patanjali in the *Yoga Sutras* as "Coalescence".

COACHING THE ESSENCE

The "Call of Self" is the reality we can experience of the eternal presence of the Self in our hearts. With continuous training we can solidify contact with the Self, thus fully experiencing the truth of human experience as a gift from the Universal Self.

Disidentification is the fundamental step toward Synthesis. Without disidentification, there can be no synthesis. We will no longer randomly identify with any psychic content or self-image, but causally with an image suitable for the evolutionary purpose, the Ideal Model for the Self that is acted upon through the SMART process. By acting through the Ideal Model we participate in creating desired and conscious effects on the path to our fundamental Authenticity..

"We are dominated by everything with which our self identifies. We can dominate and control everything from which we disidentify. The normal mistake we all make is to identify with the content of consciousness rather than with consciousness itself. Some people derive their identity from their feelings, some from their thoughts, and some from their social roles. But this identification with a part of the personality destroys the freedom that comes from the experience of pure 'I'."

— Roberto Assagioli

Coaching in general focuses on change management and excellent action designed to manifest change that procures not only the achievement of the desired result but also a certain well-being; the particular focus of Psychosynthesis is on action based on awareness in line with the Will of the Self. Combining these two approaches to will and its use in coaching is unique, since the well-being that endures emerges from being well with oneself, being in the Self as the Leader of the flow of Presence that occurs at a personal level.

As a PLC we summarize these pivotal points, always keeping in mind the quality of the direction in which the client is moving, the meaning of their goal, the motivation for them to continue, and what steps they are taking to achieve it, with emphasis on the Self that has Purpose, Values, and Meaning. The "Call of

11- From Doing to Being

Self" is related to this evolutionary, ontological driving force.

Maintaining Presence in the state of Being or Self is ultimately the constant choice to remain present with bifocal vision. This involves maintaining awareness from a different and higher perspective of Self and content simultaneously, a transcendental perspective from which, in addition to de-emphasizing inner dynamics, it is possible to access energetic virtues and strengths at the superconscious level.

This positioning facilitates responsible choice with whom or what to identify ourselves to successfully achieve a desired goal, experiencing a feeling that indicates positioning in our ontological Identity: Joy.

This Joy we know as the basic emotion, as indeed it is, in the sense that it is a constituent of our Essence, or, to put it another way, we are composed of Joy: Joy is Essential.

The Vedas confirm that *Atman*, the Spiritual Essence or Soul, is: *Sat, Cit, Ananda*. Respectively: Immortal Being, Awareness, Bliss.

Assagioli called Joy the barometer of alignment to the Self. And, not surprisingly, Assagioli was very familiar with the Vedas.

For the modern individual immersed in the hectic activities of everyday life, learning to listen to the essential inner voice that calls for manifestation requires the courage to contact and accept one's vulnerability as an instrumental passage to union with one's Source. From this perspective, vulnerability represents an opportunity to bring forth one's authenticity, veiled among the myriad superficial self-images, collaborating with Presence for change in a meaningful way through awareness of each part's "need for change and growth", training resilience to actualize and manifest the "Call of Self" and ultimately arriving successfully at the finish line of one's goal. A successful journey will have meant having "walked" together every step that led to that outcome, through manifesting and acting upon one's potentials, abilities, qualities, and any ideal aptitude to the manifestation of the propellant spiritual nuclear energy.

This is a moment to celebrate with Joy.

COACHING THE ESSENCE

To feel within ourselves that we, coach and coachee, are truly happy because we have arrived together and joyfully at the greatest achievement. Having participated in our mutual evolutionary growth enriched by contact with spiritual energy is a truly significant moment, one that remains etched in our consciousness forever and should be celebrated from the heart.

Self is the transcendental, transpersonal Reality that underlies the Leadership process, starting at the personal level and then going Beyond, to the profound heights of our Essence at the transpersonal level. Our role as Psychosynthesis Life Coaches is to ascend the path together with the coachee to this elevated awareness, reaching the ability to manifest it in action with Joy. Through this process the authentic Joy of which we are composed and which is our birthright can become ecological and globally sustainable action.

"Joy chases away the mists of depression, frees us from fear and especially from unhealthy self-pity. Joy then is communicative, it pours out, and it radiates onto others benefiting them, and creating harmonious and fruitful relationships between us and them. Therefore, joy, far from being something to be scrupulous about, constitutes a real duty to others."

-Roberto Assagioli

"In the material world, every materialist desires to obtain happiness and decrease suffering, so everyone acts in this direction. But in reality, one is happy only as long as one does not try to secure happiness; as soon as one engages in activities aimed at procuring happiness, suffering arises."

-Śrimad-Bhāgavatam 7,7,42

"Just as a deer because of ignorance cannot see the water that lies within a well covered with grass, but runs here and there looking for water everywhere else, so the individual being, covered by the material body, does not see happiness within the self but pursues happiness in the material world."

-Śrimad-Bhāgavatam 7,13,29

CHAPTER 12

WITH THE GOAL IN THE HEART
The Blessed Joy

Cris: Easton, Maryland (2022)

Happiness is the purpose of life on a personal level; Joy is the Purpose of life on a Transpersonal level; Bliss is being in the Self in all circumstances.

COACHING THE ESSENCE

This reflection of mine brings us toward the synthesis of what has been elaborated on so far.

Peace and Joy are intimately interconnected.

To speak of Joy, and the duty we have to bring ourselves into this state of Being, seems almost out of place. But in fact, the state of Peace and Joy truly exists when we are outside the place where we commonly position ourselves, that is, in the personal self, unconsciously identified with its masks, embedded in a peculiar collective, with a historical identity.

It is a fact that the personality is in chronic conflict. The "I" that dwells there is immersed in this context and can change its state of consciousness (or rather return to its natural joyful state of consciousness) only and exclusively at the moment it distances itself from this state, assuming the role of the Observer, having moved at will to another and higher psychological space from where it can observe its inner dynamics. From this positioning the subject can truly choose, in the role of Director, the best inner attitude to take to be able to obtain the maximum benefit from the experience it is about to have.

This benefit leads to well-being, to being comfortable with one's self, to savoring happiness in the moment, and falls positively on the environment in which the subject interacts.

Knowing how to put one's highest potential into action to overcome an obstacle requires going through the obstacle, experiencing it in every possible facet to learn its inherent lesson, and asking questions such as:

- *What is this situation asking me to learn as a skill?*
- *What attitude do I choose to assume in this circumstance?*
- *What psychological function is interfering here?*
- *What is my possible ally?*
- *What is the image I need to identify with at this moment to exercise the best version of myself?*
- *What past dynamics bind me to limiting beliefs?*
- *What need emerges here?*

12- With the Goal in the Heart

- *What is it that I truly desire here?*
- *What are my values in this context?*
- *Where is "Me" here?*

We can truly have the experience of interpreting obstacles as opportunities to learn skills and acquire others in a sophisticated way, for we have at our disposal subpersonalities that, once governed by the disidentified "I" and enlightened by pure original awareness, we can identify at will, becoming functional through them.

In other words, we have access to psychological functions from each functionally specialized self-image, and are able to then disidentify from it and choose another more convenient one, and so on.

Multiplicity becomes an immense resource available in our psychological realm when we know how it functions and become able to manage it to the fullest. Each part becomes functional to the whole, in a synthesis that emerges as a new element, the Ideal Model, the instrument we create at will with a specific objective to manifest the Self in daily life, moving toward achieving the coveted goal and authentically being ourselves.

In the field of psychology Psychosynthesis provides a unique approach to shedding light on what each person can truly become: a Self in expression through a personality made up of a multiplicity of self-images, that finds its "Center of Revolution in the 'I'".

The personal self or "I" represents the reflection of the Self, equal in quality and at the same time different in quantitative potency. The "I" represents the point of compromise that allows one to stand at the center of one's varied and dynamic inner system, generating harmony in one's life, having learned to transform the conflict of each part into an evolutionary opportunity. Assagioli defines this process as achieving harmony through conflict.

Actualizing oneself requires the actualization of one's potential, the ability to train innate talents, acquire others, discover one's limitations in the various spheres of life and possibilities to go Beyond, training one's resilience as an ontological capacity related to the evolutionary tension that requires the actualization of one's highest intrinsic abilities.

When I think of my life from this perspective, a feeling of nostalgic sweetness emerges from within, a feeling that I cannot precisely define but that has the perfume of a deep Joy. A Joy that when used as a "Lighthouse", illuminates the memories that reside in my unconscious, in my Egg Diagram or psychological cell. In this way, by illuminating it I can bring to the surface this joyful feeling which truly has the power to transform every other emotion related to the varied memories as if it were a powerful antidote.

And indeed it is. Joy is the transformational antidote that brings us into our Being, into ourselves, to the place where there is nothing but Joy. For everything is Joy, in different forms of manifestation.

From the Naradha Bhakti Sutra: Bhakti, Bliss, or Power of Love

The trust placed in the Self attracts the "I", inhibiting the dynamics related to identifications that bond it to the fulfillment of the their primary needs. Communion with the Self enhances the sense of Identity (transpersonal, spiritual) and of belonging to a Universal Reality.

Communion, however, does not mean confusion, in the sense of having blended the various multiple aspects, but a dynamic synthesis of them emerging from the essential energetic core present in each of us; a union of intentions and meanings that belong to the core of our deepest and highest Identity, maintaining individual identity intact.

From this communion emerges a profoundly elevated feeling in the personality belonging to the Source: The Joy correlated with Essential Bliss: which attracts one to "Fall in Love", the *Bhakti*, the Faith that Loves.

The joy that illuminates the personality from its essential core,

12- With the Goal in the Heart

the "I" in communion with the Self, is the foundation of the state of gladness which radiates from the transpersonal dimension, the Force of pure Love in Its dynamic relational expression. In this state of Being or non-dual state, we awaken to the original awareness of Being One with creation, creatures, and the Creator, maintaining our own Identity unchanged.

This state of Being is ideal for the transformation of unconscious contents through the flow of transpersonal relationships in communion with Essence.

Accessing *Bhakti*, the Nature of Supreme Love, means tapping into the highest potentials attainable when the "I" is in the neutral state maintaining, at will, disidentification from the psychic contents that incessantly impact the mental field shown in the Egg Diagram.

From this neutral space where mental field modifications are quieted through the Power of Love obstacles on the path to the realization of one's True Spiritual Nature are removed, in the sense of being transformed and regenerated in their essence. The veils of the superficial layers or material reality covering the spiritual Essential core, referred to in the Vedas as *Kosha*, are dissolved.

The 5 Koshas of the Human Being

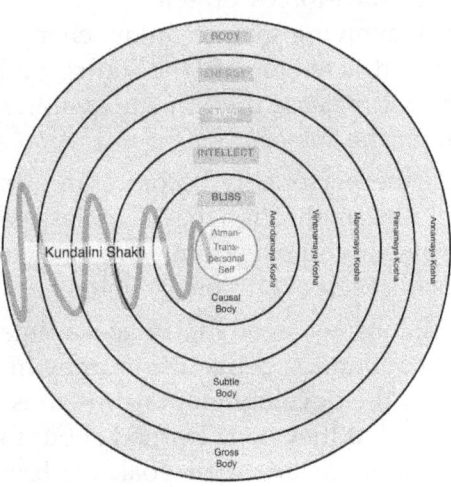

Graphic: Synthesis Coaching Associates

COACHING THE ESSENCE

The Power of Force is the energy matrix from which all emerging forms manifest, simultaneously distinct and non-distinct, from the Creator and Its creation.

Bhakti is the Essence that composes with Its expansion of the core of manifestation or *Svarūpa*, the unique form of each image in unity with Substance, from which it originates.

When we enter the neutral space of the "I", we are in the dimension of Being, equal in quality and different in magnitude from the Source.

We experience the Power of Love as a measure of the ability to remain in this neutral space and the Intention of this Loving Force that has direction and moves toward its actualization, Self-realization.

The next stage is the emergence of the awareness of Being a Self in expression through a personality composed of multiple transitory manifestations (the self-images-subpersonalities). Also the awakening of the awareness of being in constant expansion through adherence to the forms with which the subject unconsciously identifies along the path of life.

When the "I" can govern, coordinating the various parts (subpersonalities) and directing them toward meaningful goals with positive valence for evolutionary purposes, the attraction of the superficial idea-forces or self-images, transient aspects of the constantly evolving manifestation, changes. The psychic contents are now attracted toward the Source, and, irradiated by the Light of the Self, release their innate qualities as a transpersonal potential for the subject.

At this point the personality becomes an energetic catalyst: the Self goes into action through the "I", polarized in the Source, transforming psychic contents from being obstacles into opportunities, enhancing their evolutionary potential.

The coaching journey, evolving in space-time through content and related dynamics, is like the journey in life ultimately having as its goal the development of conscious awareness. By asking the client what they have learned about themself during the journey together toward their goal, we bring attention to the dimension of Being, expanding the consciousness of the "I"

12- With the Goal in the Heart

with freedom to be empathetically authentic with itself. In synthesis, it is a journey into the awareness of Being Love, mystery in the mysterious immensity of the Power of Love in its many manifestations and dynamics.

Love is not an accomplishment. Love is the quality with which the space of emptiness is filled, in which one chooses to position oneself while maintaining at will an emotional detachment from one's psychic contents, the space from which to bring forth the action that manifests the Power of the Self, grounded in Love.

Awareness that hinders Self-realization depends on the structure of content assimilated throughout life and introjected as true, truths based on impermanent foundations on which behavior is then oriented, causing actions that may lead to results that are not always satisfactory, and may even be harmful.

The consequences of actions based on values that are not one's own or introjected for various needs must be handled responsibly and sometimes make life "burdened" or cause a passing happiness that leaves a bitter taste, a painful happiness.

We tend by nature to happiness, to well-being, and being essentially Good since essentially this is our True Nature. We are created for Well-Being, being well in our Self; in our innermost core we are composed of energy constituted of Bliss (*Ananda*) and we are essentially aware that, through Self-knowledge, orientation to Well-Being is the "Destination" or "Destiny" in line with Dharma, the Universal Cosmic Order.

This tendency is facilitated when knowledge and emotional detachment jointly become the qualitative or value-based intention underlying action. The inner attitude on which to maintain Presence is grounded in being honestly authentic, an honesty that needs the coordination of the rational faculty, the psychological function of Thought. Through the wisdom of the heart, intellectual honesty full of Love and flexibility become available to transform intellectual knowledge into awareness, passing through life experience. This is the seed of Wisdom.

Life is an immense training ground for our faculties and finally, when ready to go Beyond within ourselves, tap into the

COACHING THE ESSENCE

faculties of Being, an immensely valuable resource. A knowledge that through experience is trained and grounded into the personality and enables evolution, transforming into resilient awareness as a primary skill.

The essence of *Bhakti* (faith, love, devotion, worship) can be perceived in the space of silence through maintaining control of *Vṛtti*, the modifications of the mental field. From the suspension or inhibition of the psychological function Impulse-Desire (*kama*) related to the dynamics inherent in the contact of the senses with perceived objects, the space between the *Vṛtti* emerges. This still, quiet space is *Nirodhaḥ*, from which the state of Yoga is accessed as described by Patanjali in his *Yoga Sutras*. Then the union of the "I" with the Self becomes steady.

In his writings, Assagioli defined Yoga as "the Science of Human Engineering", and viewed Psychosynthesis as equivalent to Yoga. So Psychosynthesis is "the Science of Human Engineering", the Science of Spirit in action thanks to the "machine" that the Being (*Jiva*) which has assumed a human form has at its disposal for knowing itself: a knowledge of the Truth that is not attainable by the rational mind.

In this suspended space it is possible to experience the essential Self and Joy of which we are composed at the nuclear level. Controlled breathing, slower and deeper than usual, while still maintaining a rhythm consonant with a state of stillness, focusing the mind on one point, the heart, allows the quieting of the modifications (*Vṛtti*) of the mental field. Entering the space of emptiness, basically composed of pure loving awareness and volitional dynamic energy, is now possible. Otherwise, we are in the psychological space in which subpersonalities exercise their dominance, idea-forces with attractive power over the "I".

The Void space, or *Nirodhaḥ*, is a place where time and distance are condensed, a suspended space in which active Imagination dominates, with the power to create new idea-forces and strengths and synthesize them into a pattern that can be functional for manifesting in concrete action one's Essence, building an Ideal Model for the Self.

In this place that appears magical, in which the magic follows

12- With the Goal in the Heart

the Great Cosmic Laws, the subject places themselves in a disidentified state and can observe themself while discovering internal dynamics of which they were previously unaware, expanding their awareness and power of dominion over their subpersonalities.

In practice, the subject learns to manage their inner resources as a valuable human being who has both the right and the duty to bring about meaningful changes in their own life, with joy and satisfaction, acting proudly their uniqueness in the world, because they have acted for excellence, through excellence.

In the silent space suspended from involvement with external reality, the "Personal Power" postulated by Carl Rogers emerges, the Leadership from which to exercise dominion over desires related to objective needs, and the consequent ability to actualize these needs in an evolutionary manner, from egoic to ecological inner positioning, starting from a sustainable inner ecology.

In doing so, the desire related to the subject's intrinsic project emerges: to reconnect with one's Source, the ontological need for Self-Realization and Actualization in manifest action of one's Essence. Through a well-established personality harmonized around a Unifying Center of Synthesis between the "I" and Self, the Ideal Model for the Self provides the successful instrument in pursuing any goal authentically with Joy.

Photo: "FireMaster" (Bill, 2016)

COACHING THE ESSENCE

The Ideal Model for the Self is a dynamic and ever-evolving self-image, created by a detailed project in the likeness of Substance, composed of the synthesis of multiplicity in the Unity of subjective Identity, unique, unrepeatable, valuable, generating an enduring Essential Joy that does not depend on external events, does not belong to linear time. It simply IS.

The Way of *Bhakti* moves under its own power and does not depend on the fulfillment of worldly desires. It is the engine of action par excellence as defined in the *Bhagavad-Gītā* and the *Narada Bhakti Sutras*.

To draw from the Source and choose to act for the Source, motivated by the realization of one's True Essential Nature, is to benefit from the evolutionary propelling force that finds in Love the Strength to go beyond one's limiting beliefs, beliefs which bind one to search for happiness in that which does not endure. When the mind is confused, non-ecological action emerges.

A really useful question to ask ourselves is the following:

What is the desire for this desire?

By doing so, we begin to explore starting with the objective dimension, without bypassing or denying it. It exists, it needs to be seen and accepted; it is then possible to decide whether and how to satisfy what emerges, then go beyond that. Then we can add one more piece to the question:

What is the desire beyond this desire?

...and let the desire emerge beyond objective needs. Here, too, the point of choice emerges: act to satisfy the desire that is linked to a need, or choose not to act, while still acting: action in inaction.

I remain in a state of vigilance, I act on my manifold soul, I inhibit what is not useful to my intended ends, I am in the inner action of managing my resources, I then let emerge what I have decided with deliberation, to manifest in concrete action my purpose, perhaps by remaining still, in silence, outwardly motionless, in inner motion around my spiritual center of gravity.

A mechanism that is simplified emerges as: *impulse - desire - drive - idea - word - action - destination/goal.*

12- With the Goal in the Heart

Impulse - desire - drive - idea, are movements that belong to the inner dimension.

Word-action-destination/goal belong to the outer dimension.

The overcoming of identification with a superficial self-image carrying a specific need occurs after becoming aware of it, going through the dynamics that were previously unconscious, thanks to disidentification, a process that allows one to create emotional distancing and maintain it resolutely. Disidentification leads the subject to a directional shift, from gravitating around the need of a subpersonality to following the attraction to go Beyond, into the transpersonal dimension, shifting attention to the need of the Self.

Focused attention is like a switch that turns on awareness. In proportion to the coach's ability to maintain a presence to themselves and simultaneously to their client, on whom they focus empathetically, they acquire the mastery of keeping their mind fixed on a point or *Ekagra*. By choosing to position themselves in their heart, they achieve a state of mind undisturbed by the incessant flow of content entering the mental field, facilitating access to the psychological function of Intuition.

At this point the coaching relationship occurs through Intuition, the field of the relationship is imbued with Joy and the journey to reach the desired destination becomes an opportunity for evolutionary growth for both, guide and traveler, in the Oneness of Self.

Awareness sustained by Love that illuminates to illuminate, a-spatial, a-temporal, enabling to support and be supported, leads to loving compassion for the variety of subpersonalities and related dynamics, transformed now as instrumental to the Self. Once the potentials present in the core of each part are recovered and brought into the heart, Synthesis occurs. Coach and coachee travel together on the journey of Synthesis to the Source, with the surrender of strength in the service of the Self.

We need the Self just as the Self needs us for the Great Law of Reciprocity and balancing of opposites or the Law of Karma. We have the task of learning to give and receive with love and compassion, for we are essentially Love. Through carrying out our

COACHING THE ESSENCE

life purpose we develop the ability to love responsibly, and the ability to know how to act in response to events with Love. This teaches us the Way of *Bhakti*, to love with our whole heart and to be loved from the heart reciprocally, being ultimately all Love.

It is the questions aimed at unveiling the Self that foster the embodied soul's need to reconnect with the Source. Joy is the Nature of the Self and consequently of the "I", immersed in the personality in a peculiar psychic field, constantly seeking happiness. Therefore, it is not a matter of building elements to achieve essential Joy but of removing obstacles that impede clear inner vision, through their transformation from obstacles to evolutionary opportunities.

They enable us to set in motion skills that need to be trained, others recovered, and others acquired or modulated, solidifying the personality and preparing it for the next step: accessing dimensions Beyond the personality and tapping into transpersonal potentials, the meta potentials that radiate from the Self. From the profound peaks of the meta-space of our heart every action that brings the Self into manifestation fosters and nurtures Joy. The Joy of having a Will that aspires to share Self-realization with other travelers, in the mysterious journey of life.

The spiritual nature of *Bhakti* is the essence of the human being. The path of Self-realization has as its ultimate goal the realization of our essential Joy which arises from the dynamic I-Self relationship and emerges as action acted in a non-dual state of consciousness. In the act of loving Love and acting out of this flow of Supreme Bliss, the experience of living life with Joy in the flow of the Power of Love emerges, proceeding toward Bliss generated by *Bhakti*, the source of Knowledge of the Truth, the inner Wisdom to be drawn upon.

In this state of Being, enlightening consciousness illuminates the whole psyche with spiritual light. The unconscious in its shadow resolves into awareness of the "I" on all psychological levels (pre-personal, personal, transpersonal), simultaneously mastering and managing through the Power of Love. The enlightened knowledge of the Self is transformed into a conscious experience of Being Loving Joy.

12- With the Goal in the Heart

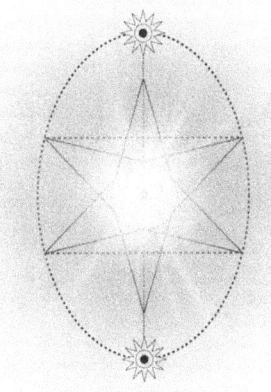

Graphic: Synthesis Coaching Associates

May the divine Spark within material coverings become the means that transforms conditionings from obstacles to resources through the positive intention they carry at their core. May spiritual nuclear energy emerge from this transformation, so that the "I" can draw on them for the arduous task of Self-realization, becoming a Self in expression through its psychophysical tools.

"Stones are found by the thousands, but diamonds are rare."
— Vedic saying

"The human form is made for the understanding of the self and the Supreme Self, God, the Sovereign Person, both of which are situated at the transcendental level. If both can be understood as soon as one has purified oneself and attained high knowledge, why on earth and in whose favor does a foolish and greedy person maintain the body for sense gratification?"
— Śrimad-Bhāgavatam 7,15,40

"Transcendentalists who have advanced in knowledge compare the body, which is due to the Will of God, the Supreme Person, to a chariot. The senses are like horses; the mind, which controls the senses, is likened to the reins; the objects of the senses are the destinations; intelligence is the charioteer; and consciousness, which is spread

COACHING THE ESSENCE

throughout the body, is the cause of imprisonment in this material world."

— Śrimad-Bhāgavatam 7,15,41

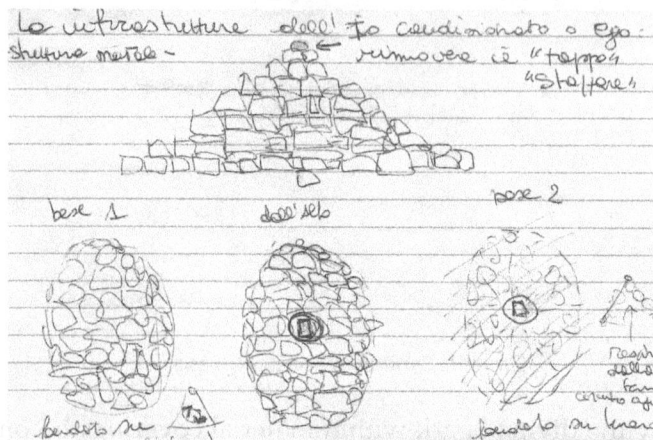

Graphic: Cristina Pelizzatti (2022)

The field of consciousness of the "I" varies according to the space with which we furnish our heart, in other words with the space we create in our heart and what we put into this space, moment by moment. In the space of the heart, we invite content at will from its intrinsic and meaningful value. When we set up this space with Bhakti, we participate in the Power of Love over the contents, which can finally be invited as welcome guests into the intimate sacred space of the heart, as they are accepted for their essential value.

When the structures supporting the personality are solidly grounded on the disidentified "I", they create fertile ground for the next step, transcending the primary needs of subpersonalities, having met them in an ecological way for their evolution. Their nuclear energetic qualities have emerged and are now present in our "backpack" as necessary elements for the next step in life's evolutionary journey: Moving Beyond.

The strenuous conquest of the lofty heights of our ontological Real Nature has begun, an endeavor that requires putting one's abilities to the highest levels and beyond, training innate and acquired talents along the path of life, invigorating the body and

12- With the Goal in the Heart

mind, solidly connected to the heart with the firm intention to reach the coveted goal.

We have been preparing for this moment all our lives, in moments of happiness and suffering we have learned to train our abilities and have become adept at crossing obstacles, without which we could not have trained resilience, an essential skill for approaching the Divine Creator, simultaneously within us and without us.

What we have longed for and trained with our will, impulsively following the various forms of the *Bhakti* Way, is now in place. We have arrived at the starting point: Be Who we have always and forever been, ourselves, our Spiritual Identity. It is a journey composed of moments of ascent, pause, descent, discouragement, interruptions, doubts and second thoughts, and exciting resumption, all of which are typical stages in the non-linear journey of life.

Thanks to this varied progression, we are required to implement previously acquired skills, some ingrained, some instinctive, and others learned along the way, all in the flow that follows an inescapable evolutionary drive. We can only move forward, moving toward a goal, whatever it may be, but we can never go backward. We can make the download from the past but still, the path is to move forward, standing, and at times to resolutely let go of what is no longer conducive to advancement and finally to move Beyond.

The "Call of Self" reveals itself as it goes, an inner voice that has strength and intention and calls to its actualization. Doubts vanish, shadows dissolve having realized that this silent voice, among the hubbub of the inner multitude, now resonating in unison, is the inner Voice that has always called us to authenticity.

The self that realizes itself as a spark of the Self, illuminating itself illuminates.

"M'illumino d'immenso" (I shine with the Immense)
- Giuseppe Ungaretti

COACHING THE ESSENCE

Illuminating the field of consciousness, the Self is now the Guide of the transformational process at the transpersonal level. It begins the subject's journey to the discovery and activation of higher potentials. Self-realization culminates in the realization that we have always and forever been a Self, sometime in expression through a certain "I"-directed personality that has "understood" or regained consciousness of True Essential Nature.

We are potentially powerful the moment we identify with our ontological Nature through the highest potentials; the human form has all the requirements to take this evolutionary step.

The Light of the Self impresses the consciousness which, from that moment, remains "positively" oriented toward the evolutionary process: impressing our path with the luminescence of Essence, illuminating the mental field shown in the Egg Diagram.

Every relationship from this internal positioning and activity emerges from the desire to create beauty, to participate in beauty with acts that manifest Love. The motivation that moves action is Love, the will to act for perfection from a small gesture, even imperfect, offered with sincere Love, emerging from heart and mind resonating in unison with the "Call of Self".

The feeling of Love purifies action and becomes the instrument of transformation for action in the Spirit of Love, toward the essential Joy of which we are composed.

Dutiful Joy

Joy is like a ray of sunshine that metaphorically descends into the personality, illuminating it as Assagioli points out in his paper: *"Individual Psychosynthesis-Lesson XVIII, Spiritual Elements in Personality V. Joy- Undeveloped Notes"*.

As the Vedas also confirm, Joy is an enlightening factor rooted in the Bliss-*Ananda*, of which we are essentially composed. Joy is a state of non-dual Being that finds synthesis in Peace. Peace is Joy, in Joy there is Peace.

12- With the Goal in the Heart

IN THE AFTERNOON

In the afternoon while doing my homework
I hear someone mumbling
I look out to see two people argue
I go into the woods where there is no silence
The birds sing, the wind whistles
In the trees, the wolf howls
I don't find silence and I think I won't
I will find it.
I go back home but the silence is not there.
Maybe I will never find it.
Night falls with silence and I sleep peacefully
In the deep silence, I dream blissfully.

- Bianco Lenatti
written in 2003 at the age of seven years.

When the "I" is freed from psychic contents, or in the state of disidentification from them, it rediscovers its essential origin of pure awareness and will, or Love and Will.

Love finds its emotional expression in Joy, which motivates to action on the path of Dharma. It emerges as an inner feeling that indicates to us that we are on the right path, the truth that we know for us to be the one that adheres to our ontological values.

Thus I ask myself the question that I then also use with my clients.

"Cristina, how do you know it is true for you?"

I just know. There are no precise words to indicate what I feel is true for me. I feel it through this Joy that is also nostalgia, a nostalgic Joy that speaks to me of a dimension deeply rooted in my heart.

COACHING THE ESSENCE

Cris, Isola d'Elba (2010)

When the "I" is unconsciously identified with the varied psychological contents, thus under the domination of the system around which it revolves, it has limited access to Joy, which is filtered and diverted toward the pursuit of goals oriented toward satisfaction of the primary need of which each self-image is the bearer and that procure only a pale shadow of this essential state.

In practice, the subpersonality that dominates the field of consciousness of the "I" at the moment seeks its own satisfaction and happiness, precluding the same process for the other multiple subpersonalities, which at this point come into conflict. Great expenditure of energy fuels dissatisfaction. The "I" binds itself to the objective dimension by constantly binding itself to the pursuit of happiness, which, however, does not last, is illusory, and leads to dissatisfaction and ultimately to suffering.

Joy at the personal level, when the subject is not conscious of themselves, is thus directed toward satisfying the primary need of

12- With the Goal in the Heart

which each subpersonality is the bearer and mingling with other elements. The result is a dilution of the power of Joy, refracting it into the will of the subpersonality in its constant search for idealized happiness as described in the Ten Laws of Psychodynamics.

This mechanism procures a numbing of the awareness of one's True Nature, which remains latent in the unconscious, but indestructible. The more it is removed, the more distorted it emerges through the dominant subpersonality in the field of awareness of the I at the moment, imprisoned in its own

This mechanism brings about a numbing of the awareness of one's True Nature, which, although indestructible remains latent in the unconscious. The more it is removed, the more distorted it emerges through the dominant subpersonality in the field of awareness of the "I" at the moment, imprisoned in its own "Ignorance / *Avidyā*". It emerges as a sense of unease, an underlying dissatisfaction, which leads the subject to search outside themselves for what actually lies latent in the depths of Self. The search for Joy through a sense of satisfaction in contact with objective reality leads to even more longing, leaving a bitter taste, like trying to quench one's thirst by drinking seawater. To desire is attached an expectation which when unfulfilled generates resentment- and the game is over.

The moment the person realizes that the desired satisfaction cannot be found in the world of things, he or she begins to look in another direction, in a different place. Awakening to the realization that the state of well-being and satisfaction cannot be separated from feeling good about oneself is often painful. It is also called a crisis.

The crisis of awakening, as Assagioli indicates in his masterful research, can lead to an ascent to the heights of one's personality, to an evolution in consciousness if well understood and contextualized. But awakening crises do not always lead to evolution: if the personality is not at least partly contextualized around an "I" in the ontological role of Observer-Director of one's inner realm, the predominance of subpersonalities is inevitable and evolutionary blockage occurs.

COACHING THE ESSENCE

The person halts their development of consciousness or realization of their ontological Reality, remaining in the dimension of doing, objectifying themself. When the subject objectifies themself by losing consciousness of their ontological Identity, the crisis that arises is not evolutionary.

The satisfaction that is confined to the need of one part of us (subpersonality) leads to so-called selfish pleasure which generally tends to separate us from others but first of all from ourselves. We become objectified. We are at the mercy of the subpersonality that enters the field of consciousness of the "I" or, to put it another way, the role we play in a certain context. Our perspective is constrained by that role/self-image and any intention is conglomerated into the need it carries, closing perception of the multiplicity of which we are composed. Even if we opened perception to other subpersonalities, they would become allies of the one dominating the "I"'s field of consciousness at any given moment.

We function well in the dysfunctionality of our psychic system, which is a closed loop that leads us to gravitate around the center of synthesis of the moment, that self-image that allows us to savor immediate pleasure but which leaves a bitter background at the end. Dissatisfaction ultimately indicates that we have strayed from the real evolutionary need.

Growing that part integrating it into a larger whole in which it exists as a nuclear quality, feeding the "I" with the Joy it carries at its core is the key step. It is not a matter of doing a spiritual bypass, not a sinking into the meanderings of the past precluding the actualizing tendency from flowing naturally, but a dynamic transformation from the Self that fosters our evolutionary process.

At this point, through the mind-heart connection, synthesis takes place. The quality at the core of the subpersonality emerges, the "I" is empowered and can act at will, motivated by the evolutionary drive that emerges from its authenticity. When an action emerges from the heart, it causes an emotional contagion: Joy. This is inspirational and involves us in the same motivation, bringing Joy.

12- With the Goal in the Heart

I choose to be a viral bearer of Joy and this choice is not easy for it requires me to make Joy the Purpose of my life. How do I feel Joy in the deep pain I carry, to truly be myself as I meet others, placing myself in the role of an Ideal Model for the Self?

To do so, I had to transform my suffering into awareness, my emotional carriers into instruments of "well-Being", recovering with constant acts of will, the positive moments experienced and full of vital, joyful emotions, of lived experiences of belonging to a greater Whole. At that point, I can consciously sustain the memory of a truly painful moment, an unbearable pain that radically transformed me and if unmanaged becomes a great obstacle to my Presence.

To do so, I have had to transform my suffering into awareness, my emotional carriers into instruments of "well-Being"; recovering, with constant acts of will, the positive moments experienced and full of vital, joyful emotions, of lived experiences of belonging to a greater Whole. At that point, I can consciously sustain the memory of a truly painful moment, an unbearable pain that radically transformed me and if unmanaged becomes a great obstacle to my Presence.

The words were spoken to me by my son Bianco, who said in his beautiful voice a few days before returning to the One Source:

"Mamma....why are you sad?....don't be sad Mamma, I am happy...I am grateful for what you are doing for me....you don't have to be sad...."

Since then, Joy is a duty for me in the knowledge that it too can be a great obstacle if pursued exclusively in the personal dimension.

"O son of Kuntī, the non-permanent appearance of joy and sorrow, and their disappearance over time are similar to the alternation of winter and summer. Joy and sorrow are due to sense perception, o descendant of Bharata, and one must learn to tolerate them without being disturbed by them."

COACHING THE ESSENCE

"O best among men [Arjuna], the person who is not disturbed by either joy or sorrow, but remains steadfast in all circumstances, is certainly worthy of liberation."
-Bhagavad-Gītā 2,14,15

I do not want to be sad and I choose to have Joy in my heart, even though sadness is in the background and sucks up my energy when I am not stronger than it is. Sadness exists in me, the unbelievable pain of loss remains, overpowering and powerful. I cannot erase it, I cannot eradicate it and, honestly, I cannot accept it from the perspective of my objective personality.

The mother part of me is not accepting, it is deeply sad and angry. However, I can live with it since I have learned that there are antidotes to it, the best of which is disidentification. Grief and sadness exist and remain where they are. I move to another psychological place from where I can observe myself, in my sadness, and from there I can truly accept from my heart that I have the right to deeply feel my sadness with anger and understand its educational value.

Graphic: Carmen Lenatti (2011)

I have a part of me that is absolutely sad and deeply wounded, that does not accept the loss of my beloved son Bianco, taken away by cancer at the age of twelve, and is so angry. I also have

12- With the Goal in the Heart

other parts of me, that existed before I became a mother and during her manifest existence are carriers of other emotions.

I can latch on to them and be strong, support my grief, once I courageously bring them into my awareness, the moment I feel the draining energy arising that tends to bring me back into angry grief.

I resolutely choose to act with my positive emotional memories, my emotional substrate, as an antidote. I do not disengage. Instead I put in place an emotional memory that allows me to stay in the moment, suffering less, decreasing the intensity and duration of the obstructive emotion.

Today that suffering has turned into a strength, an important skill. I have learned to sustain my weakness with the utmost commitment, actualizing my highest potential that allows me to position myself in my heart, to be myself and to draw strength from my Self.

On the strength of my weakness, I can be an authentic model of resilience from the heart.

Then, when I meet another human being who is going through a crisis, during the first phase of the contract I honestly communicate with delicacy that, to help support suffering, my role is not to be strong on behalf of my client, otherwise I would weaken them and I would depend on them to feel strong.

From my pain-sadness-anger dynamic I have learned that my anger is managed by pain. Grief inspires anger and, in the interactive dynamic in this "indigestible emotional soup", Joy is increasingly removed from my feeling, and I am ultimately disconnected from myself. I am identifying with the indigestible emotional state. I am afraid to feel my Joy because it emerges as a sense of guilt, certainly reinforced by a system that has a hard time accepting that there is nonetheless a right to feel content, happy if not quite joyful, especially when there is memory or presence of a significant loss. And the loss of a loved one is one of the most significant.

Fear is the boundary that allows me to handle both anger and sadness, that helps me contain my impulsive reaction at the moment of being in a non-empathetic context which would cause a chain reaction. The farther I am from my joyful core, the more I am chained in non-being, that is, in the personality identified in a single self-image that feeds on an "indigestible emotional soup".

Paradoxically, Joy can exist simultaneously with pain if we are oriented from the perspective of the Self. At the transpersonal level, there is only Bliss. At the personal level both happiness and sorrow exist. At the pre-personal level there exists mainly sadness and sorrow for not having rejoiced in joy when it was available.

Joy is the medium that the Ideal Model can bring as an antidote to illuminate the personality when it is overshadowed by a painful event. Suffering consists in adhering to the sense of separateness from one's Essence: the subject, The unconscious identification of the subject with a form that is destined to disappear feeds suffering.

Joy bridges the gap between the two dimensions. Light and Joy are intimately interconnected, bestowing the greatest benefit one can desire: "Peace untouched by events" as defined by Assagioli. Seeking Joy in that which is destined to disappear is like trying to quench our thirst by drinking water from the sea.

In To be a Leader of Myself and be an Ideal Model for my clients, I have accepted that I cannot change events anyway. Practicing "hindsight" is a waste of energy and time, and I prefer to devote time and resources to learning how to manage myself and the dynamics related to my history and choose how to propose myself in light of events. I'm free to choose which inner attitude to take given the circumstances, tap into my potential, and above all connect with my center, with my Self, getting help from direct contact with Nature of which I am an integral part. Being naturally with myself, one with my Nature reshapes my feeling and reconnects me to the One Source.

My Ideal Model is a PLC; it allows me to be authentically myself by acting from my Self and to experience an intense Joy that I wish to enthusiastically share with those who cross my path so that by mirroring themselves through me, they may access their ontological joyful feeling.

12- With the Goal in the Heart

This Joy is the antidote that emerges from the heart as transpersonal potential, the meta-potential that has always and forever resided in the metaspace of the heart, the Home of the Self. Then I can truly radiate Joy if in Joy I reside, choosing it by a volitional act. Otherwise, I can do nothing but release the emotion on which I sit comfortably, finding an excuse to do what I don't want to do: stay in the sadness of a meaningless life.

"It is not fitting that the servant of God should appear sad and darkfaced."
-San Francesco

In my work as a PLC I find a way to feel the Joy that emerges spontaneously from the heart and, on that, I establish my Presence. This is a skill that must be trained incessantly since the obstacles to maintaining this state of Being are many. First, inner obstacles come from the subpersonalities that come into play while in a personal or professional relationship. External obstacles can challenge the maintenance of presence in my center and require specific skills which may not be available at the moment.

Finally, if we honestly give an account of the situation, we realize that the greatest obstacle is the lack of awareness of our spiritual essence embedded in a bio-psychic form, and our adherence to self-images that in one way or another seek satisfaction for the basic or primary needs they carry.

As we have seen earlier, these basic or primary needs are related to subpersonalities to which, as the Samkhya philosophy teaches, the personal self or ego, the *Ahaṁkāra* (the "I" unconsciously identified with psychic contents) is attached, entangled, and unconsciously identified. Sometimes a certain attachment to suffering provides a sense of identity e.g., the rebel, the victim, the superhero, the mother, the father, the brother, the sister, the good girl, and the crusader. These are all attitudes that emerge from the way that part of us that uses the subtle sense organs (the psychological functions), performs to deal with the suffering encountered by that role.

If I let my self-image as a wounded mother intervene while I

COACHING THE ESSENCE

am in any relationship, I am aware that what happens is putting a "plug" on my suffering to avoid spilling it onto others. I am not authentically myself at that moment or rather I am authentic only to that part of me that came into play (the wounded mother) evoked by an emotional trigger that I unconsciously latched onto going into reaction mode. At that point an inner dialogue takes place between this part of me and my "I", so I tell myself, "I can't be happy". I don't allow myself to be happy, and when I do I trespass, guilt emerges, a psychic burden that is added to others, fueling my inner conflict and triggering anger, essentially toward myself.

Over time I have learned to ask myself, honestly:
- *How happy do I allow myself to be?*
- *Do I deserve to be happy?*
- *How do I celebrate my successes?*

The answer is sometimes puzzling. I don't allow myself to be happy, I don't deserve to be happy, and I don't have time to celebrate my successes. "Tristesse" emerges and immediately the angry part of me, the "Rebel", comes to the rescue and I become a driven achiever, a "Caterpillar". In the name of unexpected Joy, the inner battle begins, as in the Kurukshetra battlefield in the *Bhagavad-Gītā*.

A map we use in Psychosynthesis that I find very useful at this juncture is the False-Negative and False-Positive model:

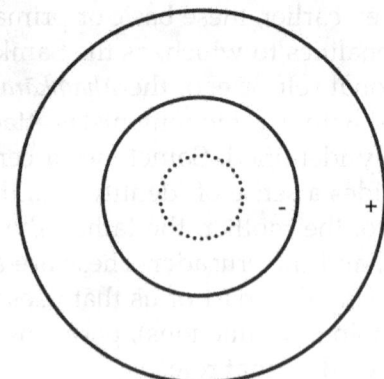

Graphic: The Synthesis Center (Amherst, MA, USA)

12- With the Goal in the Heart

I can thus visualize my essential center of Joy trapped between two opposite but related dynamics. The deep sadness that provides the framework is nonsense from a neutral perspective or has no meaning except to feed the dynamic itself by trapping me in nonbeing.

I am feeling my anger, I feel very angry because I feel deep sadness.

I, who am essentially not sad, feel deep sadness, and my anger increases. Identified with these two emotions I say to myself: I am very angry because of my sadness.

I am aware that in me there are at this moment two real dynamics in conflict. My Joy is encapsulated in a wave of emotion and I think I am this reality that I experience vividly because of my identification with it.

Resolving this conflict is a duty for me, otherwise, how can I be authentically present to another living being?

At this point, I focus on the transference and countertransference that may arise while I am in coaching as possible evolutionary tools, offering a way of being with the client and myself as these dynamics possibly arise. They would serve as a revelation of my authenticity in showing my vulnerability and knowing how to handle it masterfully, thanks to the Presence flowing from my Self.

I become an Ideal Model from my Self for the Self of the client, in a process of sincere empathic mirroring, grounded in resilience as the actualizing tendency to manifest one's authenticity.

My authentic presence as a human being who has learned to manage their inner dynamics as they emerge along the session is a gift within a partnership between two Selves. From this partnership in turn emerges the main ability to challenge these dynamics and bring out the positive intention within them: evolution in consciousness through the enactment of our highest potentials.

The state of Presence is an "inner achievement" not an "outer acquisition". How I maintain it with my clients depends on how I maintain it with myself, no matter how strong or overpowering are the waves of emotion.

COACHING THE ESSENCE

By maintaining the state of Presence, having gone through the stages of Identification-Disidentification-Self-identification, I can infuse Joy from myself into the personality overshadowed by depowering emotional waves, thereby catalyzing the feeling of happiness. Happiness is the indicator of the realignment of the "I" with the Joyful Source. The personal dimension in synthesis brings the fundamental or primary need to feel happy, the right to happiness, or the essential right to Joy, as the Self is Bliss.

The space of the coaching relationship is a living space, teeming with energies at various levels of manifestation. The ability to know how to resonate with the energetic vibration of the Self at the transpersonal level requires the subject to master the management of energies belonging to the personal dimension.

Assagioli teaches that an attitude grounded in a sense of humor allows the downsizing of a feeling that otherwise leads us to take an event too seriously, focusing exclusively on its tragic nature, and losing sight of the evolutionary opportunity that such an event embodies.

If we take our subpersonalities too seriously, making them the pivot around which our lives revolve, then we are the architects of our chronic failures, our pursuit of happiness and peace that does not endure, dissipating while leaving a bitter background taste.

By positioning ourselves at the center of ourselves, we regain the dignity of not allowing ourselves to be carried away by the emotions of the moment but go through them with an ideal attitude that allows us to find the positive intention concealed in the emotion we are perceiving thanks to a subpersonality with which the "I" is associated and that participates in an emotional event.

However, having the goal of being positive no matter what the circumstance without confronting the situation does not help us to grow as human beings, individuals searching for their ontological individuality in an objective reality which by nature is evanescent.

If I humorously observe myself in the course of the events of my life, having positioned myself in the neutral nonjudgmental

12- With the Goal in the Heart

space, and maintaining an attitude focused on the search for positive intention, I can now perceive a different emotion. This helps me transform a memory associated with an emotional event colored by a "negative" emotion, lightening it and "injecting" it with an antidote that allows me to let the quality emerge that lies within any emotion: Joy.

Joy is the bridge that connects the field of the coaching relationship, between coach and coachee. The interaction between two the psychic fields represented by the Egg Diagram of the coach and that of the coachee can, in other words, take place safely and confidently when there is a third unifying element through which the transformational process can flow. This is a transpersonal psychic field from the Self, a third Egg Diagram, engendering a micro-culture carrying Joy as the context where the transpersonal process of Self-realization takes place.

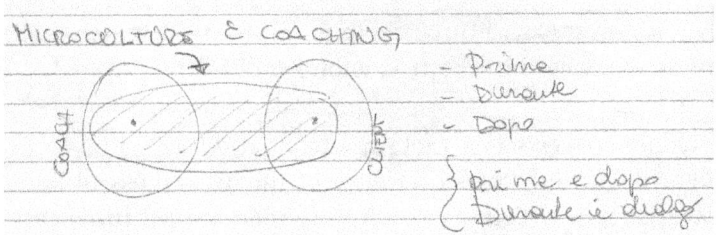

Graphic: Cristina Pelizzatti (2022)

The element represented by the third Egg Diagram emerges from the synthesis between the psychic field of the coach and that of the coachee; it is not the sum of the interacting parts between the two mental fields but an element in its own right, composed of the essence of the contents that is fed into this field, which follows the stages of sowing, nurturing, gestation, pruning, manifestation, and action of awareness. This element is managed simultaneously by the Self, by the coach, the client and Source. It is a prototyping field, where important choices need to be made, between what one needs to keep moving forward and what needs to be resolutely let go of with gratitude, aware of the intrinsic lesson that now needs to take on new idea-forms, more in line with personal growth, tending toward transpersonal development.

COACHING THE ESSENCE

It is here, in the Egg Diagram of Synthesis, that the highest potentials are contacted and redistributed into the coachee's field of consciousness, into their "I". This happens through an Ideal Model that facilitates the metabolization of such content in the coachee's "I", to bring it responsibly into SMART action.

To me, Psychosynthesis is not only a psychology of the soul but also a philosophy that educates to act from the heart. It is a highly valuable methodology, an educational model of living every moment of life with the soul, because every moment is worthwhile, unique, and unrepeatable in its evolutionary opportunity.

Living in the world, aware of Being the world and more than the world, of Being Life ever-expanding and interacting, manifest in myriad forms representing Essence, with the ability to evoke Essence, to Be Essential, a Self that has a form, a name, a momentary history: a Self that matters.

The value we, as human beings, place on the manifestation of life is what we build our existence on, in the pursuit of happiness.

Psychosynthesis is a meta-model that educates us to live in the world through the experience of the awareness of being an Observer with Directive capacities to manage our inner resources, the immense wealth of transpersonal qualities each person possesses, and with the power of choice over our behavior.

From being controlled to being the controller, mastering through governing the dynamics of inner tensions, transforming them into valuable resources to be manifested with intention toward excellent and evolutionary goals.

This in my view is truly an Ideal Model of Self-Leadership.

We can shift our identifications into resources when we are aware of their presence, and decide to stay in the flow of their dynamics, maintaining a healthy emotional detachment with an attitude of benevolence. Moreover, by adopting a sporting attitude in wanting to get to the coveted goal we are putting into action the natural tendency for excellence, the motivator of action that brings the Self into manifestation.

12- With the Goal in the Heart

We are a divine spark, equal in substance, infinitesimal in power, drawn by the Great Laws of Nature to have to remain in a specific bio-psychic form until the time has come to go Beyond, for we will have had an evolutionary experience through the abilities allowed us by that peculiar form. The time of change is natural, each season coming to its end, leaving room for the emergence of the next, in the constant cycle of renewal and rebirth to which we belong.

Choosing to live with awareness, in alignment with the Essence that underlies everything, allows us to appreciate every moment, every situation with Joy, at least that much that enables us to go Beyond. Otherwise, we remain still, stuck in the past, ruminating about indigestible food that cannot be metabolized naturally.

Paradoxically, unhappiness may be very much connected with attachment to joyful contents in the past. This can hinder the evolutionary process of awareness, locking the subject in the past, in a barren present for the future.

Being in the Self generates a perception of Peace regardless of events; a state of Being that radiates Peace and Joy, perceptible in the Silence of the hidden depths of the transpersonal dimension.

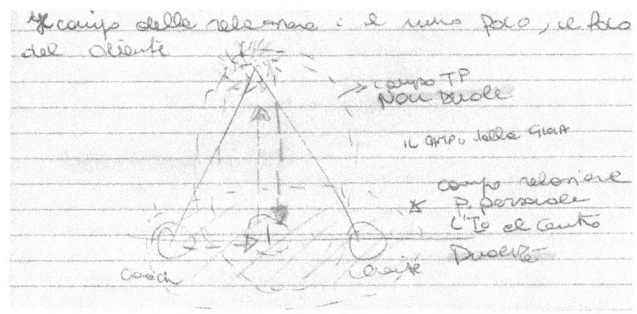

Graphic: Cristina Pelizzatti (2022)

"The unawakened man identifies with his pain and joy, but he who is awakened and feels the soul in himself independent of personality, lives in two worlds."

- Roberto Assagioli

COACHING THE ESSENCE

Following a profession that is consonant with my Essential Nature of Being a Coach practicing Psychosynthesis is essentially my Ideal Model for the Self, so that I can truly and authentically bring my uniqueness in the service of others seeking to give shape to their Essence and manifest it in actions congruent with their ontological values. The meta values are evolutionary propellants for ourselves and the environment in which we are embedded, aimed at manifesting the Beauty inherent in the work of life in all its manifestations, having Blissful Love as its goal.

In Synthesis

Serving humanity on the way to its evolution in consciousness is a source of immense Joy for me. The big question I always keep in mind to help me reconnect with my heart is suggested by Assagioli:

"Is my mind an organ of spiritual vision? And am I offering this organ to the use of the Higher Self?"

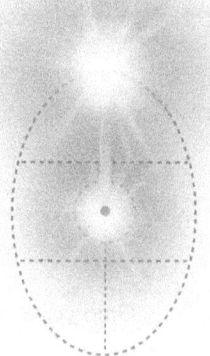

Graphic: Synthesis Coaching Associates

In the years following Bianco's departure, I devoted myself unceasingly and with passion, determination, persistence, and diligence to studying the IndoVedic Tradition from a

12- With the Goal in the Heart

psychological perspective. The encounter with Psychosynthesis that came later immediately fascinated me: in it, I saw the unique potential of being able to apply the Science of the Spirit, of which the Vedas are the highest expression, in contemporary reality.

Although Psychosynthesis dates back to the early 1900s it is still little known and sometimes not understood in its essence. A niche psychology that has Spirit at its heart, which finds in Spirit the substratum of bio-psychic form and helps to experience this Essential Reality of which we are bearers. Acting in daily life with spirit, bringing it into ecological and sustainable action, for ourselves, our planet, and adding positive valence to the Universe, means radiating Joy.

So the Light of the Self illuminates the shadows of my egg-shaped psychic cell. I become aware that I am not this subpersonality or that, and paradoxically that I am. Now I am aware that through that partial image or another, I can experience the objects of the senses through the subtle organs, the psychological functions through which it functions in a sophisticated way. Then I can by choice undress (disidentify) myself from it and identify with another one at my own convenience, adopting its functional modalities and taking advantage of its essential qualities, in the process becoming more and more resilient.

Thanks to the skills of multiplicity that I can now direct, according to the guidance of my Self, I can face obstacles on my existential path using their nuclear quality and be grateful for the great opportunity they are giving me.

I can train my capacities and tap into the transpersonal faculties that find synthesis in my Self, thanks to the tool which belongs to the phenomenal, manifested reality that bridges the two dimensions: the Ideal Model for my Self, Being a Coach, practicing Psychosynthesis and simultaneously Be Authentically mySelf.

Guided by an honest positive intention toward fulfilling my duty toward the achievement of my goal and putting my talents, personal abilities, and transpersonal strength into action to my best advantage, I root this attitude in myself, nurturing my resilience.

COACHING THE ESSENCE

I can thus honestly celebrate the achievement of my goal, having savored every moment of connection with myself and simultaneously of interconnectedness. This process nurtures the self-image I have chosen to wear, the Ideal Model that allows me to condense Doing and Being into a single point.

I can then authentically manifest my Self in action, feeling a sense of joyful fulfillment, wholeness, rightness, and worth: Being a Coach.

To be a Coach means to place myself at the service of the people who choose to work with me, being a moment-to-moment Leader of myself. I am aware that the strength of my excellence is rooted in my vulnerability and simultaneously in mastery by managing my inner dynamics, while I am roped along a precipitous trail through the psychic heights with another human being, on the mysterious "Journey" in that small juncture of Life we are traveling together.

I was told some time ago by a friend of mine: "Do you realize that the drama you have been through now makes you unable to see reason?" I have thought a lot about these words, which at the time resonated with me painfully. It is true that I no longer reason as I reasoned before what happened and I have often wondered what it means to reason at this point. The heart knows reasons that the mind does not.

Suffering breaks through the encrustations of the heart, of the mind, and by tearing them, creates space. What I put into this space is what makes a difference.

I've put in this space the transpersonal research, the universal Knowledge of the Truth that is free from dogma, moved by the desire to help understand Reality Beyond Appearances, wanting to understand the meaning behind suffering, and perceive its positive intention.

Psychosynthesis came to me, and I welcomed it when I needed it so much. It helped me and continues to help me, and for that, I am truly grateful to it. I have learned that reason must be aligned with the heart and together they must be embodied and actuated to accomplish the mission that I am sincerely passionate about. Mine is coaching and, while imperfectly, I apply

12- With the Goal in the Heart

myself to always do my best, with excellence as my goal.

Can study soothe intense suffering? It can truly do so if what we discover through study is a source of wisdom, the kind that enables us to go to the place within us and at the same time without (outside of) us, where there is neither pain nor sadness, where there is no separation but union with Everything.

Here, in this place so near and yet so far away, there is Bianco.

Love flows, and life still flows, Beyond the manifest. If sadness and sorrow come, I sit, I welcome them, I weep, then I turn away from them, I see them and from there, I watch them with detachment and a quiet mind. Seeking the Light, Peace comes, and the distances vanish. I can be serene, feeling within me that what I have seen, heard, learned, experienced, and perceived, has absolute value, and contains in its heart a great lesson that offers the possibility of leaping over the boundaries of my limiting beliefs.

If I am serene, even amid the storm, it is because I am centered in the Self, and in this positioning, I perceive courage, strength, compassion, empathy, trust, and a joyful union with the Whole.

I perceive Love.

To express Joy while feeling sadness, I use the Ideal Model, I "act as if" I am in my Self, in Bliss untouched by events. I disidentify from the sadness pressing in on my personality, center myself, and welcome and transform suffering into Joy.

I act as if Joy is all around me and in short, the sadness vanishes, and I can smile, love, and let myself be loved. From a closed heart, no Love enters- and no Love goes out.

Through the application of psychosynthesis methods to coaching we learn to shift our point of view, value what we have, know how to manage our resources and weaknesses while becoming aware of the tools at our disposal to operate constructively and consciously in the reality in which we interact.

We learn how to use good, strong, and wise will at every opportunity; to give thanks for life and the opportunity to be in this life; to recognize our role and task to offer the best of ourselves and our potential for the common good; to bear heavy burdens, for if they come it is because we can carry them.

We reach the ability to maintain active emotional detachment so we can empathize with our brothers and sisters in the world, whoever or whatever they may be. We become able to metabolize joy and sorrow as ingredients both of which are necessary for the development of our consciousness and to let go of what is no longer necessary and hinders our evolution. We no longer attach ourselves to anything ephemeral, for the only thing we will take with us when we leave is the Love we shared through the Self.

The good things we carry in our hearts are deeper than the deepest sorrow. Joy is essential, Bliss our Essence. We learn to contact the un-rejoiced Joy, the mortified Joy; to accept our "flaws" and value our virtues; to lighten the baggage of attachments to deep-seated beliefs that weigh us down and hinder our evolutionary development.

To realize the "Freedom to be our Self", that is, individual and conscious human beings, unique and valuable notes in the Greater Harmony, interconnected with other Selves, we have to learn how to tolerate the lights and shadows, the joys and sorrows, and the obstacles which are nothing more than resistances opposed by our personality to the actualization of our highest potentials. We apply a consciously good and tenacious will working to conquer the unconscious, releasing and directing the stored and compressed energies toward the Source, so that Spirit can work freely in us through Its powerful spiritual energies.

We focus on consciously "Being" in a Universe that is there and exists, building relationships of Love that leave others free to authentically BE themselves. This way builds Love and freedom in one's own ontological identity; Love that does not invade or encroach upon us, free of possessions or pretensions. Let us give others the freedom to Be that Self, as they already are, with all that they are, showing ourselves authentically as an Ideal Model for Self.

If we are positioned as observers, centered in the Self, we are no longer dominated by the multiple contents with which the unstable "I" identifies, but we dominate, direct and

12- With the Goal in the Heart

use everything from which we disidentify. This principle is fundamental and represents the transition between bondage and inner freedom.

True Love, which endures through change, is that which liberates. The relationship that allows the other to "see themself and see me as well", as I am, recognizing me, recognizing themself, in the sincere unconditioned acceptance, without masks, is true brotherhood.

As in the beautiful prayer "The Great Invocation", the "*Point of Light within the Mind of God*" is in us; the "*point of Love within the Heart of God*" is also in us. Light and Love are within our reach if we turn our gaze upward to the apex of the triangle, so dear to Psychosynthesis, connecting to the "Will of God" in a movement dictated by the "Will of Good".

Aligning the personal will with the Transpersonal Will, in the knowledge that everything happens for a reason which is causal, not casual, with courage, humility, foresight, austerity, and sincerity.

Say Yes! to the One Life.

From Personal Psychosynthesis to Spiritual Psychosynthesis, passing from the "I", in the flow through which the Spirit can guide, as the Great Invocation teaches us, "the little wills of men", being Beyond dualism, thus Unity in diversity, harmony, peace, the synergy of energies, SYNTHESIS, aimed at the ultimate goal: Love, a-mors, not death, Life, which IS: The "Joy of being in all that is".

Psychosynthesis is the wonderful promise of what we can become if we will: the Self, the source of all Blessing.

"Joy is a spiritual coffee! Joy vivifies, heals, radiates, arouses, and activates. Joy eliminates self-pity and criticism. Joy redeems."

-Roberto Assagioli

COACHING THE ESSENCE

CHAPTER 13

ORIGINAL RESEARCH
Psychosynthesis and Positive Psychology Coaching

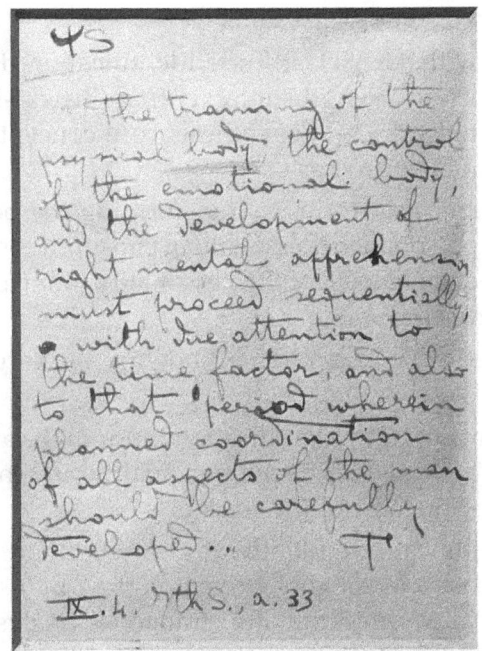

Photo: "Assagiolino"- note handwritten by Roberto Assagioli

"Training in psychosynthesis has no end."

-Roberto Assagioli

COACHING THE ESSENCE

Cristina's notes and ideas on PPC (Positive Psychology Coaching) and Psychosynthesis presented during the Advanced Practice in Positive Psychology Coaching with Dr. Robert Biswas-Diener & Dr. Christian van Nieuwerburgh- January 18th, 2022

PPC (Positive Psychology Coaching) and PSY (Psychosynthesis), Introductions & Strengths
January 18th, 2022

Levels of Sophistication in Strengths Coaching

L1: Identify and Use - Questions

L2: Name, Claim, Aim - Questions

L3: Test and Learn - Questions

In line with the AID (attitude, identification, development) approach to strengths intervention (Biswas-Diener et al., 2011) and the Psychosynthesis core concept of the Ideal Model in the process of:

Knowing - Mastering - Transforming the personal level of the personality (Personal Psychosynthesis) toward the transpersonal level of the personality (Transpersonal Psychosynthesis):

L4: (deepens the L1 and L2): Knowing by Recognition and Naming

Explore Strength Identification through the analysis (fractional analysis) of the subpersonality present in the field of consciousness of the coachee's "I".

a) Identification- Identify the Strength to identify the related subpersonality or vice versa - by using the subpersonality questionnaire, fractional analysis, and Egg Diagram in mapping the subpersonality and dynamics impacting the coachee's "I". The False-Positive and False Negative map, Triangle maps, guided imagery, and others may also be used to bring out the Potential - Skill.

b) Attitude- Making a conscious exploration of the

unconscious dynamics related to a particular Strength related subpersonality or from implicit to explicit attitude related to a specific subpersonality using a particular Strength.

As a coach I ask myself:

- *What dynamics occur while the subject is unconsciously identified with a particular subpersonality using this Strength? or identifies at will with a particular Strength used by a subpersonality?*

or:

- *By identifying with a particular Strength used by a known subpersonality, what change emerges along the process and at the end of the session?*

Examples of questions to share with the client:
- *Who are you through the lens of this Strength?*
- *What beliefs are related to this particular Strength?*
- *What do you want to accomplish through this Strength?*
- *What do others want you to be according to this Strength?*
- *What do others believe you are through the lens of this Strength?*
- *How does this Strength empower you?*
- *How does this Strength limit you?*
- *What do you really want to reach through this Strength?*
- *What would your life be if you could manage this Strength at will?*
- *What would your life be if you were not able to access this Strength?*
- *What can you do to become more comfortable with this Strength?*
- *Whom do you want to become through this Strength?*

L5: Mastery through Disidentification, the key to inner freedom

The 7 Steps of Synthesis

1- Recognize: the primary Strength, the one most commonly used on autopilot/unconsciously. Generally this is related to a dominant subpersonality or most mature subpersonality (MMSP). This can be a difficult passage for those who are unconsciously identified with a subpersonality to the point where the subpersonality completely dominates and defines their sense of self/self-identity (the 8th Law of Psychodynamics- R. Assagioli, *The Act of Will*)

Questions are to be posed to evoke the client's awareness of the presence of Strengths related to emotions, thinking, imagination, impulse- desires, sensations, behaviors of a subpersonality, and vice versa.

2- Naming: Give the subpersonality or strength a specific shape-form (metaphor, symbol, evocative image, body posture, drawing, etc.). Once recognition is reached, naming is the necessary step to make the subject conscious of this unconscious content and related dynamics. Technically Recognition and Naming allow the Strength related to the MMSP to enter the field of consciousness of the "I". There is now a conscious awareness of its presence and related dynamics over the subject (5-6-7-8 Laws of Psychodynamics). Naming also helps to ground the new awareness to move to the next step of Acceptance.

3- Acceptance: Rate it from 1 to 10. Acceptance diminishes or neutralizes the polarity of the subpersonality over the "I" because it diminishes or controls the fears associated with self-preservation (of the subpersonality, 8th Law of Psychodynamics), opening the way into the space of the "I" (reflection of the Self into the personality, pure Awareness and Will, free of contents). True Acceptance is an ideal process.

Examples of "powerful questions" associated with acceptance:

- *Which strength/ability associated with the subpersonality can help you to begin this process of acceptance?*

- *What strength/ability associated with the subpersonality is interfering with the process of Acceptance?*
- *What strength/ability associated with the subpersonality is interfering with the process of Acceptance?*

The more the subject is aware of the presence of x number of strengths/abilities related to x number of subpersonalities, the more access to a sustainable step toward more and lasting acceptance can occur. Questions will be posed to "Call the 'I'" as opposed to the subpersonalities, querying the "Who" of the client along with the "what" of the contents. By calling the "I" in the coaching conversation, we are bringing elements of the Disidentification process, the first of the Psychosynthesis core concepts, into play.

Examples of questions associated with this work are:
- *Examples of questions associated with this work are:*
- *Which strength/ability at this moment can help you to accept x?*
- *On a scale from 1 to 10, how much can this strength/ability help you to accept x?*
- *Which strength/ability is an ally for you in this process?*
- *Which strength/ability is an obstacle for you in this process?*
- *How was this particular strength/ability useful to you in the past in a similar situation?*
- *Whom do you admire who in a similar situation was able to manifest more acceptance?*
- *What particular strength/ability do you think was in play there?*

Mastery

4- Coordination: Here we begin an inner dialogue between the "I" and the subpersonalities having at their core a particular strength/ability, by inhibiting one or the other as necessary to achieve a balanced conversation among the subpersonalities in play in a particular circumstance. The outcome of the Coordination step is to manage at will the inevitable subpersonalities and inner conflict.

COACHING THE ESSENCE

This is the phase of the "I" choosing a strength/ability at will related to a specific subpersonality, in line with the process outlined in Assagioli's *The Act of Will*. Each Stage of the Act of Will is explored through the lens of a specific strength or ability.

Inhibition is a key element in the coordination phase. Generally, inhibition is immediately associated with repression or over-control. Instead, in the Will process "inhibition" represents the conscious act of controlling the drives inherent in the process of deliberation. It is important to understand that Inhibition is different from repression. Repression generates a huge amount of unexpressed, unconscious energies which are utilized to forcibly contain content. The result of this is that the unconscious energies related to subpersonalities and other contents exist and will emerge sooner or later, generally in an uncontrolled manner such as rage, anguish, or desperation. On the other hand, Inhibition is the conscious choice to resolutely hold back an impulse or tendency while deliberating the best next step in the process. The masterful utilization of inhibition involves 4 steps-

- Recognize the emerging impulse to use the strength/ability
- Examine and analyze the impulse to use the emerging strength/ability
- Direct or transmute it for the task to be reached
- Act on it (using the strength/ability) at the most appropriate time

Questions to be used here will enhance the strength/ability dynamics relative to the "I" and will be correlated with the Will Project. Each Stage will have specific questions. Each Quality will be explored together with the relative strength/ability.

5- Integration: takes place in the "I" once disidentified from contents to the point that it can direct the subpersonalities at will and use the related strength/ability accordingly.

Integration can't take place without "grounding" the awareness of the strength/ability over the "I", bringing theoretical work into action. Grounding is the essential process of integrating the awareness gained from working with subpersonalities and their relative strengths/abilities. It means bringing the various qualities and strengths/abilities of the subpersonalities into the field of consciousness of the personal self or "I", to be applied to the objectives of everyday life. In Psychosynthesis, grounding means bringing Purpose into action, and we do this through Anchoring, and Anchoring occurs through Affirmation.

- Which Quality and strength/ability do I affirm to be mine here?

6- Transformation: The subject, in the role of Director, is now able to regulate and use the strengths/abilities at will, managing those subpersonalities and related dynamics selected to successfully achieve the desired goal through the "I".

7- Synthesis occurs at the transpersonal level and is the outcome of the previous steps. Is a new element, not a sum of the previous processes but a synthesis of them with transpersonal potentialities available to the "I" to be used at will. There is now a flow of transpersonal elements (core Values, core Strengths, solid sense of self-identity) into the personality. The subject now has the ability to act in line with their Life Purpose, having the essence of the strengths and abilities of the subpersonalities as resources. The Self-Realization at the core of Psychosynthesis is a process which evolves through various stages with the intention of revealing the highest, transcendental strengths and abilities.

In the stage of Synthesis, subpersonalities emerge as essential qualities (from their essence that always has positive intention) which empower the "I" through their ontological Values.

This whole process needs to be coached repeatedly. In the coaching phase where we go to stimulate the coachee's responsibility to train the new awareness with a SMART step, we will ask questions to evoke the intention to do it for themselves, to do it now, to do it repeatedly. Repetition is related to the seventh Law of Psychodynamics and is confirmed today by neuroscience as a necessary way to solidify learning at the cerebral level.

A recent study I did entitled "Applied Neuroscience in Coaching through the lens of Psychosynthesis" can be added to this work to underline what happens in a particular Psychological Function during a coaching conversation and how, thanks to neuroplasticity, Will can be effectively and efficiently applied to change a particular limiting thinking process.

References

Assagioli, R. (1975). *Psychosynthesis- A Manual of Principles and Techniques.* Thorsons

Assagioli, R. (1974). *The Act of Will, a Guide in Self-Actualization and Self-Realisation.* Turnstone Press

Firman, Dorothy, Ed. (2018). *The Call of Self-Psychosynthesis Life Coaching: Taking Coaching into the Depths and Heights of Transpersonal Psychology.* Synthesis Center Press

Horowitz, Mark (2014), *The Dance of We: The Mindful Use of Love and Power in Human Systems.* Synthesis Center Press

Rogers, Carl (1978). *Carl Rogers on Personal Power: Inner Strength and its Revolutionary Impact.* Delta.

Some Psychosynthetic Reflections 2008-2022

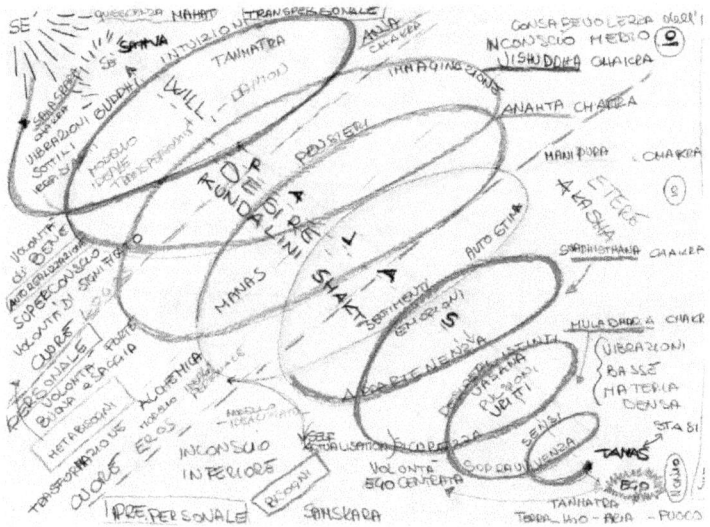

Energetic Spiral of Manifestation of the Self (2014)

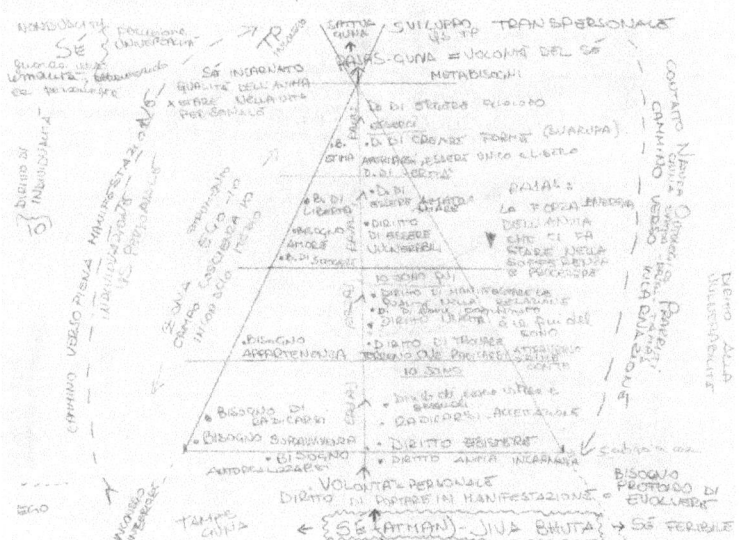

The Self at the Base of the Evolutionary Pyramid (2015)

COACHING THE ESSENCE

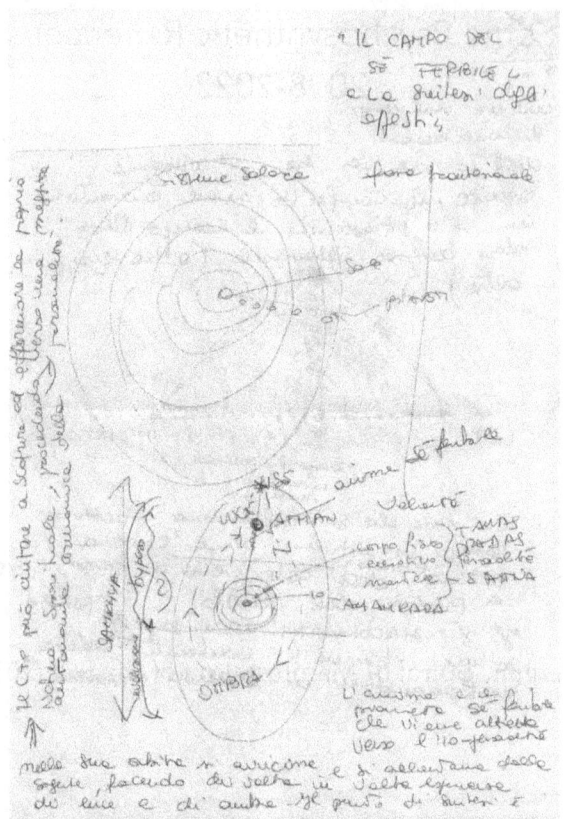

Psychoenergetics Studies (2013)

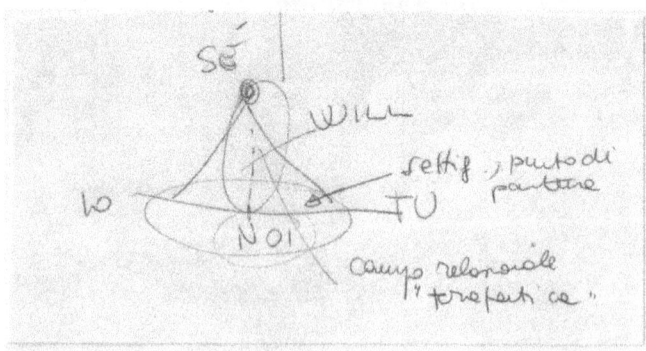

The Field of Psychosynthetic Relationships (2010)

13- Original Research

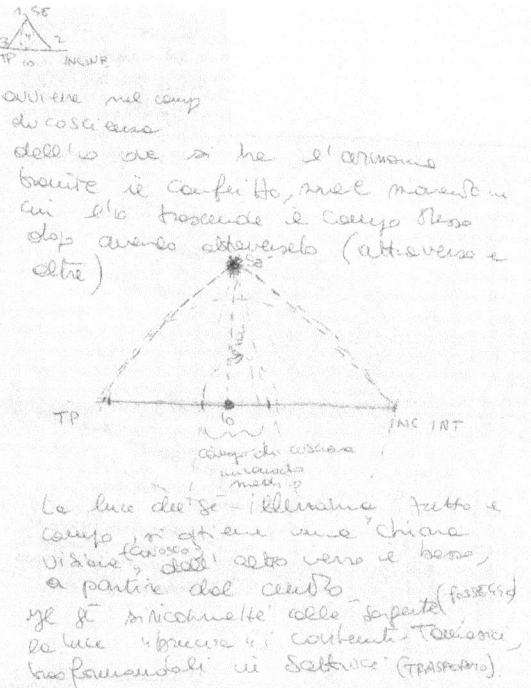

Study of Field Interactions: Personal - Transpersonal (2015)

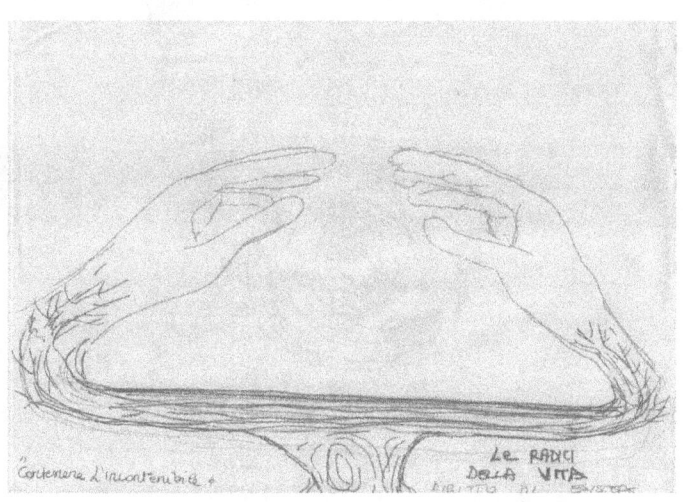

Psychoenergetics Visualization (2015)

COACHING THE ESSENCE

13- Original Research

Using a Popular Strengths Assessment within the Framework of Psychosynthesis Life Coaching

Andy Lyde, PCC, PLC, Gallup Certified Strengths Coach

The use of standardized assessments in coaching engagements is a common occurrence. The results of the assessment give the client a window of self-awareness on personality or behavioral tendencies and can often provide an anchor point in coaching conversations, pointing to changes the client would like to make or the inner resources available to them to make those changes.

One such popular instrument is Gallup's CliftonStrengths, which has been completed by over 29 million people worldwide. The assessment measures the presence of talent in 34 areas, which Gallup calls "themes." The most basic report gives respondents their Top 5 themes and the most comprehensive report gives respondents all 34 of their themes in order from strongest to weakest.

Gallup says that talent multiplied by the investment in that talent equals a strength. So the talent themes reported to respondents on CliftonStrengths reports could be seen as areas about that person that they have natural proclivities towards. It is really only when a person chooses to use the talent in service of getting a need or desire met, that it really becomes a strength.

Are Talent Themes Really Subpersonalities?

In early 2022, while I was completing the Gallup Certified Strengths Coach training, I had a conversation with Cristina about how talent themes could fit into Psychosynthesis principles. My main thought was that talent themes, especially in the way they are richly described in Gallup's literature, look a lot like subpersonalities. Themes can be talked about individually or in combination with each other and a common coaching question to ask someone working with their report is, "How does this theme show up for you?"

As I practiced debriefing with classmates during my training, I could see different levels of energy associated with different themes for each individual. One classmate had the themes of Empathy and Developer. The Empathy theme could be defined as being able to quickly sense the deep emotions of others. These people experience that emotional connection in their body, typically their gut, and they carry that deep emotion of the other with them. As my classmate spoke about how this theme shows up for her, she was sullen and hunched over with low energy. She almost teared up at several points just describing what interactions with people can be like for her, without describing to me any of the actual emotional content she carries for others.

The next talent theme for her was Developer, which could be defined as someone who can quickly see the small improvements another person can make that would make their life better. This is someone who cares about the growth of other individuals. As my classmate spoke about this talent theme, she sat upright, spoke loudly and excitedly, made large hand and arm gestures, and had a very positive energy about her.

These two experiences with my classmate in how she spoke about how these two particular talent themes show up for her occurred within minutes of each other in the same conversation. This is the same experience as working with a client with their subpersonalities. As different subpersonalities appear in the conversation, the client unconsciously changes their energy level, their tone of voice, their physical body posture, and even the words they use. Each subpersonality has its own needs it is trying to get met and has its own strategies to do it.

This led to my question to Cristina about strengths work within Psychosynthesis: Who is it that is taking the assessment? If I sit down to take an assessment and I have not consciously chosen to identify with a subpersonality, it will most likely be my Most Mature Subpersonality (MMSP) that is running the show and answering the questions, not my Ideal Self. So, the results on the assessment's reports will mostly reflect my MMSP. If that is the case, how do we use those results to help our clients with true growth rather than just reinforce the strong position of the MMSP as the director of their lives?

13- Original Research

That is when Cristina shared with me her notes on Positive Psychology Coaching that begin this chapter. I spent the next twelve months working with over 90 clients with their CliftonStrengths report with the framework Cristina lays out in her notes as the major framework informing my coaching with these clients. Some patterns emerged for me with my clients who ranged in age from their late twenties to mid-sixties, over 80% of them in a supervisory role.

Adult Development and Psychosynthesis

Research in adult development identifies stages of development that adults can move through in their life. Each higher stage offers a more complex and nuanced way of seeing oneself in the world (see Robert Kegan's Theory of Development). In Kegan's Stage 3, the identity of the individual is the identity of the group. The transition to Stage 4 can be marked by the letting go of the old, group-based assumptions that ran us and into a new period of self-authoring.

When we look at adult stage development in Psychosynthesis terms, we can see Stage 3 as the individual being run by our MMSP. Stage 3 is unconscious to the I-Self and identifies with the pieces of us that we have learned to use to be okay in our world, in our group. The transition to Stage 4 requires a dis-identification from old identities and recognition of the "I" in order to self-author.

A large coaching problem in Psychosynthesis Life Coaching is that clients must be capable of some sort of dis-identification with dominant subpersonalities in order to truly identify a goal connected to their I-Self for the transformation available through Psychosynthesis to occur. I believe that a client must be at least close to Stage 4 in order to be able to dis-identify effectively from subpersonalities. The person firmly in Stage 3 or lower cannot make sense of what there is to dis-identify from since their identity is so tied to their MMSP, which is operating at an unconscious level.

This problem compounds when we learn that only an estimated 20% of adults ever reach Stage 4 or higher. That means that 80% of adults are not reaching a level of stage development in which they can actively and purposefully, through the use of their Will, practice dis-identification which will give them access to their "I".

As a coach, I am interested in the small experiences that could reach a vast number of adults, including the leaders who are my clients, who are at Stage 3 of development. Psychosynthesis can be esoteric and the Transpersonal nature of it, though it is needed for the complexity of work in the world today, can be off-putting to those coming to coaching from a business context. So, how can we as coaches quickly and effectively engage clients with Psychosynthesis principles without ever necessarily speaking about Psychosynthesis? I believe the use of assessment, and in particular the CliftonStrengths assessment, can offer a quick and accessible path to clients.

The following is what I have learned from working with my clients over the past year.

<u>Setting Up the Assessment Results for a Psychosynthesis Framework</u>

Subtly introducing Psychosynthesis principles within the context of reviewing a client's assessment report is a stunningly simple way to prime a client's mindset for the possibility of dis-identification and identification with each of their themes. Here are the elements I cover in a short introduction to the client in working with their CliftonStrengths Full 34 Report.

<u>Focus on the Top 10</u>. Gallup's research suggests that individuals will be more successful in completing a task when they intentionally rely upon the resources reflected in their Top 10 themes than if they were to use something lower on their list. This primes the client to focus positive attention on their Top 10 talent themes and not give as much energy to themes lower in their list.

I typically point out a theme in the middle section of their results, usually the 20th theme in the list, and talk about how the client can use that theme, but that it is probably not the first they draw on. It may take more energy for them to use that theme.

Then we talk about a theme in their bottom 5, especially if the client has commented on being surprised that the theme was so low on their list. I define the theme using Gallup's definition of that theme and explain that the client can use these talent themes as well, but it would probably take quite a bit of energy to do so.

This process helps clients to start thinking about the higher uses of their themes at the start of the session. Even though their top themes are most likely being used by their MMSP currently, these are the themes that help them navigate life successfully right now and are the themes most likely to be drawn upon in constructing an Ideal Self model.

Name, Claim, Aim. Next, we talk about Gallup's Name, Claim, Aim framework and I explain that we are in the naming phase. When we name something, we can place it outside of ourselves, so to speak, and look at it from multiple angles. I often liken this to when we learn a new word and then start seeing that word everywhere. That word was in those same places we were looking before, but now that we have a container for it, a name, our awareness of it increases. It has moved into our conscious awareness.

The same is true for the talent themes. I point out to the client that I bet their top theme has helped them get to where they are today and has helped them be successful. I also say that I bet they can easily come up with scenarios in which their misuse or overuse of that same theme has gotten them results they did not want. In the second case, I explain, the theme was using them instead of them using the theme. When we have a name for this part of ourselves, we can reflect on it and, ultimately, choose to use it or not use it to get our needs and desires met.

I find these few sentences very effective in introducing the possibility for a Subject-Object shift for the client regarding very strong pieces of their personality that are typically under the unconscious control of their MMSP. The Subject-Object shift is a key element in Kegan's growth process and movement to more integrated levels of stage development. While the growth to higher stages cannot be forced, conditions and opportunities for growth can be facilitated. In this set up to viewing the report, the client has been given a framework, using what the report is showing them to be their top talent and opportunity for success, and introducing the ability to view their talents as pieces of themselves that they can choose to use or not use.

In less than five minutes, the client is introduced to a psychosynthesis framework which does not require further definition and explanation at this point. The concept of subpersonalities is introduced through phrases like, "pieces of you," and "themes that you have." Dis-identification and identification are introduced by cueing the client to think about how their top theme has been used for their success and how misuse of the same theme did not help them obtain their need or desire. After this very brief introduction, the client is invited to direct the session towards what they would like to explore.

Coping with Primal Wounds as the Birth of Strengths

In working with the questions that Cristina began this chapter with for my own talent themes and with my clients' talent themes within the context of Psychosynthesis, I have developed an insight. My insight is that our top talent themes, as presented by CliftonStrengths, are mostly the coping mechanisms we developed to deal with primal wounds earlier in life that worked for us. Since the behaviors worked in helping us cope with a loss of connection to the Self, we kept doing those behaviors and became proficient in their use. Over time, a subpersonality is formed that uses these behaviors as its strategy to get its unmet needs met.

What happens when we start to think about our talent themes, that most people identify as their greatest strengths, as effective coping mechanisms instead of some sort of innate traits about us?

When I ask most clients about how their top themes show up for them in daily life, I get responses from, what I would call, their "Business Self," who talks about getting things done. Their answer is usually told to me matter-of-factly and rarely includes any wonder or excitement about what the theme does for them or the potentials that exist within the theme. The self-awareness that is initially generated in this naming process typically reaffirms the status of the MMSP as the one running the show for the client.

Occasionally, a client will talk about how a particular theme used to show up for them and how it shows up differently for them now. I will ask the client how they knew to use the talents differently. Their typical responses are, "I had to because it just wasn't working for me anymore," or "I had a major life event (divorce, loss of a loved one, failed business, etc.) that forced me to reexamine what I was doing," or "I just learned with age." These types of responses first clued me in to the fact that the talents can be transformed from being something that unconsciously operates to something the client intentionally chooses to use differently and for their benefit.

One such conversation with a client was around her top theme of Harmony. When the client described how the theme used to work for her, she said, "I was a people-pleaser. I found it much easier to move on if I just made the other person happy. I didn't want to spend my time in a fight." When asked what had changed for her with this theme, she said, "During and after my divorce I reflected on how much of myself I had lost over the decades trying to please my husband and I had to ask myself what difference it made in the end. Now, I'm still interested in a good relationship with people, but it doesn't come at the cost of myself."

This client described several of her themes in the same pattern. The theme used to be something about her that she just thought was the way life was. She did not intentionally spend decades trying to please her husband (and bosses, by the way). She described it as something she felt she needed to do and it happened without her ever considering other options. It just was. Then, through a major loss in her life- her divorce, she had the opportunity to decide who she was going to be afterwards without the identity of Spouse.

She did not realize at the time she was developing her new identity, but she realized in our coaching how the Harmony talent theme had helped her cope with her fear of being unloved for her entire life. She realized that the skills that make up her Harmony theme helped her survive growing up in her household with a temperamental father. She became so good at pleasing people in order not to experience their anger, that she made many friends and was always well-liked. While she may have briefly become aware of the need to please her husband if he ever became angry, she said she was mostly unaware of that drive and that she thinks it was the main driver of her life for over 40 years.

This coaching session with this client was filled with questions from Cristina's L4 listed above. What beliefs are related to this particular Strength? What do others want you to be according to this Strength? What do you really want to reach through this Strength?

The realization for this client that the aspects of herself that make up her Harmony theme came out of coping mechanisms she used earlier in life and then continued to use unconsciously brought insight to her on who she wanted to be: her Ideal Model at this point in life. Because of the other personal work she had done, she was able to quickly recognize and accept the part of her that needed to feel safe to be loved. Instead of being filled with regret about being a people-pleaser for most of her life, she started to think about how those same skills could be intentionally used for the relationships she was choosing to invest in now.

For most clients I do not mention my hunch that our talent themes are coping mechanisms learned early in life. I do, however, hold that context in mind while coaching my clients. Whether I explicitly state my hunch or not, Cristina's L4 questions present many opportunities for clients to become aware of the drives beneath their talent themes.

Preventing Spiritual Bypassing

One of the traits of CliftonStrengths that makes it so attractive for clients is its foundation in Positive Psychology. The most basic message people receive from taking an assessment like CliftonStrengths is, "These are good things about you that you should invest in to make great." While this is essentially good advice, we have to consider the effect of that advice depending on the stage of development of our client.

If it is most likely the client's MMSP that completes the assessment, then the report from the assessment mostly reflects the needs and drives of the MMSP, which is not in touch with the I-Self. If we are to take the assessment results at face value and advocate to our clients that they maximize their top strengths indiscriminately, we are ultimately reinforcing the position of the MMSP in the director's chair of the client's life.

Similarly, helping the client to build an Ideal Model that is not grounded in the transformation of the energies held by the subpersonalities, especially the MMSP, that inform the report could lead to spiritual bypassing for the client.

One particular client I had was fascinated with what he saw as the higher potentials available in each of his top talent themes. He was not unhappy with his life, but he kept wondering aloud if he could "switch off the bad parts and switch on the good parts" of his themes.

Another client had a hard time finding the good in her theme of Competition, which motivates people through comparisons to measurements outside of themselves. In short, people with this theme feel the need to do better than everyone around them. She grew up in a rural community in which women were encouraged to serve others and not stick out through individual excellence.

The male client thought he could "lifehack" his way to an Ideal Model by only focusing on the parts of his talent themes he wanted to maximize and by ignoring the other parts. The female client did not want to acknowledge that Competition was one of her themes at all and felt it was a part of her that should be ignored. Both clients are in danger of spiritual bypassing by ignoring the parts of themselves they feel are unsavory, undesired, or unnecessary.

Even though clients may unintentionally view Positive Psychology and its tools as a mandate to only focus on what the client considers positive, CliftonStrengths also offers an efficient tool for clients to recognize all aspects of themselves in an accessible way. Most clients can easily answer the question, "Tell me about how this talent theme has really worked for you as a strength at different times in your life." The female client mentioned above who had a hard time accepting Competition as potentially beneficial to her was eventually able to recognize some benefits by answering, "What would your life be like if you could manage this Strength at will?"

This approach to working with talent themes is the same as the approach to working with subpersonalities. Ignoring subpersonalities or certain aspects of subpersonalities does not reduce their power. In fact, it allows their power to act on us either unhindered or manipulated by another subpersonality that manages the unwanted subpersonality. The energy remains in us un-transmuted and acting upon us negatively.

In approaching these parts of our clients through the lens of CliftonStrengths, we can ask them, within a positive framework, how certain pieces of them really work for them and when they sometimes do not. If we also keep in mind that the talent themes might be coping mechanisms developed earlier in life, we very quickly have a lot of information to help guide our clients in the possibility of transformation of their talent themes into tools they are able to choose to use at will.

Conclusion

As coaches, our most powerful tool is our self and, in particular, our own connection to I-Self which allows us to act as an External Unifying Center for our clients. We must do the work ourselves in order to hold that developmental space for our clients. The more we do the work of personal and then Transpersonal Psychosynthesis, the more we ourselves come in contact with the ineffable, the more difficult it is to describe in words to others.

It is my belief, however, that we must continue to try to simplify the language we use to give clients a taste of the essence of the I-Self connection. In my study of Christian contemplative practices, one of my teachers, James Finley, was asked by another student, "What if God is not Love at all, but something else?" He immediately answered, "God is Infinite Love, infinitely loving you into being at every moment and if God were to ever stop loving you, you would cease to exist at that very moment. It can be no other way." I find this simple statement aligns with statements by the mystics across time and cultures who have experienced the I-Self. When I have shared this statement with others, for some it has quickly and immediately touched on an inner need and provided a brief connection to I-Self.

This raises the question: can we continue to fill our toolbox with tools that give glimpses into the transformational power of Psychosynthesis?

My experience suggests we can. Assessments like Clifton-Strengths are tools that can bring Psychosynthesis to a larger audience. As we continue to progress in our personal and collective understanding of Psychosynthesis, let us work to make it more and more accessible so that, by doing so, more and more people get those moments of dis-identification with a subpersonality that allows space for something new to arise in them. In this way, seeds of possibility are planted to raise individual and collective consciousness. Not all, and maybe not most, seeds will sprout. However, some will- and that is why I am a coach.

About Andy-

Andy Lyde, PCC, PLC served for 20 years in nonprofits working on housing issues around the world, as a C-level executive for 10 of those years, and currently serves in local government. He

COACHING THE ESSENCE

received his initial coaching training in Evidence Based Coaching while completing graduate work at Fielding Graduate University in 2006. He later completed two years studying Christian contemplative practices with the Living School at the Center for Action and Contemplation. Andy studied Psychosynthesis Life Coaching under Cristina at Synthesis Coaching Associates. He is also a Gallup Certified Strengths Coach. Andy helps leaders at all levels with the emergence of their Ideal Self to transform old needs that drive current behaviors into strengths and inner resources they can choose for their self-leadership. You can connect with Andy through www.forimpactcoaching.com.

CHAPTER 14

REFLECTIONS
Experiencing Psychosynthesis

I now leave space for these four resplendent spirits who have graciously agreed to contribute their valuable experience to this paper. Their reflections exemplify the Love Force that emerges when one comes into contact with Psychosynthesis.

Thank you, Serena, Silvia, Clio, and Laura

....for Being There.

SERENA

1. Awakening

Grief can be so deep as to make reality supernatural...everything becomes superfluous, and only love remains!

COACHING THE ESSENCE

It was really the pain, felt in a very difficult moment in my life that, at the age of 50, took me by the hand and led me to embark on a path to recover my integrity, putting my Being at the center of every choice. Curious as ever, I enrolled in the Psychosynthesis Life Coach course proposed by Cristina. Almost simultaneously I started a Gestalt Counselling course at the Centro Studi Gestalt Lazio. Being a Coach or Counselor requires first of all a great deal of work on oneself to have inner clarity and purpose, to be present and focused on one's feelings that become a beacon in self-expression.

2. Self-Awareness

In my journey during these years of training, the first step toward awareness was a visualization proposed by Cristina in the first classes. Cristina led me into the depths of my being to answer the question that each of us asks, "Who am I?"

"Initially the image of my teddy bear Pingo, an imaginary childhood companion, appears to me. He is shabby, abused, one-eyed, mended, and stitched up several times. From here emerges the image of a hurricane with its devastating force of rage. A frightening hurricane that destroys everything it encounters. From the eye of the hurricane, I emerge, a victim of my rage. I plummet to the ground creating a deep imprint. From the earth thus shaken and brown comes a wonderful tree, colorful and provided with a ladder. I climb the ladder and lie down on an insubstantial cloud. Thus I plummet again creating a deeper imprint, a coffin-like pit. From the earth springs a humble, simple, fragile poppy. It is delicate, but when it withers it scatters thousands of seeds around it from which as many poppies are born. The field is filled with color, and life is reborn in its simple beauty!"

Here is a first indication for me!

The hurricane has passed...it is over. It has swept everything away and left a void...so it seems. But here is a blade of grass and now a poppy, fragile. It is an instant and the field is painted with color and beauty!

From this initial awareness, I then moved on to awareness about my subpersonalities, again through a guided visualization entitled: the subpersonality bus.

14- Reflections

"I imagine going on a picnic to a special place where I am relaxed and at peace with myself. I spread out the blanket and open the food basket. While enjoying the picnic in this wonderful place I imagine that right next to me a bus is coming. On its side is written 'Your Subpersonalities'. The door opens and my subpersonalities begin to descend. I notice how they get off, who or what gets off. They can be people, objects, or other creatures. I notice how they are dressed and what they are doing. I notice whether they get off alone or in groups. 'The flower child', 'The monster', 'The dwarf', 'The booby', 'The intellectual', 'big tits' get off my bus. They look like characters from a circus and they get off together. They all got off...now I look out the window: one is left inside. It's me as a child with my teddy bear. He needs respect and love. Driving the carriage is my father. The little girl gives me the gift of my teddy bear again, which I later find out is my driving animal."

After the visualization was over, I realized that I felt some discomfort in knowing that my bus is being driven by my father, but I still do not know the meaning of this. Only much later did I fully understand the visualization and the transformations it, along with all the work done on myself, produced. Recognizing who I had become and discerning what belonged to me from what I learned but did not recognize as my own was of paramount importance.

I was able to reintegrate my inner child that I had ousted, I carried out processes of restitution of what I did not feel was mine, and today I feel much freer and lighter. Regaining my integrity also restored dignity to people from whom I had unwittingly taken attitudes that were not congruent with me. I was also able to recognize the positive intention of my protections and learned to accept them as they were helpful to me, serving an important function.

Now I am very grateful for these protections that seemed to me to be an obstacle, and I feel the possibility of a conscious choice. This step for me was crucial in accepting those aspects of myself that I did not feel were presentable. Paradoxically, it was only when I accepted the darker sides of myself that I was able to effect real change. The transformation did not occur if I denied or tried to eliminate parts of myself but only at the moment I recognized them, gave them a voice, welcomed them, and achieved awareness of my freedom of choice as well as my responsibility and power.

Painting: Serena Matteucci

"Images: Moments of reflection, moments when images speak more than words.
Suspended on a soft tightrope of life. Poised between heights and depths, between sour and sweet. Light caresses, I no longer grasp the hand of those who will not ascend!"

Images: Moments of reflection, moments when images speak more than words.

Suspended on a soft tightrope of life. Poised between heights and depths, between sour and sweet. Light caresses, I no longer grasp the hand of those who will not ascend!"

Yes, because one of the basic things I have learned is that everything that belongs to me, even what I don't like and would like to get rid of is something that has helped me get through the various stages of my life, and for that reason it should be honored and kept, in case it can still be of use. A few days ago I repeated the visualization and finally, my father is no longer driving but I have taken over.

14- Reflections

Asserting the right to exist as I am in this world was enshrined through a ritual called "the staff of power".

"Walking in a forest, I collected some natural objects representing my qualities, resources, and gifts. I collected at least eight of them. Then I reached a secret and precious place that has symbolic value for me and laid such objects on the ground to form a circle of protection. Then I found the most beautiful staff in the forest, My Staff. I returned to the circle of protection and beating hard with the stick on the ground, I shouted my name claiming my right to Be."

Another very important work for me was the production of a self-portrait with a collage. The preparation took two days but the result was very important. Once I finished I was a little afraid of my self-portrait: I didn't like the eyes. Once I got home I took the eyes out of the portrait and changed them, then I realized that the eyes were the most real, real part of my self-portrait and that made me so tender. I saw that everything else was like a mask, a scaffolding behind which hid a frightened, guarded child. I saw my tenderness, my sweetness, and also my strength as a warrior in a battle mask. And then I was also proud of myself, of all that I was able to build, of my frailties, my will, my curiosity, and all that I am. Now I can walk with my head held high without being ashamed of myself, with the knowledge that what I am is not all bad after all.

On this journey, I also experienced my guide animal: the bear. The bear is an ambiguous animal that arouses tenderness and fear in others at the same time. It is an animal that does not let its feelings show, which if respected goes on its way but if hindered or unjustly hurt can become terrible! The bear is capable of living for long periods in solitude and needs such lethargic solitude to recharge and survive adverse environments, also it can become aggressive, especially if its cubs are threatened. But the bear is also inexpressive and so others may attribute feelings and thoughts to him that does not belong to him. And that's something I still need to work on…

3. Relationships

In relationships with others, a key moment was hearing how emotions can all be accommodated and that sometimes being close in silence to a person who is suffering, without wanting to change the situation at all costs, is very important. Being close in silence means allowing the person to understand, welcome and support their pain, gently diluting it. I did not accept pain and sadness, I fought it hard and was terrified of it, and it often turned into anger. This allowed sadness to hold power over me. I also did not accept the sadness of the people around me, thus hindering their reworking process.

Acquiring the skills of a coach was very important for me, not only from a personal point of view but also from a professional point of view as a secondary school teacher.

I understood how to help others to help themselves without interfering in their processes but simply by facilitating awareness of their inner dynamics to enable them to responsibly assume the choice of their course of action, choose their own goals and face difficulties with self-efficacy. Regenerative listening facilitates self-awareness and respects the personal power of the interlocutor. On the path to becoming a coach, I also realized that the words one uses are crucial and can heal or hurt, sometimes very deeply.

I now use open-ended questions more and refrain from the main obstacles of communication (although I do not always find it easy): evaluating, interpreting, giving pre-packaged solutions, supporting or consoling, and investigating. When we evaluate or judge we attach value labels that prevent the person from seeing themselves objectively. The person does not feel heard for who he or she is and the flow of communication gets blocked. This occurs whether the judgment is negative or positive. In interpretation, there is communicative arrogance, an intrusion that often produces a defensive reaction. Instead, giving pre-packaged solutions has the effect of devaluing the person as being unable to find personal and original solutions. Consoling makes them feel needy, unable to sustain any frustration, and generates anger and confusion. Finally, investigating has the

14- Reflections

effect of making the interlocutor feel guilty, provoking a defense mechanism.

The interesting thing about coaching is that by working on concrete, attainable, specific, and measurable goals related to a particular aspect of our lives, it is possible to work on the profound in a lighter but no less effective way. Indeed, during the sessions, the person's values, resources, and limitations emerge. The expansion of awareness achieved by the client frees up energies and makes the client feel his or her freedom of choice. By increasing resources and decreasing interference, performance improves. It involves initially focusing on what is there, then identifying obstacles and finding a solution to overcome them.

This "simple" method can also be applied in teaching with good results. Goals should be small steps toward achieving the larger goal. Attainable steps that enable us to gain confidence in ourselves and our abilities and nurture our sense of self-assurance. On the other hand, anyone who has embarked on a long journey has taken one step after another. The first step sets in motion energies that lead to reaching the goal, taking us out of that paralyzing and unproductive stasis in which we sometimes find ourselves.

On the other hand, from the work at the Lazio Gestalt Study Center, I have come to understand how sharing one's own experiences is a great drive toward meaningful change. In the relationship with others, in our experience of the here and now, in the mutual exchange, lies the core of our cognitive process of ourselves that leads to a meaningful awareness capable of mobilizing great energies. Telling others about ourselves is not at all easy; we fear not being understood, judged, abandoned, humiliated, or laughed at. Group work is a true laboratory, and even just listening allows one to contextualize, circumscribe and reframe one's problems. But it is in the feedback that the most important findings are. Feedback is not something about the other person but is something that belongs to the person giving it, so it tells something about us both when we give it and when we receive it. One has to be centered on one's feelings and be able to separate what we feel is true and useful for us from what does not belong to us and is necessary somehow to give back to the other person. Feedback is a seed that sprouts something very much alive and true and allows for stabilizing change.

This summer I took the ACC exam and will soon take the counselor exam but what I want is to enjoy the journey and the journey has just begun!

4. Eyes of the Bear

Your father used to tell you that of the three you were the one who looked most like him. He would tell you this partly with pride and partly with that contempt that you reserve only for yourself.

It was January 5, 1974, and a lady, a colleague of your mother's whom you had never seen and would later never see again, came to visit you. The lady placed two large gifts on the floor and the third, smaller one on the crystal table. In that package was me. I waited eagerly for one of you to choose me; I hoped it would be you. Your older sisters chose the stuffed animal before you did: the first a big green and white dog, the second a beautiful yellow and brown giraffe.

"I wonder if you would have liked me!" My eyes were big and plastic and I had a small red tongue hanging out of a nonexistent mouth.

"I'm sorry", said the lady glimpsing your disappointment, "the Befana found only these." You looked at that big arrogant dog and the vain giraffe and wished for them. "You are ugly! I don't want you!" you used to say. "How", I thought, "now shouldn't I be hugged tenderly, brushed and placed like a king on your bed, while you my baby, my little girl, falls asleep holding me close to her?" For a few days, you poured your anger on me, an innocent teddy bear. Then suddenly something changed: you looked into my eyes that were little brown suns with golden rays, and in that magical moment you saw you too. That was how I became your inseparable friend. Now I even had a name, Pingo, and you were my little girl. I would always be with you and you with me, we understood each other with a look and I would protect you forever…

14- Reflections

But words are like drops that cut through stone, and at some point that "you are the one among the three who looks most like me" had its effect! One day your father gave you a jacket, a green and brown plaid wool jacket. When you wore that jacket a spell enchained you. You were no longer one but divided... A part of you, the real and vital part, suddenly stopped growing and became imprisoned in childhood. I stayed by your side and tried hard to break the spell. But we both remained for a long time trapped in a kind of space-time cage, far from reality in which we could only see the flow of events without being able in any way to take part in them.

Also trapped in that cage was a part of your father, "the Commander", who by exercising his power prevented you from returning to the other part of you. A girl in a plaid jacket, who also somehow resembled you but no longer had light in her eyes, unknowingly took your place until, now an adult, she left home. No one noticed that you were no longer you and everyone called her Emmeline. Wearing the plaid jacket she was just the one of the three who most resembled your father. She could take part in real life, go to school, graduate, get engaged and go out with friends- but trapped in a role that didn't belong to her. Since I had been manufactured I knew I was inextricably linked to a real animal who could help me in times of trouble to protect the little girl I would be entrusted with. His name was Igor, he lived in Canada and perhaps he could have done something to break the spell in which we were trapped.

One July evening in 1998 Emmeline arrived right in Canada- in Calgary. The landscape looked like a postcard: towering mountains, immense green valleys, and a long straight road crossed the valley between Banff and Jasper parks, leading to Edmonton. Emmeline was 29 years old and wearing the green and brown plaid jacket her father had given her. The car was speeding through the woods when Emmeline saw Igor crossing the road. The bear gave her a look of imperturbable calm and implacable ferocity, a magical look that began to slowly undo the spell and awaken Emmeline from the stupor she had fallen into.

A few more minutes of driving and Emmeline arrived at the Luxton Museum of American Indian Culture. She parked beside the bus where Igor had directed us to arrive.

Most of the passengers got off the bus except for you and me. Emmeline caught a glimpse of you as you held me close to you. You were sad and angry, and she did not recognize you.

I am annoyed by the stern manner and the somewhat grim look that "the Commander" gives you. Even with just his gaze he terrifies you and prevents you from moving. All passengers can move freely but you cannot, you are obliged to obey him, obliged to stay. He is in charge! The Commander also watches Emmeline as she tries to peek into the bus...they somehow seem to feel the familiar air that binds them together. You dangle your legs and hold me tightly to you. Emmeline looks at us, you look at her, too. She takes a few steps toward the bus stop to join you. But the driver promptly moves the bus forward to prevent you from getting on. After a second attempt Emmeline reluctantly gives up and enters the museum. She gives you one last tender look, however, while you, dangling your legs, remain seated in your seat looking at your feet.

Emmeline enters the museum and after a few minutes we also enter, but the Commander holds your hand firmly so that you do not move too far away, as usual...As you try to move away he pulls you back toward him with his gaze or his hand. Emmeline makes her way to the center of the hall and then is magically drawn to a wooden sculpture standing in a dark corner. It is carved from a large gnarled tree trunk and exceeds her stature by about a meter. She sees that the central part may have a large cavity like those found in a century-old tree, a secret refuge protected from the gaze by fur, bear fur.

She cautiously and fearfully shifts the soft, shiny fur and leaps backward when, from it, a myriad of wild animals, hawks, panthers, multicolored butterflies, weasels, and cats invade the hall with a great commotion. She enters it and sees that she can move freely by looking through two openings: the bear's eyes. She begins to walk slowly to avoid being noticed, when she finally catches up with you, Emy. You hold me with your

14- Reflections

left hand, while your right hand is clasped in the Commander's hand...You recognize her first and it is at that moment that I go from your small, soft hand to hers! I am a little afraid but Emmeline slowly caresses me and she recognizes me too...she recognizes us. Suddenly she realizes what is happening and feels the green and brown plaid jacket she is wearing is foreign and must be returned to the Commander.

It is your task- you little Emy give it back. Emmeline no longer wants what does not belong to her, she also wants to take part in the game of life and flow with it without chains. Finally, the time has come: you can do it! Now you no longer feel the Commander's gaze on you. As he contentedly rolls up the sleeves of his jacket he appears in your eyes, for what he is: your father. He, too, had been imprisoned in the spell, and by putting on the jacket, which belongs to him, he set you free, regaining, in turn, his lost freedom.

You enter the shelter. "I'll catch you and take you away", Emmeline tells you, and you dissolve into an embrace, no longer two but one, whole. It is early July 2021 and you return home master of your life, of yourself. By now frayed, bruised, without an eye, full of stitching (the last was a few days ago and was done to repair a tear at heart level) finally I can rest on the big bed.

Your father used to tell you that of the three you were the one who looked most like him. He would tell you this partly with pride and partly with that contempt that you reserve only for yourself.

But the soul of a parent wants for a child more than what their heart or their mind tells them. And now that you have returned to him what you took from him but does not belong to you, you are not at the end of a journey whose conclusion is to write about, but only at the beginning- finding your voice again.

It is the people who accompany me on the journey of life, albeit for a short distance, who caress my soul and sometimes return portions of yourself to me. This is what happened with Cristina during the coaching course.

It is also thanks to her that I saw exactly the moment when

COACHING THE ESSENCE

I lost and forgot myself, the moment when I went from living my life to the exhausting attempt to protect myself from it in the shoes of another, albeit my father. I was just a child and that child was waiting for me to come back to her and take her away with me!

In the difficulty of recovering the sensations, the facts, I listened to the voices in which confused, intermingled generations intertwine. I began to untie some knots and walk the labyrinth in which I got lost by patiently separating them, like threads of balls intertwined with each other in search of my own. Threads vibrate differently, with different colors. Voices are distinct yet intimately connected. One of them is rough, sometimes smooth, of changing colors, sometimes gray, uncertain, ungainly, out of tune but at least it is real and it is mine! I don't know where it will take me and I am a little afraid but it is the voice that I will follow...

Through generative listening, guided imagery, focusing on my goals, and my potential, and understanding the positive intention of my limitations I know that I will be able to face the uncertainty of the future with courage, always going further, step by step.

14- Reflections

SILVIA

A Little Cabin in the Woods, the Wolf's Guide, and My Encounter with Psychosynthesis.

And so the dark night of the soul came again like a shadow into my abode.

I do not know if she had knocked on the door before entering, but one day, silent, I found her in front of me. Other times she had come to visit me and, like all the other times, I was not at all happy to meet her. She just stood there. Standing, cold, wearing that unmistakable heavy gray cloak embroidered with fabric of old dust, threads of leaden ash, stitched with drizzling November fog. And once again, like all the others, I abruptly turned my back on her, trying to ignore her piercing presence. An attempt, that of ignoring her that, as always, would prove fallacious and leave me with a bitter gall-flavored mouth, a heart pounding with fear and abysmal sadness in my chest, as I shivered under her icy gaze

"An arrow can only be shot by pulling it back first. When life drags you back with difficulties, it means it is about to launch you into something big. Concentrate and aim."

Life was taking me dizzily downward, but without my knowing it, it was also about to launch me into something big. It was precisely on one of those difficult days, one of my days

COACHING THE ESSENCE

of crisis and confusion, of disillusioned hopes and expectations that I found you and along with you, your warm welcome. I would come to understand soon after how such a sensitive and profound woman had passed through the burning fire of grief to be reborn from her ashes like a resilient, strong-willed phoenix and how of this resilience, this strength, and will she had rendered service, made it an instrument for her life mission. Through you and your attentive accompanying me to my unexplored corners I would also begin to understand and consider that person whom I did not yet know and still completely do not know, but who existed and exists within me, in power.

To you, Cristina. Splendid woman, a splendid soul. Thank you from the Heart.

We walked into the woods via the downhill path. I don't remember if it was wet with dew, but I remember vividly that the grass was a bright green interrupted here and there by the gray of eroded, uneven stones, scattered like flowers on the brown carpet of moist earth that, at times, slipped under my shoes. The same colors I could see all around on either side of the path where the trees, side by side made room, some overbearingly, some softly, to rise toward the clear sky of that warm and sunny late spring morning that, shortly thereafter, would give way to summer.

I could hear the birds chirping, moving lightly and almost stealthily, playing hide-and-seek in the arms of the plants to fly to a specific spot in the branches, with a probable, cheerful goal to reach. The further we went down the path, the closer the smell of moss mixed with resin of the underbrush became. That scent brought back to the mind and heart the fragrance of an incense known, and yet, never before encountered. Pungent like pine needles, I could feel it entering my nostrils, descending into my lungs, and reaching hidden and slumbering spots and corners of my body. Calling the attention of my cells. To awakening, to life. I wanted to bottle it as if it were precious distillate, nectar and ambrosia and take it away with me forever. Between smiles and introductions, I walked with Cristina by my side. Step by step I could feel the anxiety with which I had arrived, calming down.

14- Reflections

"Who am I?" This was the big question that thundered repeatedly inside me. A faint, weak, intermittent little voice that over time had become growing, constant. Insistent to the point of becoming deafening and whose call I could no longer ignore. A warning, an exhortation akin to the "Know thyself" recorded on the temple of Apollo at Delphi. The meaning of my days depended on an answer I could not find, and it was as a result of this overpowering desire, which had become a necessity to answer it, that had brought me there. I had no idea where I was heading, what I would find at the end of the path, nor what would happen next, what it would lead me to, but from the first moment I had been pervaded by a feeling of familiarity and trust.

A few meters from a walnut tree, in front of me and in my sight, raised a little way above the ground stood a wooden structure. Above the door, a few Tibetan flags waved. Just beyond, a wind chime seemed to act as a spirit-hunting guardian at the entrance. The setting I would sit inside shortly after would be one of the most magical and welcoming places I would ever find myself in.

Photo: Syntegrity Coaching Studio, Orobian PreAlps, Valtellina

Once inside, I would not be able to take in all the wonder that lay around me, but I would do so later. Time after time. Session after session.

COACHING THE ESSENCE

When I would go back there, again, to feed on the richness of that enchanted forest, the beauty of that small house with its wood-scented walls, the rays of rainbow light re-entering through the glass door, the pure and magnetizing smile of an angel, Cristina's son Bianco, portrayed in a photo carefully stowed just below the window and from which I could hardly take my eyes off. There where I would allow myself to be amalgamated like a color amid colors. There where I would breathe in the tempera of that timeless painting that came from the hands of a father, a man, an artist whose face I could only imagine. There where I would be motivated by the volcanic energy of the word courage, resting like a seed on the nest of straw woven by a bird. Lulled between the deep, rhythmic earth sounds from a shamanic drum, between the softer melody of a rain tube that would transport me in thought to look at the puddles in which I was mirrored as a child. Sitting there, among mysterious and symbolic maps that would be the maps to orient me on a journey, a journey to the center of myself. For yes, that was the first day of my journey as a traveler into the infinite cosmos within me. Escorted, protected, accompanied by the Wolf and by her instincts, her recklessness, and her faithfulness. Her high and other vision. Earthy like her sturdy and agile paws, transcendent like the silver color of her coat, similar to the trail left by a star when it falls in the night sky. Surrounded by the sled dogs who were not far away, often, with their howls seeming to call me back, ready to wait for me there, among them. Me, a part of the pack. Warmed and illuminated by the flame of the Self, invisible, but always inexorably present between Transcendence and Immanence.

I can hardly explain in words what happened inside that setting since any description would never reach the power of what emerged. I can simply say that deciding to take that path in the woods was one of the best choices of my life and that ever since I was a girl I had been looking for Psychosynthesis without knowing what it was, but especially without knowing that it existed, and there, in that little cabin in the woods where everything spoke to me in a dance between astonishment and perfection, between reality and enchantment I found her. Or

14- Reflections

maybe, she found me.

That experience as a coachee opened unexpected doors for me, and exactly one year ago, I decided to embark on the educational journey to become a Life Coach in Psychosynthesis.

At the end of the PLC training, I want to be at a point in my life where my highest potential, talents, and qualities have emerged.

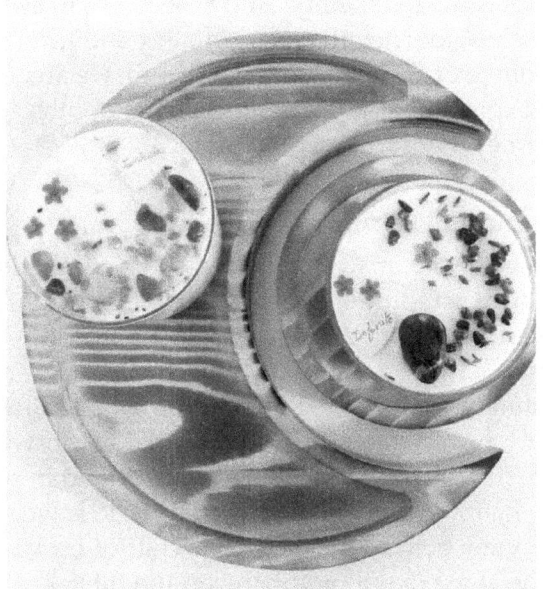

Photo: Silvia Parravicini- "Candele"

Using James Hillman's metaphor, I want from my seed, from my personal acorn, to develop the great tree to which I have been striving all my life. A big and strong tree, one that, yes, has solid roots firmly planted in the ground, but always keeps its gaze and branches turned upward, to the sky from which I come, to that vast and boundless space where everything is possible. Once a tree I will be able to give the proper shelter to all travelers who seek its comfort. Little birds will be able to build their nests and feed on my fruits. Take shelter from wind, snow, and rain or the scorching sun of too-hot days. Insects will stroll over my trunk, sucking the sap they need. Bees and butterflies will transport pollen from one to another of the flowers born from my branches. And they, through their biodiversity, will be for me tree, substance, of my perfectly imperfect and settled ecosystem in the temporal space of this life. This is my personal view of this path, which I see as a great journey within myself, within the infinite and changing space that passes through me. A satisfying journey, a great opportunity for evolutionary growth, of improvement, of knowledge, understood in its broadest sense, for understanding and putting my abilities into action. A journey that impels me to take myself by the hand, to accept myself, to love myself. A journey that is ultimately a journey back to the Supreme Source of the whole of which I am, we are, made. It is a journey of exploration of my Essence, in its depths and heights. It is my journey. For me. For the other.

Dear journeying spirit, I now turn to you.

I do not know the answers you seek, I have no advice to give you, and I have no solutions to your problems. But if, like Santiago, you want to set out on this journey of "Know, Own, Transform Yourself", I will accompany you. I will be your guide. Experienced, but humble. We will walk side by side, always. Never a step ahead, never a step behind. I will slow down when you slow down, run when you decide to run. United in partnership, allies in the heart. Whatever your life scenario is we will explore it. I will be your boat in the sea, your chariot on land, your dirigible in the sky. We will not focus on the mistakes of the past, and we will not immerse ourselves in the traumas and wounds of your experience, but we will look to the future and its infinite possibilities. In this theater that is life, we will search for ourselves among the many masks we wear and bring it out along with the potential that is already there, present, within us. We will train the will until we reach yours, your goals, and I will be there for you with respectful presence, from my Self to your Self to listen to your words or your silences, to listen to The World Within You, The World That You Are and value it.

Dear journeying spirit, we will make this journey riding a bright star. I will be Alice in your mirror. You will be Alice in my mirror. We will pass through the rabbit hole orienting ourselves

14- Reflections

on the path by following tracks of stardust, symbols and colorful crystals. We will walk the red expanse of the field of poppies in love to take us to the path of sensation. We will follow the orange of regal calla lilies to take us to the alley of impulse and desire. We will find thought in the square of yellow sunflowers gone mad with light. When our eyes rest on the green petals of cymbidium we will know we have arrived at the path of emotion. We will swim in the heady blue sea of lavender that leads to imagination. And when, along the way, we will come to discover the garden of beautiful wild violets.... then, with certainty, we will know that we have reached the magical castle of Intuition, and from there, in the circle of the whole, we will open the door to the rainbow to reach the Wonderland that resides within you.

Dear journeying spirit, this journey we will make together. You and me. When we meet. Whichever "I" you are.

My name is Silvia Parravicini. I was born to a workingman father and a homemaker mother on August 19, 1976, in Tirano, a small town located in the Alps of Valtellina, in the province of Sondrio.

A hyper-sensitive, shy and fearful child, I became a rebellious and countercultural teenager, more in feeling than in deed. Misfit, angry, and sad by turns, tending to be antisocial and shy to the point of being labeled "the antipathetic", I cultivated few but deep relationships, weaving ties with carefully selected people. My young self, characterized by high values such as a strong sense of justice, transparency, and truth, grew up amidst stirrings of inner restlessness that have led me ever since to great introspective moments and questions about the meaning of life. It was in my adolescent years that I realized that I possessed a distinct and innate gift for grasping people's states of mind and being able to help or comfort them through the power of my words.

My approach to the world of school and studies is difficult and listless, experienced as an obligatory passage and never totally accepted. Enrolled in the "Lena Perpenti" teacher training institute in Sondrio with the unclear intention of making a teacher of myself, I remain classified as what might be called "the average student", the one who never excels, although since I have known the alphabet I have at least been recognized as able to write. Fascinated by philosophy and psychology, during my school years I carried forward the conviction to study one of these humanistic subjects in depth, but after my high school studies, at the moment of choice, I underwent a change of course and at the age of nineteen I decided to enroll in a course of biomedical laboratory techniques, a 3-year degree belonging to the faculty of medicine and surgery of the University of Milan. Three years later I reached my goal with unexpected, moderate success. At the end of the thesis discussion, I was offered a job at the Besta Neurological Institute in Milan, but I refused the offer and returned to Valtellina. After some small and occasional jobs, in March 2001 I was hired at the pharmaceutical company ACS Info SA in Campascio (CH) where I worked for almost 17 years, covering diverse tasks. A worker in the production department during the first year, I spent the next six years as a laboratory analyst on microbiological quality control. In 2008 I became head of the microbiology laboratory and held that position until September 2017, when I left this job and much else for good. As a result of the events that followed, that experience will strongly change my life, triggering within me, over the years, a transformation and growth that will touch, not without pain, the professional sphere, but especially the personal sphere.

While my working career in the pharmaceutical sector proceeds without major changes visible in the eyes of others, over time, a crisis that will last for three long years begins to make its way on a large scale inside me, and while I still wear the clothes of a manager, in 2014, almost for fun and without any expectation, I enroll in the Zu Center School of Reflexology in Milan. Accompanying me on the path, enrolled in the school with me, is Pier, the person who is still my life partner today. It is during the course at the school of reflexology that the crisis becomes even more noticeable, and it does so by differentiating itself into what I might today call three clear phases:

14- Reflections

Stage 1 - doubt: "Maybe you are no longer in the right place, maybe life wants you elsewhere."

Stage 2 - realization: "The experience here is over. You gave all you could give, you took all there was to take."

Stage 3, the most difficult - letting go of the old to bring out the new: "The courage to close and take the leap into the void."

Still recurring in my mind is the image of me wearing my white lab coat as I walked through the long corridor separating the labs from the women's locker rooms on those evenings when I would tarry and my gaze would continue beyond the large glass windows to stop and stare at the mountains that rose majestically before my eyes. Those were the evenings when I prepared myself for the parting of what between joys and sorrows had been a piece of my life and of what was, after all, the only certainty I had and which, with all my limitations, I had earned with so much effort. In July 2017 I give up and resign, and two months later, on September 8, at about 8:30 p.m. my car leaves the company parking lot for the last time. Without having another job, but only dreams in my hands and a vision in my eyes, I start a new chapter in my life. About twenty days after I left, I was at the Lumen school in Piacenza to begin the two-year training to become a wellness operator. I completed the Zu school and the Lumen school in 2018 and 2019, respectively. Today, a few years later, I ironically still call myself a "work in progress". I introduce myself as a wellness practitioner and have my small clientele in tow, but I feel that I have not yet achieved what I am truly called to do. For that reason and, perhaps as a result of that empathic gift that had emerged in my teens, since last year I have been in training to become a Psychosynthesis Life Coach at Synthesis Coaching Associates, founded by Cristina Pelizzatti and William Burr and that is the reason I am here now writing.

The oak tree is growing, waiting to see the fruit that will come out of its branches.

COACHING THE ESSENCE

I will conclude by saying that I love animals, I get excited by the varied beauty of nature, I light up at the sight of a landscape, and I fall in love with a detail, a particular. I love the free expression that characterizes all forms of art and creativity. I love to read, but most of all I love to write. I have always had a special attraction to candles, and since last year I have found the space-time to devote myself to creating my candles with floral and/or crystal decorations to which I have given the name "Seeds of Light". Just recently, for the first time in my life, I feel the desire to paint on canvas, and after all ... I think I will find the courage to do it.

CLIO

The Heartbeat- A Journey in Discovery of Self

Tied to the earth or the breath of heaven?

The heartbeat as a vital vibration extends from the center of the earth. However, the beat itself is what marks the passage of time, the transmutation of emotions, as well as heavenly hymns. The beat itself is movement and everything that moves is life. But now to come to us-have you ever stopped to listen to your beat? Out of fear, I found myself going in opposite directions, closing my eyes on the highway of life so as not to bare myself and remain comfortable, unconsciously defending myself from myself. The me, who likewise wants to be a guide. This figure involves accepting that I am in a central way perfect in the eyes of the universal Self, in whom I reflect myself. A heart that beats in coordination with the will of life is a heart that can see beyond. However, the journey remains the discovery of pristine places filled with precious gems that only when seen with new eyes can be keys to a world that waits for nothing but you. With all your innate resources and gifts that you may not recognize you have, but that you have always carried with you, like your acorn (soul).

A journey that teaches, nourishes, and comforts as does the heartbeat. Don't forget to stop, even for a minute, to listen to it and give thanks. It is your Self.

COACHING THE ESSENCE

Just by traveling and looking elsewhere in a very hot Los Angeles, I discovered a treasure that will lead me to be here today. This treasure is life. Life? Yes, until that day I was not living fully. I was living a dual reality, one social and one real. I actually could not accept the fact that I was perfectly imperfect and had such a life. But, only through this introspective journey to self-knowledge, made in a place unknown to my eyes, a desert island, everything started to take a different shape. A different taste that I had never tasted before. The power of connection, a sense of belonging, and acceptance allowed my heart to be well disposed to the reception of the universal will. A good disposition of mind, a single opportunity, and a predestined place can create the right situation to induce change. Indeed, it takes a chance, a willingness to change, and a moment to induce change, which is nothing more than the spark that ignites like a fireplace burning full of ardor. So do our hearts when they are on fire driven by the desire to love. This is the joy of the heart, it is being able to see with new eyes. It is choosing the cramped and narrow door that leads to the salvation of the soul. Through change, it is possible to find joy, love, and grace. For there where you find your treasure will also be your heart.

Thus was born CHANCEMENT, from the union of 3 words: chance-moment-change. A life movement or rather a way of life that is also my vocation: *to help and support all leaders around the world to unleash their potential and take this journey of self-discovery through psychosynthetic precepts aimed at the realization of harmony and balance in the person.* And are you ready to see more to be more? It's time to take charge of your life and make it your masterpiece.

My curiosity to be able to see more to be more has always taken me to meaningful places. However, there is one inescapable trait that has marked my existence: love. The latter received in different forms and quantities and which on many occasions did not take its ordinary form. Love, at any rate, is received to be given. Love is received gratuitously. The awareness of being loved unconditionally and freely makes me look at life with different eyes: compassionate and empathetic. My journey overseas has taken me to another dimension, far from my native

14- Reflections

place but close to my nature. Docile, gentle, and determined but also aware and willing to be; to be life, to be a heart that beats in service of the other who is brother/sister and who is perhaps also traveling to discover their nature and searching for tools to find along the way.

The wandering traveler explores looking for treasures sometimes in solitude but with the freedom to choose because if listened to, it is the beating that will lead the way to other dimensions, beyond the visible. Prayer, meditation, and silence are ideal companions to lead you to your flowering field, where water gushes and the sky is blue. The invisible is thus made visible through the act, the how, and likewise, the why, which is the force that makes every how possible.

Photo: Clio Stecca- "Note"

A journey that leads to love and to love oneself more. Discovering the vocation that inspires to act to fulfill the unfinished and hear the unheard. The beating heart is the vital energy that expands beyond, where all is unity and harmony. Listening to the beat is itself a journey of life, peace, joy, and love. It is being in balance between the parts. It is letting yourself be rocked like a wave by the sea. It is awareness: I am here, I am journey, I am discovery. I can make a difference. I am a creator. The beat then becomes an antidote to life and discovery of Self.

A Self that is pure of consciousness and willing, and like a spark is free of content. Only through a great, good, wise act of will can we close our eyes, and disidentify from mind and body to enter the flow of the pulse. A pulse that is recognizing that we are bearers of the universe, perfect in the perfection of our discovery.

Now it is up to you. I invite you to close your eyes, to perform this act of courage: an introspective journey in search of Self that can only be brought to completion in sincere and compassionate listening to the pulse. At this point, let your intuition guide you.

Bio: Originally from the Tuscan Maremma, she supports people in their professional and personal growth. Her ability to feel and perceive things "beyond" and her spiritual approach prompted her to shift course from e-commerce to supporting leaders in unleashing their full potential and achieving personal well-being through Psychosynthesis. She is a Psychosynthesis Life Coach (PLC), certified by Synthesis Coaching Associates, an ICF-accredited Level 1 and Level 2 Coaching Education Provider. Clio is ICF registered; her interest in Social Psychology is a trait that has been with her since adolescence. In 2016 while earning her Bachelor's degree in Communication and Digital Technologies at Sapienza University of Rome, a book on social psychology marked her path: everyday life as representation, in which Goffman uses the metaphor of theater and social masks to investigate human action. Clio later earned a Master's degree in Marketing and Society at the prestigious SciencesPo graduate school in Paris, where she is pursuing her career as a PLC.

14- Reflections

LAURA

A Return to Self: A Journey of Self-Validation and Healing Through Psychosynthesis

In the summer of 1997, I was a 27-year-old mother with a toddler. We had moved from the Washington, D.C. suburbs the year or so before to a very rural area in Virginia's Blue Ridge. It was the first time in more than a decade I was able to take a deep breath, listen to the quiet, sit and walk in nature, and be alone. The healing vibrations of my only neighbors -- cows, donkeys, and wild animals -- harmonized intermittently with the wind, the rain, and far away in the distance on still nights, a train. The scent of the trees, grasses, and wildflowers were aromatherapy for my soul. It was a real-life Country Time Lemonade commercial of peace and tranquility.

I started working full time at 18 and by 19, I was married and supporting myself, and my husband half the time. Now approaching late early adulthood, for the first time in my life, I had both personal agency and time on my hands. I credit the former to my daughter. She reminded me what true love was. The latter was only accomplished by a desperate yearning desire, a miracle of respite, born from a void I could never fill in the suburban D.C. hellscape, which was, in reality, a cookie cutter mostly upper-middle-class postal code by 1990s standards.

I was raised a country girl in the Appalachian Mountains until age 14. It was textbook culture shock moving as a sophomore in

COACHING THE ESSENCE

high school from a region where a few kids I went to school with did not have running water at home and many had food insecurity to the East Coast equivalent of Beverly Hills 90210, where it was never quiet, and the stench of concrete, blacktop, and vehicles polluted the aether and the silence every second of every day. It proved very difficult for a young teenager on the cusp of trying to individuate her personal small self in the midst of a cultural and environmental identity crisis swallowing her whole. In pissed-off, nasty 1980s adolescent parlance, it sucked balls.

So my Child self, who was very much in close partnership with my Self, went away when I was 15. All I had left to function in the world was some Johnny-come-lately, anxiety-ridden, depressed, violently angry player at my disposal. I call her the Tough Bitch. Not because that's who she was to everyone, although she could be, if needed; but because that's who she was to me. "Toughen up butter cup. You ain't in Kansas anymore and life's not fair. You put your head down and keep marching. Keep up appearances and do what you've gotta do to meet expectations. You're a survivor, dammit! You come from tough stock, and you are not going to let your family down. They sacrificed too much and worked too hard for you to turn out a screw up or an aimless loser. And they don't need you adding more fuel to this dumpster fire by flaking out. This is the new program. Deal with it."

Set among the aforementioned scene, on top of the normal melodramatic teenage woes, was another new experience: financial troubles at home. I was adult enough to understand what was happening, but too young to help resolve it. The only thing I could do was become a fully self-supporting adult as quickly as I could. Not just to ease some burden on my parents, but for my own desperate need to try to regain some control over my life. In short, I needed money to get the hell out of town and back to a place where I could find my Self and regroup. But as is the case for many, bad decisions are often spawned from difficult circumstances. Three steps later in the wrong direction, I found myself trapped in a prison I naively agreed to enter for all the wrong reasons.

14- Reflections

For the most part, my marriage had not been happy or enjoyable. I knew on the honeymoon I had made a serious mistake. I felt it deep in my soul shortly after we got off the plane in Cancun, Mexico. A friendly and expeditious man, who didn't speak any English, greeted us with a smile, loaded up our luggage, and quickly took us directly to the bus bound for our hotel. My new husband, not having any pesos, refused to tip him. Mortified, I tried to explain to my husband that the man would gladly take a $5.00 American bill. In front of the other passengers waiting to board, my husband's raised voice cut me off mid-sentence, told me to shut up, and ordered me to get my ass on the bus, "now". It was the first of many wounds to come. My Child, who had exiled herself to some hidden compartment of my psyche the day I turned 15, released a rare spark of horror at the life contract I had just entered, "What the hell have you done!" But the Tough Bitch quickly put the smack down on her. "You are married now, dammit. This is your life. You make this work. Where else are you going to go anyway? You have no other options. Divorce is not in your family's vocabulary. Everyone will be so disappointed and angry with you for going along with that big wedding they planned. You wasted money that wasn't even available to spend." Dutifully, I did as the Tough Bitch instructed. I made the best of a mostly terrible situation for the next seven and a half years.

Finally at 27, I was at last enfolded once again by my beloved Appalachian Mountains. Not just for a superficial week of vacation, but deeply and continuously. I was being re-wombed. I'm not sure why or even how it happened exactly, but one day, after being so enticed by our surroundings, my Child self -- the girl who disappeared at 15 -- decided to return. I literally went to bed the Tough Bitch and woke up the next morning this younger, but now physically and psychologically older, version of myself. I call her the Child, although she never perceived herself to be a child. Rather, she always viewed herself a fully-grown soul stuck in a child's body, often forced against her will to do child things, like go to school, or the doctor, and generally live up to other people's expectations and definitions of 20th century success and proper societal norms.

COACHING THE ESSENCE

I must note this drastic and abrupt personality transformation was preceded by a few months of raging insomnia, an inability to eat much of anything, daily intense exercise as a way to deal with extreme anxiety, and unexpected, never-before experienced parapsychological phenomena. As an added bonus, I was in constant excruciating physical pain from the top of my head to the tips of my toes. The thought crossed my mind more than once that I might die or lose my mind completely. As the primary caregiver and only sober parent, I held it together the best I could for my daughter.

Now 25 years later, I still recall quite vividly surveying my surroundings that morning I awoke as my long-lost Child personality. As if I was seeing it for the first time, my home was pleasant and very satisfactory compared to where I had been living the prior decade. My husband, on the other hand, I regarded with visceral disgust. I can still recall the Child's inner dialogue running through my thoughts, "I would have never in a million years married someone like him! Gross!" Her admonishing shriek reverberated in my mind every time he spoke. The sound of his voice made me feel physically ill. For the first time since her creation, the Tough Bitch was uncharacteristically silent. They must have made some kind of agreement as I was sleeping that the Child would now be in charge again. My Self, who had spent most of the last decade in exile with the Child, was in a state of elation at this sacred reunion and most exciting homecoming, while my "I" was in a state of utter shock and bewilderment. Literally, I felt as if I had awoken from a 13-year-long coma. Someone else had been living in my body and had made some seriously wrong choices.

For the sake of my daughter, I spent the next six weeks trying to come to some kind of acceptable "new normal", anticipating that I could very well wake up any morning to find my old Child personality decided to skip town again and life would go back to the way it was before. I did my due diligence to see a family marriage counselor, trying to find a way forward. But each passing day further confirmed my Child personality was not going to retreat. In fact, in complete alliance with my Self, she only became more emboldened to reclaim her life. One

14- Reflections

afternoon a relatively benign quip on the emotional abuse scale from my husband sealed the decision. In that moment, I knew there was no love lost and it would certainly never be found. I packed up and left, with no desire or intention to ever reconcile.

Alone at the last counseling appointment, I related some of the experience I had just come through. I could tell by the befuddled expression on the counselor's face she had absolutely no frame of reference for the unusual story I described. I decided it would be futile to try to find any therapist or counselor who could help me reconcile what had happened to me. All would likely diagnose me with some kind of mental illness or psychotic break. Knowing the divorce and custody would be contentious, I could not risk any demerits against my parenting ability. Besides, I knew what had happened to me was definitely not a psychotic break. In fact, it had been my salvation from a very sad life in an abusive marriage. I'm averse to think about what different course my life may have taken had we not moved out to the beautiful Blue Ridge Mountains. How much longer would I have stayed trapped and miserable? The Universe delivered me into eco-psychotherapy before it ever had a name.

Since this was before broadband Internet, it wasn't until several years later that I finally pieced together what I had experienced was called Kundalini awakening, as described by the Hindu tradition. However, the description of this phenomenon did not speak to the peculiar psychological transformation that accompanied my spiritual revival. I continued my search for complete answers. I read every Humanistic and Transpersonal Psychology thought leader I could find. But it would take another ten years for my transformation to be described to me, in precise detail, by a man named Roberto Assagioli in a book called Psychosynthesis: A Collection of Basic Writings. Chapter II is dedicated to Self-Realization and Psychological Disturbances.

This one and only man wrote with such intimate and common understanding of the step-by-step psychospiritual process that can unfold, I had no doubt that (1) he knew this from his own personal experience, and (2) he was a learned genius in his ability to distill the workings of the psyche and the anima into a cohesive and cogent schematic that anyone can understand and use to reconcile themself toward wholeness and inner peace. Assagioli referred to this harmonizing as synthesis. My experience might be unusual, but it was real.

Finally, my incredible transpersonal event had been validated. And not by some random person who said something similar had happened to them, and not by an ancient spiritual text, but by a 20th century doctor and scholar of human nature; a student of Freud, a colleague of Jung, and a contemporary of Maslow and Grof. A master in his own right who understood both the spiritual and the psychological aspects of human beings. His writings made clear that thriving and flourishing cannot occur without deference to both the spirit and the psyche. This concept was nowhere on the radar of any widely accepted modern psychology modalities being used in America. I didn't need it to be. I had first-hand, experiential proof of its validity.

To me, my discovery of Assagioli and his Psychosynthesis was miraculous and, to this day, dear to my heart. If he knew this and could describe it so well, I knew the approach and tools he created to help people heal themselves would work. But yet again, life often throws obstacles in your path. Although my soul yearned to immerse myself in all things Transpersonal Psychology as a vocational calling, it would be more than a decade before I could pursue formal education in Psychosynthesis.

Fast forward to 2015, a darkness I had not experienced since the age of 14 began to creep in and upon me. But instead of naturally resolving on its own in a rapid and similar fashion to my first spiritual crisis at age 27, this one just dragged on and on, complicated by legitimate physiological dysfunction that should have been quickly and easily diagnosed, but wasn't. From 2015 onward, as any responsible adult would do when faced with such a crisis of desperation, I sought counseling, therapy, and medical intervention. Multiple counselors, therapists, psychiatrists, and doctors later, it all proved ineffective.

By 2019, I was fully sheathed in a dark night of the soul. I decided if I were not feeling better by 2026, I would end it. I had no quality of life and could not bear the thought of existing in

14- Reflections

the manner I had been for several more decades until a natural death put me out of my misery. Finally, in 2021, physically exhausted and at the end of my ability to cope, by sheer luck I found a medical specialist who, very easily and quickly, fixed my body.

Although gratefully relieved to have my physical health and mental stability restored, a year later, I realized that alone was not going to magically heal the rest of me. A lot of damage had been done in the course of six years. I also realized my dark night was not going to fade away on its own, as mysteriously and sneakily as it had come on. Both my soul and my psyche had been beaten, battered, and were now demanding my undivided attention. This was going to require me doing some work. This was going to require commitment and hard choices, such as ending a career that I had worked to hard to attain and sacrificed too much to enjoy, with absolutely no clue as to how I would support myself. This was going to require psychospiritual guidance I could not get with an American trained LCSW, LPC or Clinical Psychologist. This was going to require Psychosynthesis. In early 2022, I found a program- Synthesis Coaching Associate's ICF-accredited Level 1 "Practitioner" program- that resonated with me and enrolled for the deep experience, Psychosynthesis Life Coach (PLC) training.

Nearly a year later, I am pleasantly surprised and very satisfied with my progress. I still have a few more hurdles to jump, but I am confident with Psychosynthesis, I will get there. I am on a journey back to my Self again. The last time, it was effortless, seemingly instantaneous, and miraculous. This time there is much intentional effort and a lot of time involved. But I am quite certain, in years to come, I will regard it as no less miraculous than my first Self-recovery. I know that I will be a practitioner of Psychosynthesis for the rest of my life. Exactly what capacity that will take, I cannot predict. But that doesn't matter to me. With the help of Psychosynthesis, I am confident that I will gracefully traverse any difficult seas ahead. For I am now and will forevermore be guided by my North Star -- my Self -- my Will made into a strong and beautiful keel, my I, the adroit captain of my vessel, and my crew of Subpersonalities all work-

COACHING THE ESSENCE

ing in unison as they sing a harmonious tune.

Thank you, Dr. Assagioli, for being my lighthouse. Your light and wisdom are needed now more than ever.

EPILOGUE

"This Self of mine, situated in the heart, is smaller than a grain of rice, barley, sesame, or millet, or the core of a grain of millet. This Self of mine, located in the heart, is bigger than the earth, bigger than the atmosphere, bigger than the sky, bigger than all the worlds."

Chāndogya-Upaniṣad 3.14

"But the eyes are blind. One must search with the heart."

- Antoine De Saint-Exupéry

Drawing by Bianco, December, 2008

Bianco Lenatti: 13 February 1996 - 30 January 2009